# A HISTORY OF CYPRUS

# A HISTORY OF
# CYPRUS

## From the Ancient times to the Present

## KYPROS TOFALLIS
BA, MA, PhD, DipEd, FIL
Director of the Greek Institute
Formerly Lecturer in Modern Greek Studies
at North London College and University of North London

*A History of Cyprus*

First Published in 1983 as "A Short History of Cyprus".

3rd Revised and updated edition as "A History of Cyprus" 2016.

ISBN: 9780905313238

**Published and Distributed by
The Greek Institute
29, Onslow Gardens,
London N21 1DY**

# CONTENTS

## Part 4. Cyprus since Independence

## Part 5. Cyprus from 1974 - 2002

## Part 6. Cyprus from 2002 - 2016

# PREFACE

This *"History of Cyprus"* has been written by a Cypriot whose village called *Styllos*, situated near the ancient cities of Alasia and Salamis, the historic monastery of St Barnabas and the modern town of Famagusta, has been invaded and occupied by Turkey since 1974. As a result, this author and his family who live in the U.K. have not been able to visit their village. Whenever they visit Cyprus (their home country), they are just like all other tourists in the sense that they are forced to stay in hotels or hotel apartments because they are not allowed to go back to their own home. There are about 200,000 other Cypriots who are in the same situation and are deprived of this basic human right.

Today, most holiday brochures portray Cyprus as the romantic island of Aphrodite with a blue sea and sandy beaches and a very long and colourful history. This is indeed true, because, for its eventful history and the variety of its cultural pattern, few Islands in the world can rival Cyprus. This perhaps explains why the Island of Cyprus has been regularly visited by nearly three million tourists every year, from Britain, Europe and other parts of the world. The large influx of tourists in the past few years, together with Cyprus's application to join the European Union and the existence of large Cypriot Communities in many parts of the world, especially in Britain (about 300,000) have all contributed not only towards an awareness about Cyprus as a tourist resort, but also about Cyprus's political and geographical division which began in 1974 when Turkey invaded and occupied the northern parts of the Island.

My interest in the History of Cyprus goes back to my childhood years. When the EOKA struggle began in 1955, I was 11 years old and a primary school pupil. I came to London in 1958 where I continued my Secondary, Further and Higher Education. In 1965 when I was still a student at the University of London, I

9

published a booklet entitled *"The Cyprus Problem"*. In 1983 I wanted to expand the content of my original booklet and I wrote the "*Short History of Cyprus.*"

During my 30 years of teaching at College and University I met a number of people who were directly or indirectly connected with Cyprus: Archbishop Makarios, Glafcos Clerides, Ploutis Servas, Spyros Kyprianou, Andreas Fantis, Dr. Vasos Lyssarides, Demetris Christofias, Michael Foot, Lord Brockway, Lord Caradon, Christopher Woodhouse, Sir Hugh Rossi, Norman Atkinson, Tim Eggar, Dr. Ian Twinn, Pauline Green and many others. As a result of these personal contacts, I was able to listen to their views and also exchange ideas about the Cyprus problem, which was helpful to me when preparing this book.

The attempt to write a *History of Cyprus* has not been an easy task. Cyprus has a History of well over 9,000 years. To attempt therefore to present 9,000 years of history in a condensed format of some 400 pages has been very difficult to say the least. In the end, I came to the conclusion that most readers would be interested in the modern and the most recent period. I have therefore attempted to provide a brief outline of the Island's past history until 1878 when Cyprus came under British rule. The emphasis has been on events from 1878 to the present. It is my hope that this work will provide some insight and understanding about Cyprus' more recent and tragic events and will enable many people to understand the Cyprus Problem. I very much hope that it will also motivate many people to show further interest, hence the Bibliography at the end of the book.

It may sound astonishing as well as amusing that two persons, both religious leaders and *both born in Paphos,* one born in the 12th century B.C. and the other in the 20th c. have left their mark and influence on Cypriot History. These two Paphians were *Kinyras* and *Makarios*. The first was a king and a High Priest at the temple of Aphrodite back in the 12th century B.C. The second started as a monk at Kykko Monastery and eventually became an Archbishop and led the struggle for liberation, or more correctly, the struggle for **Enosis** from 1955 to 1959. He ended up by being both Archbishop and President of the Republic of Cyprus. It can be fairly said that he dominated and influenced the course of Cypriot history in the second half of the 20th century.

Turkey's invasion and occupation in 1974, drove some 200,000 people out of their homes and turned them into refugees in their own country. **Nicosia is still the only divided capital city in the world.** The United Nations have passed numerous resolutions calling for the withdrawal of foreign troops and for the refugees to return to their homes. Turkey still refuses to abide by the U.N. Resolutions.

The Independence of Cyprus was guaranteed by Greece, Turkey and Britain in 1960. Yet **all three guarantors** and **the leadership of both communities** are to blame for the existing tragedy. The **first guarantor**, Greece, through the military Junta and the EOKA B' organisation staged the military coup which ousted President Makarios and the Cyprus Government on July 15th 1974. The **second guarantor**, Turkey, used the military coup as an excuse to invade and occupy 37% of the territory of the Island. The **third guarantor**, Britain, with two military bases on the Island, chose not to intervene! Finally, the **nationalist leadership** of both communities, from the very beginning, were diametrically opposed to each other. Although they both compromised and accepted Independence, they were too nationalistic and too suspicious of each other, and they were greatly influenced by their "mother" countries, i.e. Greece and Turkey. They were Greek and Turkish first and then Cypriot.

What is also astonishing is the fact that in 1974 there was a military dictatorship in Greece, a so-called "socialist" Government in Turkey under Mr Bulent Ecevit and a Labour Government in Britain under Mr Harold Wilson. Most people could understand the terrible behaviour of the fascist dictatorship in Greece but they could not understand nor explain the attitude and behaviour of two supposedly "progressive" Governments in Turkey and Britain.

In 1974 Turkey occupied 37% of the territory of the Republic of Cyprus and created a "pseudo state" in the north, ruled by Mr Rauf Denktash and by an army of occupation of some 30,000 Turkish troops. This "pseudo state" is only recognised by Turkey. The legitimate Government of Cyprus has made numerous attempts especially through the mediation of the United Nations to negotiate a fair and peaceful settlement in order to re-unite the Island but has met with intransigence from Mr Denktash and the Turkish Government.

Some Greek and Turkish historians will no doubt present events from the "Greek" and "Turkish" point of view. I hope that my attempt to portray events has been impartial and not biased towards anyone. I must admit that for the last twenty five years or so, i.e. for the period from about 1977 to 2001, I provide a *record of events which may not be necessarily described as "history"*. I am conscious of this, but I have decided to keep the reader informed of the latest developments.

I wish to express my many thanks to my son-in-law Charalambos Karaolou, for checking the proofs and for making valuable suggestions; to my son Aristos, for his patience and help with the "computer side" preparation of this work. My thanks are also due to my family, many of my friends, my former colleagues and students at College and University for their constant encouragement and support. Needless to say, if there are any errors in the book, these are entirely my own. Finally, my many thanks are also due to the Cyprus Press and Information Office, for their kind permission to use many of the photographs that appear in this book.

*Kypros Tofallis*                                            *April 2016*

# INTRODUCTION

It has become traditional to start works of this kind, by giving some basic geographical and statistical facts. Cyprus is the third largest Island in the Mediterranean Sea. The name "*Cyprus*" probably derived from the Greek word for copper, because in the ancient times there was an abundance of this mineral in the Island. Another derivation was from the Greek word *Kypros* which translated the Hebrew "Kopher", meaning "Henna", a plant which flourished in the island. The Island was also known by other names in antiquity: *Makaria, Aeria, Alasia, Paphos, Aspelia, Kilinia, Amathusia, Ophiousa and Akamantis*.

Cyprus has an area of 9,251 square kilometres and a coastline of 776 kilometres. The greatest breadth from north to south is 96 kilometres and the greatest length from east to west is 224 kilometres. The *de jure* population in 1999 was 755,000. The ethnic composition of the population is as follows: Greek (80%), Turkish (18%), Armenians, Maronites, Latins and British (2%). The island is situated about 64 kms off the coast of Turkey to the north, 72 kms off the coast of Syria to the east, 400 kms from Egypt to the south and 480 kms from the Greek islands to the west.

There are two mountain ranges: The *Troodos* range which is in the centre and is about 80 kms long and 25 kms wide. The highest peak is Mount Olympus (Chionistra) which is 1,951 metres above sea level. The *Pentadaktylos* (Five Fingers) or Northern range is about 128 kms long and the highest peak is Kyparissovouno, near Lapethos, which is 1,024 metres. Between these two mountain ranges lies the fertile plain of *Mesaoria* (the Greek word which means "between the mountains") which extends for some 96 kms from Morphou in the west to Famagusta in the east. Mesaoria has been described as the "bread basket" of Cyprus.

The two longest rivers are **Pedieos - Yialias** flowing into Famagusta Bay and **Kouris** flowing into Episcopi Bay. There are other smaller rivers but all of them are dry during the summer period.

Cyprus has the following towns: Nicosia (the capital), Limassol, Famagusta, Larnaca, Paphos, Kyrenia and Morphou. Of these towns, Famagusta, Kyrenia, Morphou and part of Nicosia have been under Turkish occupation since 1974.

The Cyprus Republic was born on the 16th August 1960 after a bitter struggle of four years (1955-59). The original struggle which was led by the EOKA movement was for **Enosis** i.e. Union with Greece. In 1959 Archbishop Makarios the religious and national leader of the Greek Cypriots and Dr Kutchuk the Turkish Cypriot leader who was in favour of Partition both compromised on Independence.

The first Presidential elections were held in December 1959 and Archbishop Makarios was elected as the first President and Dr Kutchuk, the Turkish Cypriot leader as the first Vice-President of the new Republic. The Zurich and London agreements of 1959 excluded both **Enosis** and **Partition.** The agreements were signed by the Prime Ministers of Britain, Greece and Turkey (Harold Macmillan, Karamanlis and Menderes) and by Archbishop Makarios and Dr Kutchuk representing the Greek and Turkish

Cypriots respectively.

As we shall see, the reasons for the animosity and mistrust between the two communities originate from the time when the national leadership of both communities were struggling for different goals: the Greeks for **Enosis** and the Turks for **Partition**. There was no co-operation nor a common struggle from the start for an Independent Cyprus. The protagonists fought for different goals and when in the end they compromised for Independence, they were still "prisoners" of their earlier ideals and suspicious of each other. The Constitution was also divisive and contained the seeds of discord and unrest. When President Makarios proposed amendments to the Constitution in late November 1963 the Turkish Cypriots objected and inter-communal riots broke out in December 1963. The three Turkish Cypriot Ministers and the 15 M.Ps. withdrew from the Government. A United Nations Peace Keeping Force was sent in 1964 and is still there to this day. In an effort to find a lasting solution, inter-communal talks took place which lasted for a number of years.

In April 1967 there was a military coup in Greece. Grivas and his followers revived their ambition for Enosis and in 1971 formed a new organisation called the EOKA B' this time fighting not the British but the Government of Makarios! Grivas died in January 1974 but his followers supported by the Military Junta in Athens, staged a military coup on the 15th July 1974 and ousted Makarios. On the 20th July Turkey invaded the Island. A second invasion took place in August 1974 and 200,000 people became refugees in their own country. To this day, 37% of the territory of Cyprus is still under Turkish occupation.

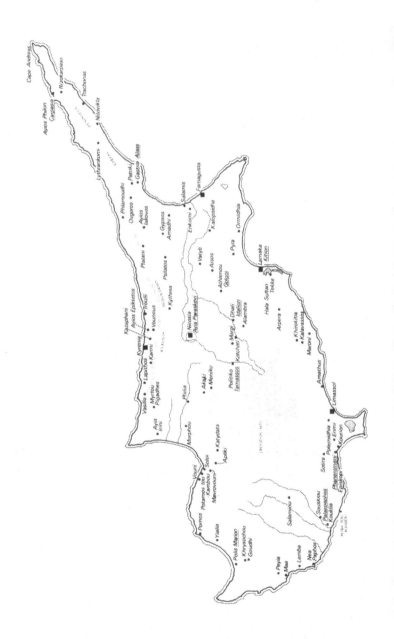

*Map of ancient and medieval Cyprus*

16

# PART 1 - ANCIENT CYPRUS

## THE NEOLITHIC AND BRONZE AGE
## (7000 - 1050 B.C).

Ancient Cyprus, like all ancient societies was a slave-owning society. It may sound strange to "modern ears" but the system of slavery when it first appeared was a progressive development because previously, all captives of war were killed, whereas now the war captives were used to carry out all forms of production. As the system of slavery was the first form of human exploitation, it led to the division of society into social classes for the first time in history. Ancient Cyprus was therefore, a society of slave-owners and slaves. The ancient civilizations and the ancient monuments such as the Pyramids in Egypt, the Parthenon in Athens, the Hanging Gardens in Babylon, the palaces and temples in Cyprus, would not have existed if it was not for the thousands of slaves who worked often in chains and in all kinds of weather, in the quarries, in the fields, in the mines, in harbours and in other places.

The position of the slaves in Cyprus perhaps was the worst because Cyprus was often conquered by the neighbouring powers, such as Assyria, Egypt, Persia and later the Romans. The rulers or kings of Cyprus were therefore often the puppet rulers of these powers. It may be said that the slaves in Cyprus were "twice slaves" in the sense that they had to work in order to create not only the wealth for their native masters but also the wealth of their masters' masters. (This was also true of Cypriot serfs, peasants and labourers in later centuries when the Island fell to the Franks, the Venetians, the Turks and finally to the British).

Cyprus has one of the richest and fascinating histories of Europe and the Middle East. The recent excavations have brought to light a Cypriot civilization dating back to the 7th millennium B.C. The earliest neolithic settlements were found at Khirokitia, Troulli, Erimi, Sotera and Kalavasos. The excavations at Khirokitia have shown that the inhabitants lived in "tholoi" or circular huts. These were located mostly near the coasts. For their weapons, tools and utensils, they used stone and constructed their dwellings with mud. Examinations of skeletons indicate that early Cypriots came from Asia Minor. Neolithic settlements were also discovered in the northern coast at Petra tou Limniti and in the centre at Ledra ( in Nicosia).

*Neolithic settlement at Khirokitia c. 5800 - 5250 BC*

The discovery of copper during the third millennium B.C. affected the course of Cypriot history. According to some, even the name of the island is associated with the existence of copper. The settlements at *Soli*, *Limni* and *Tamasos* produced an abundance of copper. This led to new settlements in other parts of the island. Their new houses were now rectangular. Such houses were discovered at *Alambra*, near Dhali village and at *Kalopsida* (in the Famagusta district).

In the Neolithic Age, the custom was to bury their dead where they had lived . During the Bronze Age, a common burial ground came into use. Such a necropolis was found near *Ledra* (Nicosia) and one was found at *Vouni* (Bellapais) near Kyrenia.

During the same period (Bronze Age), a wave of Achaeans-Mycenaeans had arrived in the 2nd millennium B.C. The most famous Mycenaean settlements were those of *Enkom*i (ancient *Alasia*) and of *Salamis*. Mycenaean tombs, vases, golden royal sceptres and royal diadems were discovered. Egyptians and Hittites also tried to dominate the native population but in the struggle for mastery the Achaeans-Mycenaeans emerged victorious. A strip of land in the northern coast is known to this day as the "*Achaion Acte*" (Coast of the Achaeans).

When Cyprus became a flourishing centre of copper production, her trade expanded to a great extent. A navy was built and trade connections with neighbouring Syria, Egypt, the Aegean Islands and the Greek mainland were established. Cyprus exported copper, timber and even perfumes. Many Cypriot perfume bottles were found in *Tel-el-Amarna* in Egypt.

It was the flourishing economy of Cyprus which most probably prompted the Egyptian Pharaoh **Thotmes III** to conquer the island in 1470 B.C. and force the Cypriots to pay tribute to him. Evidence of this are the letters which were found in Tel-el-Amarna in Egypt where we are told that the King of Alasia (Cyprus) sent gifts to **Akkenaden** the Pharaoh. This indicates that Cyprus was some kind of a vassal state of Egypt during his reign.

A splendid civilization must have flourished in the Island during the 14th and 13th centuries B.C. Evidence of this are the silver cups and other utensils which were discovered at **Alasia (Enkomi)**. The Cypriot writing which was discovered at Enkomi in the form of inscriptions date back to the 16th c. B.C. and is yet to be deciphered. Similar clay tablets were discovered in other Mycenaean regions in Greece and there is a striking resemblance to the tablets found in the palace of Pylos.

*The ancient city of Alasia ( Enkomi)*

# THE EARLY SETTLEMENTS

*Alasia* was the leading settlement during the 15th c. B.C. Other cities of this period were **Kition, Kourion** and **Old Paphos**. After the Trojan War (1194 - 1184) the influx of Mycenaean Greeks to Cyprus had increased. **Kinyras** was a High Priest at the temple of Aphrodite in Paphos and a King of Cyprus during the 12th century BC (i.e. at the time of the Trojan war). According to Homer, Kinyras made a valuable gift to King Agamemnon, leader of the Greeks in the Trojan war.

*Silver cup from Enkomi, 14th c. BC.*

*Bronze statue of Apollo from Alasia, 12th c. BC*

**Clay tablet inscribed with Cypro-Minoan script from Enkomi, 13th c. BC.**

The Cypriots attributed the origins of their cities to some of these Greek heroes who either fought in the Trojan war or came from Greece. Thus, Tefkros, half-brother of Ajax, son of King Telamon of the Island of Salamis was expelled by his father for not preventing his brother's death and came to Cyprus and founded the city of **Salamis** in the east of Cyprus.

**Praxandros** from Sparta founded **Lapethos** and **Kypheas** from Arcadia founded **Kyrenia** in the north. Although many believed that **Kinyras**, a native Cypriot was the founder of **Paphos**, others believed that **Agapenor** also from Arcadia established **Paphos** (New Paphos) in the west. **Demophon** established **Aepeia** in the north-west (near Morphou). **Chytros** gave his name to **Chytroi** (near Kythrea). **Chalcanor** established **Idalion** (between Larnaca and Nicosia). **Akamas** settled in the North-West part of Cyprus (north of Paphos) which is known after his name.

The Greek historian Herodotus states that the population of Cyprus consisted of Athenians, Argives, Arcadians, Salaminians and others. Besides the above, there were also many Phoenicians who lived mainly in Amathus and in Kition.

## RELIGION IN CYPRUS - THE WORSHIP OF APHRODITE

The ancient Cypriots like other people were polytheistic - that is they worshipped many gods and goddesses and followed many rituals and sacrificed to their gods. Excavations at **Vouni** have brought to light the rituals of sacrifices. The Assyrian and Phoenician gods Astarte and Baal were worshipped.

The arrival of the Achaeans from the 13th c. onwards also meant the introduction of their gods. The Cypriots accepted the Greek gods many years later. In Salamis, for example, the people worshipped Zeus; the Goddess Athena was worshipped at Idalion and Apollo at Kourion. For the Cypriots, the most important Goddess was Aphrodite. Legend has it that Aphrodite was born in Cyprus, in Paphos. Homer refers to her as "**Aphrodite the Cyprian**".

According to Homer, Aphrodite was the daughter of Zeus and Dione, and the wife of Hephestus. Hesiod tells a different tale, based on the supposed derivation of her name from **aphros** 'foam' by which she emerged fully-grown from the sea at Paphos in Cyprus or on the island of Cythera. For when Cronos had cut off the genitals of his father Uranus, he flung them into the sea; the foam gathered round them and they were transformed into a woman. When Aphrodite landed, flowers grew in her path and she was attended by **Eros**. She was known as **Anadyomene** (she who emerges) and **Kypris** (the Cyprian). According to the legend, however, she was not a "faithful" wife to Hephestus!

Aphrodite had the power to make all the gods fall in love or be overcome with desire, with the exception of Athena, Artemis and Hestia. She had a passion for **Adonis**, over whom she quarrelled with Persephone. When Adonis was killed by the boar, Aphrodite made the red anemone grow from his blood. She loved mortal men, such as **Anchises**, to whom she bore **Aeneas**, a Trojan prince, who later founded the city of Rome. She "sparked off" the Trojan war by offering **Paris** (the Trojan prince) **Helen, the Queen of Sparta**. She punished both gods and mortals who caused her offence or boasted of being superior to her.

## MYTH OR HISTORY - WHO WAS KINYRAS?

There is no historical or archaeological evidence to suggest that **Kinyras** was the founder of Paphos. According to **Pausanias,** the founder of Paphos was king **Agapenor** of Tegea in Arcadia, who after sailing home when the Trojan war was over, was blown off course and settled in Paphos.

According to **Tacitus**, the founder of Paphos was a native called Kinyras. According to legend, he was a rich king of Cyprus who sent Agamemnon a beautiful breastplate as a present for use in the Trojan war. He was, according to one account, the son of Pygmalion's daughter **Paphos**, after whom the city of that name was called. He married **Metharme** who bore him a daughter, **Myrrha**.

When Myrrha grew up, she conceived a violent infatuation for her father: this was a punishment from Aphrodite, either because the girl had neglected her rites, or because her father had boasted that she was more beautiful than the goddess. Myrrha confessed her incestuous love to an old nurse who, during a festival when the married women of Cyprus had to abstain from their husbands' beds, induced Kinyras to sleep with his daughter under the pretence that she was a girl of Myrrha's age who had fallen in love with him. After several incestuous nights, Kinyras brought a lamp into his room and saw the girl's face. When he recognised his daughter, he tried to kill her. But she fled, coming eventually to the land of the Sabaeans in South Arabia where the gods turned her into a **myrrh tree**. She was pregnant and the goddess of childbirth released her baby **Adonis**, from the treetrunk, or else a wild boar charged the tree and the baby was born through the cleft its tusks had made.

Another version of Kinyras' ancestry makes him the son of the Syrian **Sandoces**, a descendant of **Tithonus** and **Eos**. He was also sometimes called a Cilician who migrated to Cyprus. It was believed that when Agamemnon sent Menelaus, Odysseus and Talthybius to the city of Paphos to enlist Kinyras' support in the Trojan war, he offered a fleet of fifty ships but then cheated by making forty-nine of the boats little clay models manned by clay sailors. One ship commanded by his son **Mygdalion** set sail, but the clay models which were launched after it naturally sank.

.There are two traditions about his death. Either he killed himself after his incest with Myrrha, or he lived to a great age, favoured by Apollo and devoted to the worship of Cyprian Aphrodite, whose priest he was.

*Statue of Aphrodite found at Soloi, 1st. c. A.D.*

# THE PHOENICIANS AND THE ASSYRIANS

The location of Cyprus in the Eastern Mediterranean meant that it had close trade links with the neighbouring countries. The existence of copper mines and the developed shipbuilding facilities on the island, were added factors to attract the interest of the more powerful neighbours. One such neighbouring country was **Phoenicia** (what is **Lebanon** today). The Phoenicians were a commercial and seafaring people who travelled and created trading posts in many coastal parts of the Mediterranean. Cyprus's close proximity to their homeland encouraged many Phoenicians to go and settle in Cyprus, especially from the 10th to the 8th century B.C. Most of them settled in **Kition** (Larnaca) but others settled in **Tamasos, Idalion, Lapethos** and **Amathus.**

Cyprus came under the domination of the Assyrians in the 8th century B.C. (709 - 650 B.C.). The Assyrians were a people who lived in Northern Mesopotamia (what is **Iraq** today). A commemorative tablet which was found in Kition states that Cyprus was occupied by **King Sargon II of Assyria** in 709 B.C. This tablet states that Cyprus had seven city kingdoms and these kings went to Babylon and offered their submission to King Sargon. According to another tablet the names of ten cities and kings are mentioned. Some of these are: **Salamis, Paphos, Soloi, Kourion, Tamasos, Ledra, Idalion** and **Chytroi.** Three Greek names of kings are recognised, those of **Eteandros, Pylagoras** and **Damasos**.

The Cypriot kings retained most of their freedom in domestic matters during the Assyrian rule. The Assyrian influence can be seen in statues which are exhibited at the

Cyprus Museum. The Assyrian domination came to an end in 650 B.C. The period from 650 to 570 BC when  the Cypriot kingdoms did not  have to pay  tribute to any foreign power  is marked by great progress in the arts and poetry. It is during this period that **Stasinos** lived, the author of the **Cypria Epics**  that are connected with Homer's **Iliad.**

## UNDER THE EGYPTIANS AND THE PERSIANS

The growing power of Egypt during the 6th century B.C. came to direct conflict with Assyrian interests. **Hophra**, the king of Egypt (588-569 BC) defeated the Cypriot and Phoenician fleet but did not succeed to capture Cyprus. Hophra's successor, king **Amasis** succeeded  in 560 B.C. and the kings of Cyprus became his vassals and had to pay him  tribute.   According  to  the  ancient  Greek  writer **Diodorus  the  Sicilian**,  the  Egyptian  king  Amasis who conquered  the  Cypriot  cities,  offered  many  artistic decorations to their shrines. Many items which show the Egyptian influence especially on Cypriot sculpture have been discovered and are exhibited at the Cyprus Museum.

In the year  540 B.C. Cyprus was taken over by the Persian ruler **Cyrus the Elder**. During the Persian rule the Cypriot kings enjoyed autonomous status and were able to issue their own silver and copper coinage. The Cypriot people were now obliged not only to pay tribute and maintain  their own city kings, but to pay additional tribute to the Persians and  also  supply  armies  and  ships  to  help  the  Persian military campaigns. During  **Darius'** reign Cyprus became a fifth satrapy and the local kings became his "local agents" raising additional taxes on his behalf.

*Evelthon* the king of Salamis (560 - 525 BC) struck his own silver coins in Cyprus and tried to maintain good relations with the neighbouring kings of Cyrene. The Ionians, like the Cypriots, were also under Persian rule. The Ionians revolted in 500 B.C. and burned down the city of Sardis. Their revolt had encouraged some of the Cypriot city kingdoms to rebel against Persian rule and obtain their independence.

At the time of the Ionian Revolt (500 B.C.), *Gorgos* was king of Salamis . According to Herodotus, *Onesilos*, the younger brother of Gorgos, headed an anti-Persian party and tried to persuade his brother to rebel against Persian rule. Gorgos, however, fearing the consequences, refused to participate in a rebellion against the Persians. When Gorgos was away, Onesilos and his anti-Persian supporters staged a coup and seized the throne. Gorgos fled to the Persians seeking their support. Onesilos succeeded in persuading the other city kingdoms (except for Amathus) to declare their independence from Persian rule. Onesilos then marched against Amathus in order to besiege their city for their refusal to comply with the other city kingdoms.

The Persian king sent a strong force under the command of *Artybius* in order to crush the revolt. The deposed king Gorgos accompanied the Persians. Again, according to Herodotus, the Persian forces crossed from Cilicia on Phoenician ships and landed in the Karpas peninsula and then made their way towards Salamis. The Ionians had earlier sent their ships to Salamis to support Onesilos. A fierce battle took place in 498 B.C. but Onesilos was killed and so was *Aristokypros,* the son of Philokypros the king of Soli. The revolt failed because the army from Kourion and some troops from Salamis deserted the battlefield. As a result, the Cypriot city kingdoms who enjoyed about a year of independence returned back to Persian rule until the time of Alexander of Macedon.

## THE PERSIAN WARS 479 - 449 B.C.

In his efforts to expand the Persian empire to the west, since he was already a master of Asia Minor and Cyprus, *Darius,* the king of Persia invaded Greece in 490 B.C. but was defeated by *Miltiades* at the Battle of Marathon. Ten years later, in 480 B.C., *Xerxes*, his successor, tried once again, this time with even larger numbers, to invade Greece. It was during this campaign that Cyprus contributed 150 ships to help the Persians. Xerxes also failed and was defeated by *Themistocles* at the naval battle near the Greek island of Salamis.

The victory of the Greeks over the Persians in 490 and in 480 BC had encouraged them to try and expand their influence in the Eastern Mediterranean. *Kimon* was the son of Miltiades the hero at the battle of Marathon. He was a distinguished Athenian commander and was elected General in 479 B.C. He helped to consolidate Athenian power in the Aegean.

During the second half of the 5th century BC, some pro-Persian kings were dethroned and kings favouring the Greeks of the mainland were appointed. Kimon, together with *Anaxicrates* organized an expedition in 450 B.C. in order to exert and expand Athens' influence in Cyprus. They sailed with 200 ships but soon after their arrival Kimon died in 449 B.C. near Kition (Larnaca). His military fame was such that his death was kept secret for a while and it was later said that *"even dead he was still victorious"*. The Athenians (the Attic League) made peace with Artaxerxes and the Island remained once again under Persian rule.

*The Theatre of Salamis built by the Romans in the 1st c. A.D. probably on the site of an older theatre. It was destroyed by earthquake in the 4th c. A.D.*

# EVAGORAS KING OF SALAMIS
## 435 - 374 B.C.

*Evagoras* was born in Salamis in 435 BC and described himself as a descendant of Tefkros, the legendary founder of Salamis. The city was then ruled by a Phoenician king who was murdered by a certain **Abdemon** in 415 and declared himself as the new king. Evagoras was in exile in Cilicia but four years later he returned to Salamis in 410 B.C. and with fifty loyal supporters staged a coup during the night and ousted Abdemon. He declared himself as the new king. Since Salamis was only a naval city and produced neither copper nor gold he set about to implement a plan and fulfill one of his ambitions: to unite all the city kingdoms of Cyprus under the hegemony of Salamis. He believed that in order to achieve local expansion it was necessary to use force and therefore embarked on a series of wars which lasted for 12 years. Some kings accepted him as their leader but others such as the kings of Kition, Amathus and Soli, who preferred their independence, resisted his plan and asked for Persian help in order to foil his plans. These prolonged wars left Cyprus economically impoverished.

During the Peloponnesian War (431-404 B.C) Evagoras was on the side of Athens. The Athenians showed their appreciation by making him an honorary citizen of Athens in 410 B.C. Evagoras also minted his own gold and silver coins. When the Athenians were defeated at the **Aegos Potami** by the Spartans in 405 B.C., **Conon**, the Athenian General, sought refuge at Salamis with some of his ships.

Evagoras maintained close links with the Athenians and encouraged the arts in his native city. According to

*Isocrates*, the Athenian orator, Salamis was second to none among the Greek cities in civilization. Isocrates was also the tutor of Evagoras's son **Nicocles**. According to **Theopompus**, Evagoras and his son Pnytagoras were murdered by the eunuch of **Nicocreon** in 374 BC. Evagoras was succeeded by his son Nicocles who ruled from 374 to 361 B.C. Nicocles was in turn succeeded by **Evagoras II**. In the year 351 B.C. Evagoras II was dethroned by **Pnytagoras.**

*Salamis. The Gymnasium built by the Romans in the 1st c. B.C. on the ruins of a Hellenistic Gymnasium destroyed by earthquake in the 4th c. A.D.*

# ALEXANDER OF MACEDON 356 - 323 B.C.

Alexander of Macedon (356 - 323 BC) after conquering the Greek city states began his campaigns, first against Asia Minor and Egypt and then against Persia. He then proceeded further into Central Asia. Alexander's dream was to conquer the world. He was so ruthless and power hungry that he even considered himself as the **13th Olympian God** and expected his subjects to worship him as such! Alexander razed to the ground the Greek city of Thebes and destroyed the democratic institutions of the Greek city states. He may be described as the first *"European imperialist"*. At the time of his death (323 BC) his empire had stretched from the Indus River in the East to the Adriatic coast in the West and from the River Nile to the Aral Sea. Through his military campaigns Alexander succeeded in establishing numerous Macedonian colonies and opening new trade routes to Asia.

According to **Arrian's** work **Alexander's Anabasis,** some 3,000 anti-Macedonian Greeks had landed in Cyprus in order to resist Alexander's influence and expansion. The city kingdoms of Cyprus were divided in their allegiances and these "fugitives" from the Greek city states left for Egypt because they did not get any support in Cyprus.

In 333 BC at the **Battle of Issus** Alexander reduced Tyre and Phoenicia before pursuing King Darius into Mesopotamia. Eventually most of the city kingdoms of Cyprus sided with Alexander and led by Pnytagoras, the king of Salamis, Androcles, the king of Amathus and Pasicrates, the king of Soli they sailed with 120 ships to offer their assistance during the siege of Tyre. Alexander appreciated this naval support from Cyprus and confirmed the Cypriot kings to their thrones and rewarded the king of Salamis with the copper town of Tamassos.

*Alexander of Macedon 356 - 323 BC*

## ZENO OF CITIUM 334 - 265 B.C.

**Zeno**, the founder of Stoic philosophy, was born in Kition (Citium) in 334 BC. He went to Athens where he studied at Plato's Academy and other philosophical schools. He opened his own School at the "Painted Porch" (**Stoa Poikile**) which gave the Stoics their name. He taught that:

*"Virtue is necessarily good, that most things in life are morally indifferent, e.g. most objects of desire such as goods, honours, children, wife, and that these are at best only relatively good".* He wrote 18 books including the anarchical *Republic*. None of his many treatises survive, but his main contribution seems to have been in the area of ethics which was always central to the Stoic system. He supposedly committed suicide. Athens honoured Zeno with a public funeral, as a man who *"had made his life an example to all, for he followed his own teaching".*

**Zeno, the Stoic Philosopher**


# CYPRUS UNDER THE PTOLEMIES
## 294 - 58 BC

When Alexander died in 323 B.C., at the age of 33, **Perdiccas** succeeded Alexander as regent of the empire and tried to maintain the Macedonian dynasty but he was murdered two years later in 321 B.C. **Antigonos** was appointed as commander of the royal army. **Seleucus** became Governor of Babylon and **Ptolemy** was in charge of Egypt. Cyprus was for many years the subject of dispute between Alexander's successors **Antigonos** and **Ptolemy** and was used as a battleground by Alexander's generals to inherit his empire. The city kingdoms of Salamis (under Nicocreon), Paphos (under Nicocles), Soli (under Pasicrates) and Amathus (under Androcles), sided with Ptolemy. The city kingdoms of Kition, Lapithos, Marion and Kyrenia sided with Antigonos. A strong force was sent to Cyprus led by **Menelaus**, brother of Ptolemy and the city kingdoms which sided with Antigonos were defeated, their kings were arrested and either murdered or banished. The city kingdom of Marion was razed to the ground.

**Nicocreon** of Salamis, who was a despotic ruler, was designated as *"strategos"* and became the most powerful ruler in Cyprus. The alliance between Ptolemy and Nicocreon did not last for many years. After the death of Nicocles, the king of Paphos, Nicocreon, the last king of Salamis, is said to have committed suicide.

**Ptolemy I** and his brother **Menelaus** eventually consolidated their power over the whole island. The institution of the city kingdoms which enjoyed some autonomy under the Persians and which lasted for about one thousand years had come to an end. Cyprus remained under the dynasty of the Ptolemies from 294 to 58 B.C. when the Island fell to the Romans.

Cyprus became part of the large Hellenistic state of Egypt and was ruled by a **strategos** - a Governor General who was responsible to the King of Egypt. When the city-kingdoms were abolished the cities were governed by city commandants who were members of the Ptolemaic court.

Although Aphrodite and other Greek Gods were worshipped, the Ptolemies introduced their own dynastic cult. **Arsinoe Philadelphus** , the wife of **Ptolemy II** was deified when she died in 270 B.C., she was identified with Aphrodite and cities were founded in her name.

It was during the Ptolemaic period that the League of the Cypriots (**To Koinon ton Kyprion**), i.e. a league or a federation  of autonomous communities was formed. Similar **Koina** (Leagues or Federations) existed in **Phocea, Lycia, Syria, Cilicia** and elsewhere.  This **Koinon** was more of an association of the leading  representatives, religious and educational leaders as well as leading merchants  from the different cities.  During the 2nd century the Ptolemies had transferred the capital from **Salamis** to **New Paphos**. When **Ptolemy XII Auletes** died in 51 BC, by the terms of his will, he appointed his daughter **Cleopatra** (69 - 30 BC) as joint successor with her younger brother as **Ptolemy XIII** (who was also her husband in name, in the Egyptian manner). Cleopatra was ousted by Ptolemy's guardians but when **Julius Caesar** arrived in Egypt he took her side and after the Alexandrine war he restored her to the throne in 47 BC. She was Caesar's mistress and she claimed that  Caesarion, a son born to her was his. She followed Caesar to Rome in 46 BC but left after his assassination.

After the Battle of Philippi (42 BC), according to Plutarch, **Mark Antony** summoned Cleopatra  to Tarsus and immediately established a relationship with her. Two years later in 40 BC,  Antony  married Octavia, (Octavian's sister). He acknowledged  the paternity of Cleopatra's twins (a son and a daughter) born in 40 BC and a third child was born in 36 BC.  **Octavian** considered Cleopatra as a threat to

Rome and declared war against her. At the Battle of
**Actium** in 31 BC, Antony and Cleopatra were defeated.
Cleopatra opened negotiations with Octavian in the hope
that she would save her dynasty. Antony misled by a false
report of Cleopatra's death committed suicide by falling on
his sword. Cleopatra realised that she could not move
Octavian and rather than bear the shame of being taken to
Rome to be paraded in Octavian's triumph she is said to
have killed herself by causing an asp to bite her breast.
Cleopatra was the last of the Macedonian dynasty of the
Ptolemies.

## CYPRUS UNDER THE ROMANS
## 58 B.C. - 395 A.D.

It was during the reign of **Julius Caesar (102 - 44 B.C.)**
that Cyprus fell to the Romans. The rule of the Ptolemies in
Cyprus came to an end in 58 B.C. when the Roman
**Claudius** together with Cilician pirates occupied Cyprus.
The first Roman governor was **Cato**, who confiscated the
treasury of the island. Cyprus became part of the province
of **Cilicia**. In 51 B.C. the Roman orator **Cicero** succeeded
**Appius Claudius Pulcher** as Governor of Cilicia and
pro-Consul of Cyprus. **Cicero** was very critical of Pulcher
saying that for Cyprus he was "a wild beast" and that he
brought financial ruin to the Island because he imposed on
the people additional taxes for his own benefit.

It was during the quarrels between **Julius Caesar** and
**Pompey** and later between **Antony** and **Octavian**, that
Julius Caesar returned Cyprus to the Ptolemies in 47 B.C.
In all probability **Cleopatra**, his mistress, received the
revenue from the island. When Cleopatra died the island
was re-occupied again in 30 B.C.

During the Roman occupation, Cyprus was divided into four districts: **Paphos, Salamis, Amathus and Lapethos**. Many important public works were also carried out. Theatres, gymnasia and stadia were built in various parts of the island. A bronze statue of Emperor **Septimius Severus** (193-211 A.D.) was found at Kythrea, the ancient town of Chytroi. Also some wonderful mosaics dating from the 3rd century A.D were discovered in Paphos and Kourion depicting various scenes of Greek religious worship.

When **Constantine** moved his capital to Byzantium, the New Rome -Constantinople in 330 AD and established the Byzantine empire, Cyprus became administratively part of the Eastern Roman empire.

*Roman Emperor*
*Septimius Severus*
*(193-211)*

*Cicero - Governor of*
*Cilicia and Pro-Consul*
*of Cyprus*

*Leda and the Swan, floor mosaic, from the House of Dionysus, Paphos 3rd c. A.D.*

*Floor mosaic representing the legend of Pyramus and Thisbe, from the House of Dionysus, Paphos 3rd c. A.D.*

# THE NEW CHRISTIAN RELIGION

According to the **Acts of the Apostles**, in the year 45 A.D., **Barnabas**, a Cypriot Jew from Salamis, **Paul** and **John Mark** began preaching in the Island and tried to convert many people to the new Christian religion. On their way to Paphos, Paul and Barnabas consecrated **Lazarus** as Bishop of Kition and **Heracledios** as Bishop of Tamassos. In Paphos, Paul and Barnabas met the Roman Governor (Pro-Consul) **Sergius Paulus** (in 46 AD) who desired to hear what they had to say. In Sergius Paulus' presence, Paul struck the magus **Elymas** with temporary blindness, and Paulus seeing that admired and believed the new doctrine and was converted to Christianity. Paul and Barnabas left Cyprus for Pamphylia and John Mark returned to Jerusalem. Later Barnabas retuned to Cyprus but was stoned to death by the Jewish community in 75 A.D. and was buried near Salamis with a copy of the Gospel of St Matthew.

It took many years to convert the Cypriots to Christianity. There was strong resistance from those who worshipped the Olympian deities for centuries. There was also resistance from the strong Jewish community in the Island, (many Jews had arrived in Cyprus after the destruction of Jerusalem in 70 AD). The new religion was established by the 4th century. The success of its establishment was due to the work of Paul and Barnabas. **St Barnabas** later became the patron saint of Cyprus. The work and preaching of other people was equally important: **Heracledios**, Bishop of Tamasos, **Lazaros** Bishop of Kition, **Spyridon** of Trimithus, **Philon** of Karpasia, **Trifyllios** of Ledra, **Tychon** of Amathus and **Epiphanios** of Constantia laid the foundations of the new religion.

# PART 2 - MEDIEVAL CYPRUS

## THE BYZANTINE PERIOD 395 - 1191

The Roman Empire was split during the 4th c. with **Rome** dominating the Western part and **Constantinople** dominating the Eastern part of the empire. Constantine the Great, appointed **Calocairos** as Governor of Cyprus but he tried to rule independently. According to tradition, **Helen**, the mother of Constantine, visited the Holy Land and is said to have found the Holy Cross. On her return journey, she stopped in Cyprus and established a Monastery at **Stavrovouni** (Mountain of the Cross) near Larnaca. There she left a small piece of the Holy Cross.

*Stavrovouni **Monastery***

A terrible earthquake in 342 AD destroyed the cities of Paphos, Kition and Salamis. Salamis was rebuilt later during the reign of **Constantius II**, son and successor of Constantine the Great . The town was then re-named **Constantia** after him and became the new capital of Cyprus. Constantia also became the new seat of the first bishop of Cyprus.

The **Church of Antioch** wanted the submission of the Church of Cyprus to its authority but at the Ecumenical Council of **Ephesus** (AD 431), the Cypriot bishops resisted Antioch's claim. An end to the problem came about in 488 when the Byzantine Emperor **Zeno** recognised **Anthemios** the Bishop of Constantia and Archbishop of Cyprus after the latter had presented to the Emperor a copy of St Matthew's Gospel, which according to tradition, was found in the tomb of St Barnabas.

Emperor Zeno confirmed the autocephalous status (independence) of the Church of Cyprus and conferred upon the Archbishop, the following imperial privileges:

1. *Wearing a purple cloak, during official ceremonies.*

2. *Carrying a sceptre in place of the pastoral staff.*

3. *Signing documents in red ink.*

4. *To attend the Ecumenical Synods with the other four Patriarchs.*

# THE ARAB RAIDS 7th - 10th c.

During the early centuries of the Byzantine Empire, Cyprus came under the administration of Antioch. Later the Empire consisted of provinces and during the 9th c. *Emperor Vasilios of Macedon* (AD 867-886) recognised Cyprus as a separate province. Generals were appointed to rule the various parts of the Empire.

The seventh century A.D. saw the rise and spread of the Arabs. The Arabs began their raids of Cyprus in the 7th c. and it was during one of these raids that *Umm Haram*, a relative of the *Prophet Mohammed* fell from her mule near Larnaca and died in 647. She was buried at the spot where she died and later the Turks built the present mosque in her honour. The *Hala Sultan Tekke* or the *Tekke of Umm Haram* is situated to the West of the Salt Lake in Larnaca, and is one of the most important Moslem shrines.

*The Hala Sultan Tekke near Larnaca*

A further raid took place in 743 when **Walid II** was **Caliph** and many Cypriots were taken to Syria as slaves. Towards the end of the 7th c. (692-698) many Cypriots, headed by **Archbishop John**, emigrated to **Ioustinianoupolis** (Justinian city) on the shores of the Hellespont after the Arab raids. The Archbishops of Cyprus to this day bear the title of **"Archbishop of Nova Justiniana and all Cyprus"** in commemoration of this period of exile. The raids on Cyprus continued until the reign of Emperor **Nicephoros Phocas** (965 AD).

## CYPRUS IN THE 11th AND 12th c.
## THE BUILDING OF MONASTERIES

The town of Nicosia which is situated in the centre of the Island became the new capital in the 11th century . During the 11th c. Cyprus was no longer ruled by **Generals** but by **Dukes**. Some of these tried to proclaim Cyprus as an independent state. **Theophilos Eroticos** made the first attempt in 1042 while **Rapsommatis** made a further attempt fifty years later in 1092. Both attempts failed. **Constantine IX** and later **Alexios Comnenos** restored the Island back to the Empire.

During the 11th and 12th c. some great monasteries and churches were founded, most of them dedicated to the Virgin Mary: **Kykko** Monastery was founded in 1100 AD during the reign of the Byzantine Emperor Alexios Comnenos. The icon of the Virgin Mary with the Child is believed to have been painted by St Luke. Kykko Monastery became the wealthiest monastery in Cyprus.

In Kiti, near Larnaca, the Church of the *Panayia Angeloktistos*, originally built in the 5th c. and destroyed during the Arab raids in the 7th c., was rebuilt in 1000. *Chrysorroyiatissa* Monastery dedicated to the Virgin Mary of the Golden Pomegranate was founded in 1152. *St Neophytos* Monastery was founded in 1159 by St. Neophytos, a native from Lefkara. *Macheras* Monastery (dedicated to the Virgin Mary) was founded in 1190 AD. *Troodhitissa* Monastery (dedicated to the Virgin Mary) was founded in 1250 AD. There are many other Monasteries of course such as *St. Barnabas* (near Famagusta), *Stavrovouni* (near Larnaca), *St. Andreas* (near Rizokarpaso) and others which were founded at different times.

*Panayia Angeloktistos, Kiti, near Larnaca*

*Kykko monastery founded in 1100, Troodos mountains,*

*Macheras Monastery founded 1190, Troodos mountains*

# THE CRUSADES AND RICHARD I
# THE LION HEART

The 11th century saw the commencement of the Crusades. The First Crusade took place from 1095 - 1099. Some rulers of Western Europe who wanted to expand their power and influence in other parts of the world, especially in the Mediterranean and the Middle East, used the excuse that pilgrims to the Holy Land were persecuted by the Arabs. They therefore made several efforts to liberate the Holy Land from the Arabs but their main mission was to expand and establish their influence in the region. Their actions showed the true nature of their mission, as in the case of Cyprus which was taken over by *Richard I* in 1191 (during the Third Crusade 1189 - 92) , and in the case of Constantinople when it was taken over by the Franks in 1204 during the Fourth Crusade. Neither Cyprus nor Constantinople had anything to do with the persecution of Christian pilgrims in the Holy Land, yet both countries were taken over by the "liberating" Crusaders!

*Richard the First*, better known as *Richard the Lion Heart*, took part in the Third Crusade to free the Holy Land. The crusading fleet carrying Richard's fiancee *Berengaria of Navarre* and his sister *Joan* was forced to put into Limassol for shelter after severe storms. The ruler of Cyprus was *Isaac Comnenos* who tried to induce the ladies to land. Richard's ship arrived soon afterwards on the 6th May 1191 and Richard's remonstrances and Isaac's defiance led to the former's landing his forces and occupation of Limassol harbour. Isaac then retreated at *Kolossi Castle* but again he was forced to escape to save his life. He eventually surrendered at *Tremetousia* (in *Mesaoria*).

49

*Richard the Lion Heart 1157 - 1199*

It was in Limassol, at the chapel of St. George, that Richard married Berengaria, daughter of the King of Navarre on the 12th May 1191 and where Berengaria was crowned Queen of England. Richard succeeded in ousting Isaac and became master of the Island for a very brief period.

*Kolossi Castle near Limassol*

# THE FRANKISH RULE 1192-1489
## Introduction of the Feudal system and attempts to convert the Island to Catholicism

### The Lusignan Dynasty 1192 -1489

| | |
|---|---|
| Guy de Lusignan 1192 -9 | Peter I    1359 - 1369 |
| Aimery    1194 - 1205 | Peter II   1369 - 1382 |
| Hugh I    1205 - 1218 | James I   1382 - 1398 |
| Henry I   1218 - 1253 | Janus     1398 - 1432 |
| Hugh II   1253 - 1267 | John II    1432 - 1458 |
| Hugh III  1267 - 1284 | Carlotta (Queen) with |
| John I    1284 - 1285 | Louis of Savoy    1458 - 1460 |
| Henry II  1285 - 1324 | James II  1460 - 1473 |
| Hugh IV   1324 - 1359 | James III  1473 - 1474 |
| | Catherine Cornaro (Queen) 1474 - 1489 |

The English rule of Cyprus was short-lived. Richard I sold Cyprus to the **Knights Templars** for 100,000 **byzants** (the gold currency of Europe in the Middle Ages). The Templars in their turn, who needed their money urgently, asked Richard to buy back the Island on the same terms. Richard refused but he induced another Crusader, the French nobleman **Guy de Lusignan** to buy the Island.

Guy de Lusignan had become king of Jerusalem in 1186 because he was married to Sybilla, daughter of Amalric I. When his wife died in 1190 the throne of Jerusalem passed to Conrad of Montferrat and Guy received Cyprus as compensation where his family ruled until 1474. Guy de Lusignan bought Cyprus in May 1192 but he died two years later in 1194 and the kingdom of Cyprus was taken over by his brother **Aimery (Amalric)** 1194 - 1205. The Frankish Kingdom of Cyprus lasted from 1192 until 1489.

The Franks were now the new ruling class. They introduced the *feudal system* and the lands of the Cypriots were distributed among the *barons* and the *knights* . The ruling class spoke French and the masses spoke Greek. The Greek population became *serfs* or labourers. The Lusignans also made great efforts to impose the Latin faith on the Greek Orthodox population. Gothic style Cathedrals were built in Nicosia and Famagusta. At about 1200 the Abbey at Bellapais was built by *King Aimery* as a house of Augustinian canons. When Aimery died in 1205 he was succeeded by his son *Hugh I,* who ruled until 1218.

*The Abbey of Bellapais near Kyrenia (founded in 1200)*

It was during the Lusignan period that large numbers of Maronites (from Lebanon) came and settled in Cyprus. At one stage the Maronites were a flourishing community with a population of some 80,000 people. Towards the end of the Frankish rule their numbers dwindled to about seven or eight thousand and lived in about thirty villages. They had, however, their own Bishop in the small town of Dhali.

During the reign of **Henry I (The Fat)** 1218 - 1253, the son of **Hugh I,** Genoa was granted trading privileges that led to Cyprus' stormy relations with the Italian Republics. In July 1260 **Pope Alexander IV**, through the **Bulla Cypria**, forbade the election of a new Orthodox Archbishop of Cyprus and confirmed the superiority of the Latin (Catholic) Church. This was resented by the Greek population who were Greek Orthodox. The property of the Greek Orthodox churches was confiscated by the new Latin masters and some Orthodox bishops were burned accused as heretics. In 1231, 13 Greek Orthodox monks were cruelly killed at **Kantara** because they refused to accept certain Catholic dogmas.

During the years 1348 - 1349 there was a serious plague, later described by historians as **Black Death**, which wiped out about a third of the population. There were more plagues in later years. The plague which began 1438 lasted for 17 months.

The **Sultan of Egypt** invaded Cyprus in 1424 and at the Battle of Khirokitia on 7 July 1426, the Cypriot forces were defeated and **Janus**, the King of Cyprus, was taken prisoner. According to the Cypriot Chronicler **Leontios Machairas**, who was Secretary to King Janus and an eye witness of the Battle of Khirokitia in 1426, the peasants revolted against their masters. The **Peasants' Revolt** set up revolutionary organisations in Lefka, Limassol, Orini, Peristerona, Morphou and Lefkoniko. These organisations joined forces and proclaimed a serf called **Alexis** (from Kato Milia) as the new King with headquarters at

*Lefkoniko*. The leaders of the revolt were later arrested and hanged. Alexis himself was captured and was hanged in Nicosia on 12th May 1427.

King Janus was later released but died in 1432. He was succeeded by his 18-year old son *John II* (1432 - 1458). The hopes of large sections among the Greek Orthodox Cypriots were raised in 1441 when John II married the Greek Princess, *Helena Paleologos.* They believed that through her influence on her husband, one day their Island will become part of Byzantium - the bastion of the Orthodox faith. Their hopes however were dashed because twelve years later, Constantinople fell to the Turks, on the 29th May 1453.

John II had an illegitimate son called *James* and at the age of 16 he appointed him as the *Latin Archbishop of Nicosia*. The Greek sympathies of Queen Helena and her daughter Charlotte were not in full accord of the Latin rulers of the Island. They succeeded in arranging the marriage of Charlotte with the Catholic Prince John, grandson of the King of Portugal. John however died soon after the marriage and some believe that he was poisoned.

*Queen Helena* died in April 1458 and her husband King John II died a few months later in July 1458. *Charlotte (Carlotta)* became Queen at the age of 17. In 1459 she married her cousin *Louis, Count of Geneva*, son of the Duke of Savoy.

Charlotte reigned for six years, but James, the Archbishop of Nicosia, her treacherous half brother, never ceased plotting against her from the Archbishop's Palace. When he finally planned to overthrow her, his plot was betrayed and fearing for his life left for Egypt. Such was his lust for power to become King, that as a Christian Archbishop he stooped so low as to beg for the support of the "infidel" Sultan to support his claims against those of his half-sister Queen Charlotte!

History seems to repeat itself: In the 5th c. BC some Greek city states were prepared to form an alliance with the Persians against other Greek city states! In this case, a Christian Archbishop was offering homage and suzerainty and a higher tribute to the Moslem Sultan of Egypt in order to achieve his goal. In September 1460 James, supported by an Egyptian army invaded Cyprus and Queen Charlotte and Louis sought refuge at the Kyrenia fortress. The civil war lasted four years. The Genoese, who for many years had ruled the sea-port town of Famagusta and had supported Louis surrendered the town.

*James II* was one of the most ruthless rulers of Cyprus. He reigned from 1460 - 73. Through the "mediation and influence" of the **Republic of Venice**, James II married **Catherine Cornaro**, daughter of Mark Cornaro, a Venetian aristocrat. The Genoese influence and interest on the Island was now replaced by those of Venice. James II died soon afterwards (his death is attributed to poison) and he was succeeded very briefly by his son **James III** (1473 - 74). James III was also poisoned and Catherine Cornaro was the last Lusignan Queen of Cyprus (1474 - 1489).

In 1489 Queen Catherine renounced her rights in favour of the Republic of Venice. Cyprus was to remain under Venetian rule from 1489 until 1571.

*Catherine Cornaro - the last Queen of Cyprus*

It was during the Frankish period that some magnificent Latin Cathedrals and castles were built. The **Cathedral of St. Sophia** in Nicosia was built on the same design as that of **Notre Dame of Paris** in 1209 and was completed in its final form and consecrated on the 5th November 1326. The Lusignan kings were crowned in this cathedral as *"Kings of Cyprus"*. The Cathedral was later converted into a mosque when the Turks captured Nicosia in 1570. (Later In 1954 the Turks renamed the Cathedral as "Selim Mosque" in honour of the Sultan Selim II, who conquered Cyprus).

Another Gothic style Latin Cathedral, that of **St Nicholas**, was built in Famagusta in the 14th century, almost identical to the St Sophia Cathedral in Nicosia. At this Cathedral the Lusignan Kings of Cyprus were crowned *"Kings of Jerusalem"*. (Later, after the Turkish occupation, the

Cathedral was converted into a mosque and is now called *"The Mosque of Lala Mustafa Pasha"* after the man who captured Famagusta in 1571).

*The Gothic style Latin Cathedral of St. Nicholas, Famagusta. The Lusignan kings of Cyprus were crowned here.*

*The Gothic style Latin Cathedral of St. Sophia*
*(exterior and interior)*

58

# THE VENETIAN RULE 1489 - 1571

*The Republic of Venice* was a naval power and dominated the Mediterranean Sea from the 12th to the 17th century. Soon after the fall of Constantinople to the Franks in 1204 (during the Crusades), the Venetians took over *Euboea* which they ruled until 1470, the *Cyclades* which they ruled until 1566 and the Island of *Crete,* which they ruled until 1669. They also ruled the Island of *Corfu* from 1386 and the other Ionian Islands from 1483.

The Venetian rule in Cyprus was mainly a military one. For the ordinary people there was hardly any difference from Frankish to Venetian control. The feudal system remained intact. The serfs remained serfs and the nobles remained nobles. The only change in the administration was that Cyprus no longer had a King but a *Venetian Governor*. The Governor was assisted by two Counsellors who formed the so-called *Regimento* (the Government). They were elected (by the nobles) for two years only. This *Regimento* was supported by a *Captain* (better known as the *Captain of Famagusta*) and was the *Commander-in-Chief of the Army*. Schools were closed down. Financially and culturally Cyprus fell into a sad decline. The Venetians were interested in collecting taxes and constructing stronger fortifications, such as those of Famagusta and Nicosia.

*Shakespeare's* tragedy *"Othello"* is related to the Venetian occupation of Cyprus. The tragedy is said to have taken place in the tower of the old town of Famagusta. The tower where Othello murdered his charming and innocent Desdemona, is known as *"Othello's Tower"*. The poverty that existed as well as Venetian misrule had forced many people to leave the island and as a result the population during this period was reduced to about 180,000. According to **Martin von Baumgarten**, who visited Cyprus in 1508, "all the inhabitants of Cyprus were slaves to the Venetians and were obliged to pay the state a third of their income or their products."

*The Lion of St Mark, the emblem of Venetian rule. The tower of Othello, Famagusta, Cyprus*

The 15th and 16th centuries was a period of Ottoman expansion. Constantinople fell to the Turks in May 1453 and the rest of Greece and the Balkans a little later. The Sultan **Suleiman the Magnificent** died in 1566 and was succeeded by his son **Selim II** (1566 - 1574). The Grand

Vezir Mehmed Sokolli had advised Selim II to maintain friendly relations with Venice. Selim II however was greatly influenced by two military persons: **Lala Mustafa** and **Piale Pasha** who had advised him to take over Cyprus in order to establish his absolute authority in the Eastern Mediterranean. A messenger named Kubad was sent to Venice in March 1570 with the following ultimatum:

*"In the name of Seilm II, Ottoman Sultan, Emperor of the Turks, Lord of Lords, King of Kings, Shadow of God, Lord of the earthly paradise and of Jerusalem demands the cession of Cyprus willingly or perforce..."*

Selim II was claiming Cyprus using the pretext that once it was conquered by the Arabs. The **Signori** - the Venetian Oligarchy, rejected the ultimatum and prepared for resistance. The Pope, the Duke of Savoy and the King of Spain also advised for resistance and offered their support. In the desperate situation that the Venetians had found themselves they promised to free the serfs in Cyprus in order to secure their support. They even tried to arrange through the Greek Patriarch, for a revolt of the Greeks of the Peloponnese in order to embarrass the Turks. They even tried to encourage the Russian Czar Ivan the Terrible to attack the Turks from the north. These things were momentary decisions and were doomed to failure from the start because they were not properly planned in advance.

When the Venetians refused to surrender the Island, Selim II sent Lala Mustafa with 100,000 soldiers and Piale Pasha with 300 ships to take the Island by force. The Ottoman fleet arrived in Larnaka (near the Salt Lake) which was one of the main ports on the 1st July 1570. The Venetian administration of Cyprus, which was under the control of Governor **Nicolo Dandolo** (a weak and incompetent person), decided not to offer any resistance to the Turks at that particular moment. The Turks were therefore able to freely disembark their cannons, their horses and their military equipment.

Lala Mustafa and his troops spent the next three weeks resting and planning in Larnaka whether to attack Famagusta or Nicosia first. He decided that Nicosia should be attacked first and on 25th July 1570 the siege had commenced. It lasted for a few weeks and Nicosia was taken on the 9th September 1570. After their victory, the Turks embarked in a series of atrocities killing some 10,000 defenders of the town and about 20,000 women and children. Nicolo Dandolo the Venetian Governor was also beheaded.

On the 3rd October 1570 hundreds of young captives (mainly girls) loaded on three galleys were about to be sent to the Sultan as a gift. One of the galleys was blown up, off the coast of Famagusta, destroying the other two. It has been said that either **Arnalda**, daughter of Eugene Sinklitikos Count de Ruchas, General of the Cypriot cavalry or **Maria Sinklitiki** (niece of Sinklitikos) deliberately set fire to the powder magazine that destroyed the galleys.

Meanwhile on the 21st September 1570, the re-enforcements (some 17,000 soldiers) from Venice, Spain and the Papal states, which had reached the small island of Castellorizo (near Rhodes), contemplated what action to take. Their mission was to save Nicosia the capital but since it had already fallen to the Turks, it was decided by the naval commanders that it was pointless to sail any further and consequently Famagusta was left to defend itself against the numerous forces of Lala Mustafa.

According to **A. Calepio's** account (Calepio was a Doctor of Divinity and head of a Dominican Convent) he had witnessed the fall of Nicosia and was taken a prisoner, a few days after Kyrenia had fallen on 14 September 1570 with no resistance. Paphos, Limassol and Larnaca did not offer any resistance to the Turks either. Lala Mustafa then sent a messenger to Famagusta with Dandolo's head demanding its surrender.

**Marc Antonio Bragadino**, who was the Captain of Famagusta, refused to surrender the city. The siege of Famagusta was a fierce one and lasted from the end of September 1570 until its final capitulation on the 1st August 1571. It was estimated that some 80,000 Turkish soldiers were killed during the siege. An agreement was eventually reached whereby: (a) All Venetian officers with their wives and children were to be allowed to leave for Crete on Turkish ships. (b) Any Greek soldiers or civilians who wished to leave could also go to Crete. (c) The Greek civilians who wished to stay in Cyprus were allowed to do so. The agreement however was not kept by Lala Mustafa.

On the 5th September 1571 Bragadino dressed in ceremonial clothes and accompanied by some 300 Venetians had visited the tent of Lala Mustafa in order to surrender the keys of the city. Although they were welcomed at first, Lala Mustafa accused them that during the truce, the Venetians had put to death certain slaves. He immediately ordered them to be bound and they were led to the square. There, Bragadino's men were executed and Lala Mustafa himself cut off Bragadino's nose and ears. Bragadino was later flayed and stuffed with straw.

*(Cobham: Excerpta Cypria, pp. 156-157).*

In the struggle for supremacy and control of the island, the role of the Cypriot masses (who were in effect powerless), was mainly that of indifference. Some of them saw the Venetians as cruel masters and hoped that the Ottoman Turks might be better by imposing lesser taxes. Others, especially the very religious, had the opposite view and feared the worst because the Turks practised the Islamic religion. Some feared that the presence of the Ottoman Turks might lead to their conversion to the Islamic faith as the Franks had tried to convert the population to Catholicism when they took over the Island.

The vast majority of the people did not want any masters at all because they saw them as tyrants, irrespective of whether they were Franks, Venetians or Turks. They wanted to be left alone to lead a peaceful life. At an age however, when the might of the foreign ruler was the determining factor, the poor peasantry who were deprived of their land and were at the mercy of their masters for their very survival did not have much choice. For most of them, it was irrelevant whether their master was called Nicolo Dandolo or Lala Mustafa, i.e. whether he was a Venetian or an Ottoman Turk.

The population of Cyprus when the Venetians took over the island in 1489 was 106,000. When they left it was 200,000.

# THE OTTOMAN RULE 1571 - 1878

After the conquest of Cyprus, Lala Mustafa returned to Constantinople expecting a hero's welcome. His return however, was overshadowed with the news that the Turkish fleet was destroyed at the *Battle of Lepanto* (in Greek waters near Naupactos). The allied fleets of Venice, Spain, Genoa and the Papal states destroyed the greater part of the Turkish fleet on 7th October 1571. In the Sultan's court some people had blamed Lala Mustapha for this naval defeat because he had advised the Sultan to go ahead with the conquest of Cyprus.

After their establishment in Cyprus, the Sultan appointed *Muzaffar Pasha* as the first Governor of Cyprus. The Turks deprived the Latins of their rights and privileges and restored to the Greek Orthodox Christians their rights, which had been removed by the Franks and the Venetians. The Moslems had to pay a tenth of their produce as a form of tax and the Christians anything between 20 and 50%. Corruption was widespread. The Sultan had also appointed the Cypriot Church to help collect the taxes from the population.

## Archbishops of Cyprus during the Ottoman occupation

1. Timotheos 1571 - 79
2. Lavrentios 1579 - 86
3. Neophytos II 1586 - 92
4. Athanasios I 1592 - 98
5. Veniamin 1600 - 04
6. Christodoulos 1606 - 39
7. Parthenios 1639 - 40
8. Nikeforos 1641 - 74
9. Ilarion Kigalas 1674 - 79
10. Iakovos I 1679 - 89
11. Germanos II 1690 - 1705
12. Athanasios II 1705 - 07
13. Iakovos II 1707 - 18
14. Silvestros 1718 - 33
15. Filotheos 1734 - 59
16. Paisios 1759 - 61

17.Chrysanthos 1768 - 1810
18. Kyprianos 1810 - 21
19. Ioakim   1821 - 24
20. Damaskinos 1824 - 27
21. Panaretos 1827 - 40

22. Ioannikios II 1840 - 49
23. Kyrillos I   1849 - 54
24. Makarios I   1854 - 65
25. Sofronios II 1865 - 1900

In 1660 the Sultan recognised Archbishop Nikeforos (1641 - 1674) and the three Bishops as the unofficial guardians of the *rayahs* (Greek Cypriot population) and granted them the right to petition him directly. In 1754 the Porte issued a firman (Decree) appointing the bishops as the official representatives and supervisors of the people. It was further decided that as from 1754 the taxation should be 21½ piastres per head on 10,066 assessments. The bishops were therefore responsible to collect this money and should the population decrease then they should make sure that they paid the fixed amount.

This recognition of the Archbishop and the three Bishops as *political leaders and representatives* of the Christians was very significant because it affected the subsequent role of the Church.   The Church had now acquired official status.   Some   Archbishops   visited   the   Sultans   in Constantinople and spoke about the problems of the Cypriot   population. The Archbishop was therefore recognised as   the *Ethnarch* (the national leader) of all Greek Cypriots. In later times (in the 1950s) Makarios used this position as Ethnarch to speak on behalf of all Greek Cypriots and negotiate with the   British about the future of Cyprus.

Through the influence of the Cyprus Church, some Greek Cypriots rose to prominence and were appointed as *Dragomans*. A *Dragoman* was originally an official interpreter at the Sultan's Court but eventually became one of the important offices of state. The main role of the Dragoman (who worked closely with the Pasha) was mainly that of an administrator and a tax collector. The Dragoman himself was exempt from paying taxes and wore a distinctive uniform. He also had the right to communicate with the Sultan.

One very unpopular Dragoman during the period 1669 - 1674 was Markoullis, who imposed such heavy taxes that forced many Greek Cypriots either to emigrate or to accept the Islamic faith in order to avoid the heavy burden of taxation imposed on the Christian population.

*Nicosia; Lacroix-Lemaitre after Cassas; steel engraving 1853*

## Social and Economic Unrest
## The 25th October 1764 Uprising

In 1764 **Chil Osman Agha**, was appointed as the new Governor of Cyprus. He used his position to make as much money as possible and so decided to double the taxation. The taxes in 1754 were 21 ½ piastres and Chil Osman decided to raise it to 42 piastres. This cruel decision offended the already desperate population, because, in the early 1760's many people were at the point of starvation. Others were seriously affected by the plagues and others saw no other solution but to emigrate.

When the Bishops protested about the unfairness, Chil Osman had them arrested and placed under guard at the Archbishop's house so that they may not attempt to send a delegation to the Sultan and complain about this matter. Many Turkish notables also protested and a certain Hadji Vasilis from the village of Mia Milia was secretly sent to report this to the Sultan. The Sultan had issued an Order not to raise taxes and sent a messenger to investigate the matter. A meeting was arranged at the **Saray** (the Governor's Palace) on 25 October 1764. This was attended by Chil Osman, the Archbishop and Bishops, the Sultan's messenger and other leading Turks and Greeks.

As Chil Osman was speaking, saying that he was wrongly accused to the Porte, part of the floor collapsed and those attending found themselves in the basement. As it was the eve of St. Demetrios annual fair, large numbers had gathered near the Saray. When news soon spread that the floor had collapsed, the people immediately suspected that it was a plot to kill their religious leaders. Greeks and Turks attacked the Palace and although the Governor's bodyguard fired upon them, they broke into the Saray, killed Chil Osman and eighteen of his men, including the Sultan's representative. The Saray was then looted of its treasures and set on fire.

The Sultan sent Commissioners to Nicosia to investigate and the administrators promised them to re-build the Saray and restore all the looted treasures. The new Governor, in order to recover the damages, imposed a tax of 500,000 piastres and demanded that the Greeks should pay fourteen and the Turks seven piastres per head. The Greeks began to pay this new tax but the Turks refused, blaming the Greeks for what had happened.

In April 1765 the military commander of Kyrenia, *Khalil Agha*, together with three hundred of his supporters captured the Water Mills at Kythrea and demanded that the tax should be abolished. In August 1765 Khalil Agha issued orders to Greeks and Turks to refuse to pay this additional tax. He also wanted to punish the Aghas of Nicosia and the bishops because he blamed them for what had happened and demanded that they should be handede to him. He tried unsuccessfully to capture Famagusta and Nicosia.

Many Church leaders feared for their lives. Archbishop Paisios together with the bishops of Kyrenia and Paphos went to Constantinople where they reported to the Sultan of what had happened. A force was sent to Cyprus, Khalil Agha was arrested and executed and two hundred of his supporters were beheaded. Khalil's rebellion collapsed.

In 1771, an illiterate, notorious one-eyed Turkish peasant called *Abdul Haji Baki* rose to prominence through bribes, first as Chief of the Treasury.  In 1775 Haji Ali Agha was appointed as Governor and wanted to get rid of Haji Baki but the latter succeeded in persuading the Governor's doctor to poison him.  When Haji Baki succeeded in eliminating Haji Ali's deputy as well, he persuaded the bishops and the other Turkish officials to recommend him to the Porte to be the new Governor. He became Governor in 1777 and ruled until 1783 when he used his position to amass great wealth. The bishops went to Constantinople to complain about his corruption and cruelty. They were supported by the Greek Dragoman *Hajigeorghakis Kornesios* and eventually Baki was recalled,  tried, found guilty and had to pay a very heavy fine.

### *Hajigeorghakis Kornesios,  Dragoman for 30 years 1779 - 1809*

Hajigeorghakis Kornesios was born in Paphos and  was married to Archbishop Chrysanthos' niece. He became a Dragoman during Haji Baki's notorious governorship in 1779 when Abdul Hamid I was Sultan. In 1796 he was made by the Sultan Selim III  a Cyprus Dragoman for life and answerable only to the Sultan. Kornesios succeeded in persuading the Sultan to remove Haji Baki from his position in Cyprus because of his cruel methods in exacting taxes from the population.

Kornesios' position as the Greek Dragoman and the main Tax Collector of Cyprus meant that he was in sole control of the economic life of the island.  Kornesios like all his predecessors committed excesses and injustices and amassed great wealth.  His Mansion in Nicosia (which still survives) became  the centre point of meetings for the Aghas, Pashas and other dignitaries. His wealth was such that he was able to contribute towards the building of three Greek churches in Nicosia and also funded the Monastery at Chrysoroyiatissa.

*Hajigeorghakis Kornesios*

*Hajigeorghakis' Mansion in Nicosia*

## The 1804 Uprising

By the Treaty of Kutchuk Kainardji in 1774, Russia had been given the right to protect Orthodox Christians in the Balkans, which were under the Ottoman Empire. The Greek Church in Cyprus looked for support from fellow Orthodox Russia. The growing authority of the Archbishop and the Greek Dragoman was greatly resented by many Turkish Aghas in Cyprus. In 1804 the increase in taxation had prompted angry crowds to attack Kornesios' Mansion (who managed to escape to Constantinople) and also Archbishop Chrysanthos. Kornesios appealed to the Sultan who sent 2,000 troops to crash the rebels. This was the first time that the Ottoman Empire were punishing Turks in Cyprus at the request of the Greeks! Hajigeorghakis Kornesios, who was Dragoman for thirty years, was accused of being corrupt and was beheaded in April 1809.

In order to make tax collection easier, the Turks divided the Island into *17 Districts*: *Nicosia, Kythrea, Mesaoria, Famagusta, Limassol, Larnaca, Koilani, Avdemou, Kyrenia, Morphou, Pentayia, Lefka, Paphos, Chrysohou, Kouklia, Karpasia and Episkopi*.

Later in the 19th century Cyprus was divided into six districts, the districts which exist to this day, i.e. Nicosia, Famagusta, Larnaca, Limassol, Paphos and Kyrenia.

## The "Philiki Etairia" (1814) and the Greek War of Independence (1821)

When the French Revolution broke out in 1789 and the French people were demanding *Liberty, Equality and Fraternity*, their demands were destined to influence the peoples of the rest of Europe. The people of Greece who were ruled by the Turks for nearly four hundred years rose against the Ottoman Empire in 1821 demanding their freedom and national independence.

In 1814 a Secret Society called the *"Philiki Etairia"* (Friendly Society) was initially formed by Greek emigres in Odessa (in Russia) in order to prepare the Greek War of Independence. The revolution broke out in March 1821, first in the Peloponnese but soon spread to the islands and the rest of the country.

The rebellion of the Greeks had infuriated the Sultan *Mahmoud II.* He feared that their example would soon be imitated in other parts of the Empire, especially in the Balkans. He was therefore determined to crash both the Greek rebellion and any signs of disturbances in the Empire.

In 1810 Archbishop Chrysanthos died and was succeeded by Kyprianos. The new Archbishop was keen to promote Greek education and founded next to the Archbishopric, the *Hellenic School* (which later became known as the Pancyprian Gymnasium). The new Archbishop was contacted by the *Philiki Etairia* and promised to offer financial and moral support. There is no evidence however to show that he was actually a member of this Secret Society. In the spring of 1821 the Cypriot merchant

*Theophilos Theseas* came to Cyprus from France and distributed revolutionary proclamations and managed to escape arrest.

The Turkish Governor of Cyprus, **Kuchuk Mehmet** , had his own suspicions and fears that the Greek people of Cyprus would soon rise against the empire like their fellow Greeks in the mainland and the islands. He therefore informed the Sultan that there was an impending revolution and asked for permission to execute all the leading Greeks of the island including the Archbishop. The Sultan who had already hanged the Greek Patriarch Gregory V on Easter Sunday (1821) and executed the Grand Dragoman Mourouzes and other leading Greeks living in *Fanari* (in Constantinople) agreed to send additional troops.

Fearing the consequences of bloodshed on 16 May 1821 Archbishop Kyprianos issued an encyclical advising the Greek Orthodox population in Cyprus to remain calm. Kutchuk Mehmet however was not convinced about the sincerity of the Church leaders.

On 9 July 1821 Archbishop Kyprianos and the three bishops **Lavrentios** of Kyrenia, **Meletios** of Kition and **Chrysanthos** of Paphos were summoned at the Governor's Palace. They were accused of plotting for a revolution. The Archbishop was hanged on a mulberry tree in the Square in front of the Palace. The three bishops together with other leading Greeks were beheaded. The summer of 1821 was a period of terror. Hundreds of people young and old, from all walks of life were put to the sword; villages were burnt, churches were turned into mosques or stables, women were raped and it is estimated that some 20,000 Greeks left the island.

The Cypriot poet **Vasilis Michaelides** wrote a moving narrative poem in the Cypriot dialect entitled **The Ninth of July 1821** where he describes the tragic events.

**Archbishop Kyprianos hanged on 9 July 1821**

The success of the Greek War of Independence and the establishment of the new Greek state gave new hope to the Greek people of Cyprus. The Greek population of Cyprus being Christian Orthodox looked not only to the new Greek state but also to fellow Orthodox Russia for support and for deliverance.

**Cypriots with traditional holiday dress in the 19th c.**

# PART 3 - MODERN CYPRUS

## THE BRITISH RULE 1878 - 1960

### Administrators

Garnet Wolseley 1878
Robert Biddulph 1879
Henry Bulwer      1886
Walter Sendall    1892

### High Commissioners

William Haynes-Smith 1900
Charles King-Harman  1904
Hamilton      Goold-Adams 1911
John Clauson 1915
Malcolm Stevenson 1920

### Governors

Malcolm Stevenson 1925
Ronald Storrs 1926
Reginald Stubbs 1932
Herbert Palmer 1933
William Battershill 1939
Charles Woolley 1941
Reginald Fletcher 1946
Andrew Wright 1949
Robert Armitage 1954
John Harding 1955
Hugh Foot 1957 - 1960

In 1878  the Russo-Turkish war ended in a complete disaster for the Ottoman Empire. The Sultan signed the treaty of **San Stefano** which gave Russia many advantages in the region. The Russian victory and the terms of the treaty worried the British government and a new treaty was called for at  **Berlin** (1878). **Benjamin Disraeli**, the British Prime Minister, was determined to reduce the Russian influence in the region.

On  4 June 1878 Disraeli signed with  the Sultan the *"Defensive Alliance between Great Britain and Turkey"* whereby Great Britain agreed to protect the integrity of the

Ottoman Empire and in return the Ottoman Empire had offered Cyprus to Britain in order to allow the latter to carry out its obligations.   Britain also agreed to pay the Sultan £92,799,   *11 shillings and 3 pence* (!)   per annum, an amount  which was later collected from  the Cypriots in the form of taxes. On the 12 July 1878 the first British troops arrived in Cyprus and Disraeli had gone to inform Queen Victoria that   *"Cyprus is now our key to Western Asia"*.

**Cartoon in Punch (1878) showing Disraeli carrying the Sultan**

# SIR GARNET WOLSELEY (1833 - 1913)
## First British Administrator 1878 - 1879

When the British took over the Island in 1878, the Cypriots were described on all official documents not as Greek Cypriots or Turkish Cypriots but as **Moslems** or **Non-Moslems.** The Turkish Cypriots naturally did not object to be described as followers of their Prophet but the Greek Cypriots resented the fact that they were described as Non-Moslems.

The first British Administrator was an Army Officer **Sir Garnet Wolseley**, who was later made a Field Marshal. Before his appointment as British Administrator of Cyprus he served in the Crimean War (1854) where he lost an eye, the Indian Mutiny 1857-59, the Chinese War 1860 and the Ashanti War 1873-74. In July 1878 he was appointed as the first British Administrator of Cyprus where he served for just over a year. In 1882 he was appointed as Commander in Chief of the expedition to Egypt. In 1884 he commanded the Sudan expedition that arrived too late in Khartoum to save General Gordon.

When he arrived in Cyprus he was welcomed by **Kyprianos**, the Bishop of Kition who said that the Cypriots accept the change of administration and expressed the hope that Great Britain will help Cyprus, in the same way as they did with the Ionian Islands, in order to unite with their Greek Motherland. A little later **Archbishop Sofronios** addressed Sir Garnet Wolseley as follows:

" We hope that from now on, a new life begins for the people of Cyprus; a new great period, which will become memorable in the annals of the island. We hope that all *shall be instructed without distinction of race or creed, that law is the king of all; that all shall have equal rights and equal responsibility before the law, for equality of rights implies also equality of responsibility; that all shall be used to treating the good road, that is to say, the road of truth, of duty and of liberty."*

When Sir Garnet Wolseley replaced the Turkish Governor in 1878, he nominated six British officers to take the places of the Turkish **Kaimakams** to be in charge of the six administrative regions. According to C.W.Orr, when the British took over the island there were no roads, the harbours silted up, the peasants were apathetic, agriculture was languishing, trade and commerce undeveloped, and a general paralysis prevailed. *(Cyprus Under British Rule, p. 66).* The author attributes this great apathy and lack of incentive due to the fact that 80% of the money the Cypriots paid was taken out of the island to fill the coffers of their Ottoman masters in Constantinople.

In a Report that he sent to the Foreign Office, Sir Garnet Wolseley proposed the introduction of a railway line because, he argued, that such a line will be useful and beneficial for British military operations. The establishment, however of British bases in Egypt in 1882 led to a considerable delay and it was not until 1905 that the first railway line was introduced.

In 1879 Wolseley was replaced as Administrator by **Robert Biddulph.** It was during Biddulph's administration (1879-1886) that a uniform system of currency was introduced because various currencies were in use in different parts of the island.

*The first British High Commissioner Sir Garnet Wolseley*

The value of the English sovereign was fixed at 180 piastres in 1879 and copper coins was struck for Cyprus bearing the effigy of Queen Victoria and consisting of piastres, half piastres and quarter piastres. In 1900 a silver coinage was issued, consisting of pieces of 18, 9, 41/2 and 3 piastres, equivalent to 2s., 1s., 6d., and 4d of English money. (*C.W. Orr: Cyprus Under British Rule, p.67*).

In 1880 the political and administrative affairs of Cyprus were directed by the Colonial Office instead of the Foreign Office. In the autumn of 1881 a Colonial official, G. Fairfield, was sent to Cyprus to report upon the administrative requirements of the island. As a result of Fairfield's Report a number of administrative reforms were introduced. A Constitution was granted in 1882 which provided a Legislative Council of 12 elected members and gave the people a direct voice in the management of their affairs.

*Archbishop Sofronios 1865 - 1900*

Britain took over the Island in 1878 mainly for strategic reasons. Four years later in 1882 Britain took over Egypt which served as a military and naval base. As a result, Cyprus was of lesser importance and consequently the economy and construction works were neglected.

*Greek Cypriot priests blessing the British flag*

# THE RISE OF GREEK CYPRIOT NATIONALISM

## The First Move Towards *"Enosis"* but Opposed by the Greek Government

In 1879, i.e. a year after the British took over the island, some Greek Cypriot secret organisations were founded in order to promote the cause of **Enosis**. In Larnaca, which was the town with the foreign Consulates, the newspaper called **Enosis** appeared for the first time and openly propagated the union of Cyprus with Greece. Many Greek Cypriots were encouraged by the example of the Cretan struggle to unite with Greece.

In April 1899 **Spyros Araouzos** and **N. Katalanos** went to Athens to petition the Greek Government to take up the issue of Cyprus and to appoint Prince Nicholas as *"High Commissioner"* for Cyprus in the same way as Prince George (the King's elder son) was appointed for Crete. The visit of the Cypriot delegation was only two years after Greece's crashing defeat in the 1897 war against Turkey. **G. Theotokis,** the Greek Prime Minister, consulted **King George I** on this matter. The King who owed his position (his throne) to the British (they had appointed him as King of Greece in 1863), naturally opposed the patriotic activities of the Cypriots. The recent crashing defeat of Greece in 1897 prompted Theotokis to advise the Cypriot delegation with these words:

*"Return back to Cyprus and back to your work. Crete has created numerous problems for us and nearly ruined us. For God's sake do not rebel. The English will destroy you*

*and will turn your island into a bloodbath. The Greek state is not in a position to help you. Even if it was, it would not dare create a "Cyprus Problem". You must understand that we are not in a position to clash with Great Britain. In any case, Cyprus is far away from the other Greek islands and I doubt if ever it will separate from the British Empire."
(Yiannis Kordatos: A History of Modern Greece, Vol. 5. p. 21).*

In 1907 Winston Churchill, then Colonial Secretary, visited Cyprus. A delegation of Greek Cypriots visited him with a petition for *Enosis.* Churchill's response was the following:

*" I think it only natural that the Cypriot people, who are of Greek descent, should regard their incorporation with what may be called their mother country as an ideal to be earnestly, devoutly and fervently cherished. Such a feeling is an example of the patriotic devotion which so nobly characterizes the Greek nation.... I say that the views which have been put forward are views which His Majesty's Government do not refuse to regard with respect."*

## THE ROLE OF THE CHURCH
### Archbishops of Cyprus during British rule (1878 - 1960)

Sofronios 1865 - 1900
Kyrillos II (Papadopoulos) 1909 - 1916
Kyrillos III (Vassiliou) 1916 - 1933
Vacancy   1933 - 1947

Leontios Leontiou 1947 (June-July)
Makarios II (Myriantheas) 1947 - 1950
Makarios III (Mouskos) 1950  - 1977

As we have seen in the previous chapter, the privileges accorded to the Orthodox Church by the Ottoman Empire had helped to make the various Archbishops both religious and political leaders of the Greek Cypriots. Thus, when the British took over Cyprus in 1878, the Greek Orthodox Archbishop of Cyprus, **Sofronios**, welcomed the first British Administrator on behalf of the people. Sofronios was Archbishop for 35 years, i.e. from 1865 to 1900. During the Administration of **Henry Bulwer** (1886 - 1892) Sofronios led the first mission to London in 1889.

Sofronios went to London in order to plead with the British Government to show understanding and leniency, especially on the heavy taxation imposed on the Cypriot people. He also expressed his concerns about education, the constitutional powers of the Legislative Council, the condition of the Orthodox Church and other matters. During his visit, Archbishop Sofronios was received by Queen Victoria and was also awarded the Degree of Doctor of Divinity by the University of Oxford. The Archbishop also held the view that British rule will constitute "*the golden bridge which will unite Cyprus with Greece*". The Conservative Government of Lord Salisbury was not very sympathetic to the requests of Sofronios.

Sofronios died on 22 May 1900. His death however, had left a nine year vacuum in the archiepiscopal position which was caused by the rivalry of two Bishops: the Bishop of Kition **Kyrillos Papadopoulos** (called by the people as **Kyrillatsos** because he was heavily built) and the Bishop of Kyrenia **Kyrillos Vasiliou** (called by the people as **Kyrilloudhi** because he was small built). As a result of this rivalry the position of Archbishop remained vacant for nine years, until 21 April 1909, when the Bishop of Kition, Kyrillos Papadopoulos **(Kyrillatsos)** was elected Archbishop as Kyrillos II. The Bishop of Kition was elected under the Archiepiscopal Election Law whilst the Bishop of Kyrenia was appointed as Archbishop by the Patriarchate at Constantinople. The dispute between the two contestants lasted for ten years and was finally resolved when two new Bishops were elected in Paphos and Kition and the Bishop from Kyrenia accepted Kyrillos II (*Kyrillatsos)* as the new Archbishop.

*Kyrillos II* died in 1916 and was succeeded by his previous rival Kyrillos Vasiliou *(Kyrilloudhi)* as *Kyrillos III* who remained Archbishop until 1933. From 1933 until 1947 the Archiepiscopal position was vacant. In 1947 *Leontios* was elected but he died two months later. The Bishop of Kyrenia Makarios Myriantheas succeeded him (1947 - 1950) as *Makarios II.* When Makarios II died in June 1950 he was succeeded in October 1950 by the Bishop of Kition Michael Mouskos as *Makarios III* (1950 - 1977). When Makarios III died in August 1977 he was succeeded by *Chrysostomos*, the Bishop of Paphos and the current Archbishop (2001).

*Archbishop Chrysostomos (1977 - )*

# BRITAIN ANNEXES CYPRUS 1914
## The First World War and the Treaties of Sevres 1920 and Lausanne 1923

When the First World War broke out in 1914 and Turkey joined the war on the side of Germany, Britain used this opportunity to annexe Cyprus. On 5 November 1914, the British were not only celebrating "Guy Fawkes Day," but also for adding Cyprus as part of their Empire! On 10 August 1920, the *Treaty of Sevres* (near Paris) was signed. The three specific articles on Cyprus are Articles 115, 116 and 117 and state the following:

Article 115: *"The High Contracting Parties recognize the annexation of Cyprus proclaimed by the British Government on 5 November 1914."*

Article 116: *"Turkey renounces all rights and titles to Cyprus, including the right to the tribute formerly 'paid' to the Sultan."*

Article 117: *"Turkish nationals born or resident in Cyprus will acquire British nationality and lose their Turkish nationality."*

On 24 July 1923, the *Treaty of Lausanne* (Switzerland) was signed. Articles 16, 20 and 21 are of particular interest because they specify the following:

Article 16: *"Turkey hereby renounces all rights and titles whatsoever over or respecting the territories situated outside the frontiers laid down in the present Treaty and the islands other than those for which her sovereignty is recognized by the said Treaty."*

Article 20: *"Turkey hereby recognizes the annexation of Cyprus by the British Government on 5 November 1914."*

Article 21: *"Turkish nationals ordinarily resident in Cyprus on 5 November 1914 will acquire British nationality subject to the conditions laid down in local law and will thereupon lose their Turkish nationality. They will, however, have the right to opt for Turkish nationality within two years from the coming into force of the present Treaty, provided that they leave Cyprus within twelve months after having so opted."*

The Turkish Government opened a Consulate in Larnaca and appointed Assaf-Bey as Consul in order to help those Turkish Cypriots who wanted to move to mainland Turkey. In fact by 1927 only 3,000 Turks opted for the Turkish nationality.

The same Treaty (Article 15) had in fact betrayed Venizelos and the other Greek nationalist aspirations because it gave Rhodes and the other Dodecanese Islands to Italy.

In 1925 Cyprus became a **Crown Colony**. **Sir Malcolm Stevenson**, who was the British High Commissioner since 1920, became the first **British Governor**.

During the First World War, in 1915, the British Government, anxious to enlist the support of Greece on the side of the Allies in order to support Serbia, made the following proposal offering Cyprus to Greece. The British Foreign Secretary **Sir Edward Grey**, sent the following telegram on 16 October 1915 to **Sir Francis Elliot**, the British Ambassador in Athens, in order to convince the Greek Government to join the war :

"His Majesty's Government are asking the support of Greece for Serbia believing that it is especially in the interests of Greece to prevent Serbia from being crushed. If Greece is prepared to give support as an Ally to Serbia, now that she has been attacked by Bulgaria, **His Majesty's Government will be prepared to give Cyprus to Greece**. Should Greece join the Allies for all purposes she would naturally have a share with them in advantages secured at the end of the war, **but the offer of Cyprus is made by His Majesty's Government independently on condition that Greece gives immediate and full support with her army to Serbia.**"

On the same day (16 October 1915) the Colonial Secretary **Bonar Law** sent the following telegram to **John Clauson** the High Commissioner in Cyprus in order to get the Archbishop to urge the Greek Government to accept the offer:

"His Majesty's Government feel that in the present emergency no effort must be spared to induce Greece to go to the help of Serbia in accordance with her treaty obligations. They have therefore **offered to give Cyprus to Greece on condition that Greece gives immediate and full support with her Army to Serbia**. Please communicate this fact to the Archbishop or other leading personages in Cyprus and suggest to them that if they wish to take advantage of this opportunity for securing the union of Cyprus with Greece, **which is unlikely to recur**, they should immediately proceed to Athens and press their demand on the King and Parliament."

Greek politics, as well as politicians ever since the Independence of Greece, were divided and reflected either pro-British, pro-French, pro-German or pro-Russian interests. At the time when the offer was made, the Government of **Zaimis** was in power and the offer was refused by the pro-German government.

A few months earlier, when the Allies were offering Northern Epirus to Greece in order to induce her to join in the war, the pro-German **King Constantine** rejected the offer much to the protestations of **Eleftherios Venizelos** the Prime Minister (who was pro-British) and who resigned in protest. Earlier, the pro-German Queen also protested about the Allies' offers to get Greece involved in the war against Germany and said that *"if a single German soldier was killed by a Greek she would immediately leave Greece for ever"*.

In February 1919, the leader of the Labour Party **Ramsay Macdonald** speaking to 102 delegates from 26 countries at the Socialist International Conference in Berne, Switzerland, stated that the Labour Party supported the Cypriots' right of self-determination and promised that if they came to power they would fulfil this pledge. Five years later in 1924, Macdonald was the first British Labour Prime Minister but had already forgotten what he had promised!

In December 1918 a further deputation led by Archbishop Kyrillos III with the 8 Greek members of the Legislative Council went to London to press once again for the same demand, i.e. the *Union of Cyprus with Greece*. The British Government who three years earlier were offering Cyprus to Greece now did not want to know.

After the defeat of Greece in Asia Minor in 1922 the Greek

**"Grand Idea"** to incorporate various Greek speaking regions in the Eastern Mediterranean had collapsed. In 1923 under the **Treaty of Lausanne**, signed by Britain, France, Italy, Japan, Greece, Romania and Turkey, the annexation of Cyprus by Britain was recognised (article 20) and Turkey renounced all her rights on the Island.

In February 1925 the membership of the Legislative Council was increased from 19 to 25. The Greek elected members were increased from 9 to 12, the British non-elective members (appointed) were increased from 6 to 9 and the number of Turkish elective members remained the same at three. There was also one position, that of the Governor.

In November 1925 the 12 Greek Members of the Legislative Council presented a petition to **Governor Stevenson** demanding the union of Cyprus with Greece. The members were told that the **"Enosis"** Union issue was closed. The Government in Greece was not prepared to take on the cause of **Enosis** because the British exerted great influence in Greek foreign policy and did not wish to upset the Anglo-Greek "**entente cordiale**" which existed since Independence. Furthermore, the recent terrible disaster in Asia Minor in 1922 with the influx of about one and a half million refugees was an added factor for the Greek Government not to pursue adventurous policies which might lead to further disasters.

# THE GOVERNORSHIP OF SIR RONALD STORRS 1926 - 1932

In November 1926, *Sir Ronald Storrs* replaced Malcolm Stevenson as Governor of Cyprus. Storrs described himself as a *"philhellene"*. In his book *"Orientations"*, he wrote:

*"The Greekness of the Cypriots is, in my opinion, indisputable. A man is of the race which he passionately feels himself to be."*

Although he was a lover of Classical Greece and he often recited verses from Homer to some leading Greek Cypriots, he said that *he was not appointed to give away portions of the British Empire!*

During official ceremonies the *Mufti,* who was the leader of the Moslem community (Turkish Cypriots), always sat on the right of the Governor indicating (according to protocol and custom) his great importance. The Greek Cypriot Archbishop was considered less important and sat on the Governor's left side. Storrs "reversed" this custom of "seniority" in order to reflect the importance of the ethnic leader of the larger community (the Greek Cypriots). In order not to upset the Mufti about this new "re-arrangement" Storrs told the Mufti very cunningly the following:

*"In all future official ceremonies I will have you sit on my left because that is where my heart is. Even the Koran states that the heart is the most important part of the body!"*

Storrs was a staunch anti-communist and in 1928 he used the Seditious Publications Law of 1921 to ban 15 publications. The Communist Party of Cyprus K.K.K. (*Kommounistiko Komma Kyprou*) which was formed in 1926 was made illegal and its newspaper *Neos Anthropos* (New Man) was forced to close down in 1929.

In 1928 Storrs wanted to celebrate the 50th anniversary of the British occupation (1878 - 1928) and sporting activities and other celebrations were arranged. Eleftherios Venizelos, the pro-British Greek statesman advised the Greek Cypriots to take part in the events. The Communist newspaper **Neos Anthropos** in a leading article in January 1928 called upon the Cypriots to boycott these jubilee celebrations because, it said: *"the conqueror has been milking for fifty years the Cypriot cow which has therefore ceased to yield"*. As a result of harsh treatment, the vast majority of Cypriots boycotted the celebrations.

The economic depression which prevailed in most parts of the world was particularly severe in Cyprus where people had to rely on agriculture which was affected by the long drought periods. The poor people were forced to sell their land to money lenders. As if the Cypriots' economic suffering was not enough, the Colonial Government wanted to raise more money through taxation. It could only do this through the approval of the **Legislative Council**. The membership of this Council consisted of 25 people: 12 Greeks, 3 Turks and 9 British non-elective Members plus the Governor.

In September 1931, Sir Ronald Storrs, the Governor, wanted to introduce a new **Customs Tariff**. He expected to win in the Council by using the 9 British non-elective (appointed) Members and also expected the 3 Turks to vote with him and together with his casting vote he could have the majority (i.e. 13 out of 25). It so happened however, that one Turk, **Nejati Bey**, voted together with the 12 Greeks because he sympathised with the economic plight and suffering of the people.

The Governor was furious for losing this vote (13 : 12) and in order to raise the taxes he issued a **New Order** so that he could override the decision of the Council. Later, in his Memoirs, entitled **Orientations** (p. 590), Sir Ronald Storrs described Nejati Bey the Turkish Member of the Council who voted with the 12 Greeks as *"the little Turk - who became the 13th Greek and voted with his traditional enemies"*. The Governor's decision to impose the further taxes not only infuriated the people but it exacerbated the situation.

## THE OCTOBER 1931 UPRISING
### Nicodemos Mylonas

On 30 May 1929 the Labour Party in Britain won the General Election for a second time (the first Labour victory was in 1924) with a very small majority. In June a minority Government was formed under Ramsay MacDonald. The victory of the Labour Party had revived the hopes of the Greek Cypriot Nationalists who believed that the new British Government will be more sympathetic to their cause.

One of the leading members of the Cyprus Legislative Council was **Nicodemos Mylonas**, the Bishop of Kition who was a fiery orator. He was the cousin of Archbishop Kyrillos III. Bishop Nicodemos was such an eloquent speaker that even Sir Ronald Storrs commented in his "Orientations" that *"the Legislative Council would not be the same without the presence of Bishop Nicodemos*

*Mylonas."*

In October 1929 Nicodemos Mylonas led a three-man delegation and came to London to put the case of Cyprus to the new Labour Government. The delegation met with the Colonial Secretary **Lord Passfield** and told him that it is the Cypriots' aspirations to unite with Greece because they have the same language, religion, culture and traditions. The Colonial Secretary listened to their demands and replied a month later stating that *"His Majesty's Government are unable to accede to these demands."*

When Governor Storrs imposed the Customs Tariff and ignored the majority wishes of the Legislative Council, Nicodemos Mylonas summoned the Greek members to **Saittas**, a village in the Troodos mountains in order to decide what action to take. The members met again at the beginning of October 1931.

On 17 October 1931, Nicodemos Mylonas tendered his resignation from the Legislative Council and issued a fiery manifesto which advocated resistance to British rule. He stated among other things that:

*"Subjugated people are never liberated by pleas and begging to their masters because they would only ignore them. Our salvation can only be our national freedom. The reason for the presence of the foreign rulers in our country is to maintain and preserve their interests at the expense of our moral and material wretchedness".*

On 20 October 1931 Nicodemos together with **Nicholas Lanitis** and **Zenon Rossides** addressed a crowd of some 3,000 people in a sports stadium in Limassol.

*The Government House burnt down in the October 1931 uprising*

News of the Bishop's passionate speech for the struggle of *Enosis* and to disobey the colonial laws, was conveyed by telegram to the Secretary of the National Organization in Nicosia.

Members of the **National Union** met in Nicosia on 21 October 1931 and urged people to ring the church bells in order to summon people. **Dionysios Kykkotis**, a priest at the Phaneromeni Church in Nicosia, made another pro-Enosis speech and he was presented with the Greek flag. He urged his congregation to defend the Greek flag. It was at this point that the crowd shouted to march to the Government House.

At about 7.00 p.m. the crowd carrying the Greek flag headed for the Government House. Police re-enforcements arrived. The crowd chanted slogans of *Enosis* and demanded to see the Governor. Stones were thrown. At about 11.00 p.m. the Government House (which was a wooden bungalow) was set on fire. Shots were fired by the police and an 18 year old, **Onoufrios Clerides**, was killed and 15 others were injured.

News of the uprising in Nicosia spread and demonstrations took place in all the other towns, especially outside police barracks. Schools were closed and business suspended. Two days after the uprising (23rd October 1931) the Greek statesman Eleftherios Venizelos condemned the riots, thus showing once again his pro-British sentiments. In a statement issued soon after the events, Venizelos declared that *"there was no Cypriot question between the governments of Britain and Greece, but only between the British Government and the people of Cyprus."*

Venizelos was too dependent on British Foreign policy and was not prepared to pursue an "adventurous" policy over Cyprus and thus risk the excellent ties he maintained with the British Government. Greek nationalists and passionate supporters of **Enosis** however, described him as a modern Pontius Pilate "who washed his hands" over the Cyprus issue.

As a result of the **21st October 1931** uprising 2,952 people were arrested and tried and 2,679 were convicted. The following ten people were deported:

1. *Nicodemos Mylonas*, Bishop of Kition.
2. *Makarios,* Bishop of Kyrenia (Later as Archbishop Makarios II)
3. *Dionysios Kykkotis*, Nicosia priest.
4. *Theofanis Tsangarides*, Trade Union leader.

5. *Theodoros Kolokasides*, Trade Union leader.
6. *Savvas Loizides*, Trade Union leader.
7. *George Hadjipavlou*, Member of the Legislative Council.
8. *Theofanis Theodotou*, Member of the Legislative Council.
9. *Haralambos Vatyliotis (Vatis)* , Communist leader.
10. *Costas Skeleas*, Communist leader.

In November 1931 the Governor abolished the **Legislative Council** and stricter dictatorial measures were imposed. In 1932 Ronald Storrs was replaced by **Reginald Stubbs**, and Stubbs in turn was replaced in 1933 by **Herbert Palmer**.

**Nicodemos Mylonas, Bishop of Kition**

Nicodemos Mylonas, the passionate Bishop and advocate for **Enosis** decided eventually to leave London (from his exile) and go and retire in Jerusalem. The ship he was travelling stopped at Pireas and according to Ploutis Servas, he wanted to disembark and *"kiss the soil of the*

*Greek motherland*," but the pro-British Greek Government of Venizelos, which was so sub-servient to British interests, would not even grant him this basic wish, for fear of upsetting the British Government! (P. Servas: *Efthynes,* Vol. 1. pp. 92 - 93). Nicodemos who so passionately tried to unite Cyprus with Greece, *was not even allowed (by Venizelos), the Greek Prime Minister, to disembark for even a few minutes!* He died in Jerusalem in 1937.

# HERBERT PALMER 1933 - 1939
## Palmer's Dictatorial Measures and Post-war developments

Some of the dictatorial measures imposed on the Cypriots soon after the October 1931 uprising, remind one of the dictatorial legislation which was imposed on the British people itself some 120 years previously, especially after the riots on Manchester in 1819, which became known as the Peterloo Massacres. At that time the Government of Lord Liverpool, at the insistence of Lord Sidmouth, introduced the notorious **Six Acts** of 1819 which came to be known as the "Six Gag Acts". In the case of Cyprus the following measures were introduced:

1. Press censorship was introduced.
2. In August 1933 the Communist Party (KKK) was proscribed.
3. Meetings of more than five people were prohibited.
4. The flying of the Greek flag was prohibited.
5. Ringing of Church bells was restricted to church services.
6. Municipal elections were abolished.
7. Trade Unions were forbidden.

8. Tax imposed on land to collect £34,315 to cover the cost of damages to property.

These measures remind one of similar ones imposed on the British people in the late 18th and early 19th centuries. When the Second World War ended in 1945 and Fascism and Nazism were defeated, the Cypriots like all other colonial people believed that it was now the time to be granted their national independence. They had high hopes because many thousands fought on the side of the British and many of them lost their lives fighting for the same cause: **For Freedom and Democracy**. Their hopes and aspirations were raised especially since there was a new Labour Government in Britain under Clement Atlee. These proved to be short-lived however, even though India was granted Independence in 1947. This was seen as a good starting sign that the "*snow of the colonial rule was beginning to melt, but it was melting very slowly.*"

## THE RISE OF SOCIALISM

The success of the Bolshevik Revolution in Russia in 1917 and the ideas and teachings of *Karl Marx* and *Vladimir Illich Lenin* had encouraged the formation of Communist parties in many parts of the world. The idea of forming the *Communist Party of Cyprus (KKK)* began in 1925 by *Dr. Nicholas Yiavopoulos* who studied Medicine in Athens and was a member of the *Greek Communist Party (K.K.E.)*. Dr Yiavopoulos and his son-in-law *Dr Vassos Vassiliou* published the fortnightly newspaper *Neos Anthropos* (New Man). Dr. Yiavopoulos was later expelled from the Party accused as a "*Trotskyist*".

The first Party Congress was held on the *14th August 1926* and *Costas Skeleas* was elected as the first General Secretary. Later *Haralambos Vatyliotis (Vatis)* took over as leader until 1931. Skeleas and Vatyliotis were exiled soon after the October 1931 uprising and both of them lived and worked in the Soviet Union where they both died.

After the departure of Skeleas and Vatyliotis, *Costas Kononas* (supposedly a moderate) took over as the General Secretary until the KKK was proscribed in August 1933. Kononas eventually left the party and abandoned his ideology and helped to find the right wing Trades Union (SEK) and many years later worked as editor of the right wing newspaper called *"Patris"* (Fatherland).

*Haralambos Vatyliotis and Costas Skeleas two pioneers of socialism in Cyprus in the 1920s*

*Ploutis Servas* (1907 - 2001) took over the leadership of the KKK in 1936. He believed in giving the party a broader base and a wider appeal and in 1941 he helped to amalgamate the KKK with the new Party called AKEL.

# SOCIAL AND ECONOMIC CONDITIONS DURING THE FIRST HALF OF THE 20TH CENTURY

*Living Conditions.* C.W. Orr's book provides a vivid picture of the living conditions of the Cypriot peasants:

*"When a peasant wants money .... he is compelled to have resource to the usurer, who usually lends him money with the following condition: Interest to be 24%; the payment to be made in kind, with a discount of 15% from the current price; the interest to paid entirely, even if the ingathering of the produce is approaching; a juggling theft at the time the produce is weighed; and moreover when the entries are made in the book, if the produce that is given to the peasant or credit is barley, which is worth one piastre the kilo it is put down at three piastres; if it is worth 3d the oke, at 9d, and so forth in the same proportion, the capital being also charged with interest." (Cyprus Under British Rule, p. 149).*

Although the above was a reference to 1889, similar conditions prevailed during the first thirty years of the 20th century. There was poverty in most parts of the island. In the villages most of the houses were built of mud bricks and there was no sanitation. Very few villages had electricity or water supply and the roads were mainly dirt tracks. It was after the Second World War that things gradually began to improve. Working conditions were very harsh, people used to work from sunrise to sunset all year round and **Sunday was not made a day of rest until 1907.**

**Medical Care**: Medical care during the first quarter of the 20th century was almost non-existent. The infant mortality rate before the 1950s was very high. Children often died from meningitis and other diseases. Eye infections were common, especially with *trachoma*. Sanitation was almost non-existent and people often used the public baths

**Education**: Primary education before the Second World War was similarly almost non-existent and was not compulsory. As a result, the rate of illiteracy among the poorer sections of society was very high. There were very few Secondary Schools, which were mainly in the towns and Secondary Education was not free. Only those children who could afford to pay the fees could attend and there were many instances where poorer pupils were sent home because they were unable to pay their fees.

**Agriculture**: The vast majority of the population during the first half of the 20th century worked on the land. In the 1920s and 1930s some poor people often worked with farmers and their only reward was just food and clothing. Very rarely they were paid one or two pounds for the whole year! The frequent droughts and poor harvests had left the poorer farmers often at the mercy of the money lenders and they were often forced to sell their small plots of land at ridiculous prices in order to repay their loans. As a result many of them found themselves bankrupt and many more agricultural workers found themselves out of work. From the 1930s onwards there was a gradual move from the villages to the nearby towns in search for work. Most of them worked for very long hours and lived in derelict conditions.

**Forced Unpaid Labour:** In the late 1920's, it was a well known fact that forced unpaid labour was in operation, especially for road-making. The Labour MP, **Fenner**

*Brockway* (later Lord Brockway, a well known anti-colonialist and a great friend of Cyprus), asked Dr Shields the Under-Secretary for Colonies about this very issue in June 1931 and was told that: "Amending legislation has been enacted to put an end of compulsory labour for village road construction."

*Transport*:: As mentioned previously, there were no proper roads in 1878. A Road Network programme had commenced in 1881 and was extended in 1904. The arrival of the car came late in Cyprus. Before the Second World War donkeys and mules and carts were used as means of transport. Some farmers took their vegetable products to sell to the markets in their nearby towns. Apart from the Famagusta-Nicosia rail line (which closed down in 1951) public transport was practically non-existent before 1945. Many people never visited other towns apart from their nearest. For example, some people who lived in some villages in Famagusta and had no connections with Limassol or Paphos or Polis would never see these places in their lifetime. (*This is also true of the present writer: I never visited Larnaca town until 1952 when my elder brother took the boat to come to England!*). Pilgrims to some of the Monasteries often took days to get there and back.

*The Railway in Cyprus 1905 - 1951*: The first railway line commenced in 1905 and connected Nicosia the capital with the port town of Famagusta in the east, a distance of some 36 miles. In 1932 the line was extended to Morphou, to the west of Nicosia. The railway line however, was not destined to last for long and with the advent of the motor car, the whole railway system closed down in 1951, 45 years after its introduction.

**Annual Fairs**: These were held in many larger villagers on the name day of the patron saint of the village. At these village fairs all sorts of products would be sold. At the village of Peristerona (in Famagusta) for example, at the feast of St Anastasios on the 17th September, in addition to the usual sale of various goods they would sell and buy livestock. There, one could buy and take back to their village a horse, a mule or a donkey.

**Social Life:** Cypriot society during the first half of the 20th century was very patriarchal. The male domination was visible everywhere. The village cafes existed for the benefit of men. Women stayed at home. Even in churches men stood in the front part of the church and women at the back. Amazingly, even today (2001) in many churches men stand in the front of the church and women stand at the back!

Education was a male priority. The wealthy parents would encourage their sons to study but not their daughters. When it came to marriage, matchmaking was very common. It was also customary for the parents of the girl to give a dowry to their future son-in-law. The village priest would be invited by the parents of the future groom and bride and be a witness to the "Dowry Agreement". This was a valid and legal document and if the father of the girl refused to provide what was listed in this Agreement the son-in-law had the right to take his father-in-law to court.

# THE RISE OF TRADE UNIONISM

The Trade Union movement came about at the same time as the Cypriot Communist Party was founded. Cyprus was still an agricultural society and in 1920 there were about 6,000 people working in industry. The vast majority of the population worked on land as farm labourers. The gradual growth of industrialism led to a rapid growth of small trade unions. By 1940 there were 62 such small trade unions. On 6 August 1939 the first Trade Union Conference was held at the Haji-Hambi theatre in Famagusta and was addressed by Ploutis Servas, the General Secretary of the Cypriot Communist Party. On 16 November 1941 the second Trade Union Conference was held in Nicosia and was attended by 194 delegates representing 7,500 members. It was at this meeting that the *Pancyprian Trades Union Committee (P.S.E.)* was officially founded to act as the co-ordinator of these small Trade Unions. **Andreas Fantis** (born 1919) was elected General Secretary of P.S.E. and when he joined the Second World War as a volunteer, he was succeeded in June 1943 by **Andreas Ziartides** (1919 - 1997). The *P.S.E.* was eventually replaced by the *Pancyprian Federation of Labour (P.E.O.)* in 1946 and again Ziartides was elected as the first General Secretary.

Andreas Ziartides became actively involved in the trade union movement at the age of 18 (1937) and joined the K.K.K., the Cypriot Communist Party in 1939. He once described working conditions as follows:

*"Almost in all professions people had to work from sunrise to sunset. This was particularly true with shoemakers and tailors whereas in some other professions people had to*

*continue their work beyond sunset. People in such cases had to work with the poor lighting from the oil lamps. As regards wages, I need only mention that the workers had no say and this was always decided by their employers."*

Through the PEO Trade Union which he led for about 45 years, he had contributed considerably in improving the working conditions of the Cypriot working class. He was also a Member of the House of Representatives as an AKEL deputy from 1960 - 91.

In April 1988 when Ezekias Papaioannou the General Secretary of AKEL died and the leadership was assumed by Demetris Christofias, Ziartides left the leadership of the PEO Trade Union and AKEL. Avraam Antoniou took over as General Secretary of PEO. Ziartides together with Andreas Fantis, Pavlos Dinglis, Michalis Papapetrou and some others formed the splinter party known as ADISOK.

***Andreas Ziartides 1919 - 1997***

The ideological differences among Trade Unionists and the establishment of New Trade Unions in the towns led to the formation of the *Confederation of Cyprus Workers (S.E.K.)* in 1944. Paradoxically, although both Trade Unions supported and promoted the Workers' interests they were (and still are) divided along ideological lines, the *P.E.O.* following the socialist ideology and the *S.E.K.* the conservative and neo-liberal ideology.

## AKEL - A NEW PARTY IS BORN 1941
### Ploutis Servas (1907 - 2001) the first General Secretary

When the KKK went underground during the 1930's *Ploutis Servas* became the General Secretary in 1936. He studied Political and Social Sciences in Moscow. Servas (his real name was Ploutrarchos Loizou Savvides) was born in Limassol in 1907. He was elected Mayor of Limassol from 1943 - 1949. It was Servas's idea to form a new broader party of the Left in order to promote the right of self-determination for Cyprus as well as the ideals of socialism. Servas invited 36 delegates to attend a meeting in order to set up a new political party and also to merge with the existing KKK. The 36 delegates (Journalists, Mayors, Barristers, Trade Unionists and others) met on the *14th April 1941* at the village of *Skarinou* (a village situated between Nicosia and Limassol). It was at that meeting that *AKEL (the Anorthotiko Komma Ergazomenou Laou - Progressive Party of the Working People)* was founded. Ploutis Servas, the former leader of the KKK was elected as the first General Secretary (1941 - 45).

In 1943 Servas was elected Mayor of Limassol but the central committee of AKEL insisted that he could not hold two positions, i.e. be both a Mayor and General Secretary of the party, and insisted that he should move to Nicosia from Limassol. In 1945 he was deposed from his position and during the 5th Congress of the party held in September 1947 **Fifis Ioannou** was elected General Secretary.

(As we shall see later on, something similar happened to Archbishop Makarios. Three bishops tried to defrock him and insisted that he should resign his post as President if he wished to remain an Archbishop or resign his position as Archbishop if he wanted to remain President. He could not, in their view, hold two positions, i.e. be both an Archbishop and a President at the same time. In the case of Makarios, he was able to resist the opposition and he succeeded in defrocking his opponents).

In 1948 Ploutis Servas expressed his differences with Nikos Zachariades (the Stalinist leader of the KKE - the Communist Party of Greece) and with the leadership of

*Ploutis Servas 1907 - 2001*

AKEL. In 1952 he was expelled from the party. He spent the rest of his life writing books and articles in Greek newspapers and magazines. He died in Nicosia on the 14th February 2001 at the age of 94 and was cremated a week later at the New Southgate cemetery in London.

Two years after the establishment of AKEL, in the first Municipal Elections held in 1943 (they were banned previously because of the October 1931 Uprising), AKEL won the Municipalities of Limassol (with *Ploutis Servas* as Mayor) and Famagusta (with *Adamos Adamantos* as Mayor) as well as other smaller towns. In the 1946 Municipal Elections AKEL increased its strength even more and was able to spread its influence in many parts of Cyprus.

*Ezekias Papaioannou 1908 - 1988*
*General Secretary of AKEL 1949 - 1988*

109

# CYPRUS AND THE SECOND WORLD WAR

*Cypriots who joined and fought with the British army
against fascism during the Second World War*

When the Second World War broke out in September 1939
and Britain with the Allies were fighting Hitler's fascism, the
Cypriots showed their full solidarity because it was a War
for Freedom and Democracy. When Mussolini tried to
invade Greece on 28th October 1940 many Cypriots
enlisted and fought together with the Greeks driving the
Italians into Albania. Sir Winston Churchill was so
impressed by the brave resistance of the Greeks that he
declared:

*"From now on we should not be saying that the Greeks fight
like heroes but the heroes fight like the Greeks!"*

When the Soviet Union joined the Allies in June 1941

against Hitler, the British Colonial authorities relaxed the emergency measures which were imposed in Cyprus in 1931. About 35,000 Cypriots volunteered and joined the British army and fought with them against Hitler's fascist tyranny in order to preserve Freedom and Democracy. In fact many of them died at the Battle of El Alamein in Egypt in 1942.

When the War ended in 1945, the Cypriots together with the other Colonial peoples of Asia and Africa who had fought with the British and their allies and had given their lives for the cause of Freedom, had expected that they would be granted their own "freedom" from British Colonial rule. They were led to believe that they were fighting for Freedom, Democracy and Justice but when it came to asking for their own Freedom, the Colonial powers turned a deaf ear to their demands. Their national aspirations were shattered by those same Colonial powers who a little earlier were preaching different things! Sir Winston Churchill at a meeting with Stalin in Moscow in October 1944 and later together with US President Roosevelt in another meeting at Yalta in February 1945 had decided the fate of Europe. They had agreed to divide Europe into "spheres of influence". Greece and Cyprus were to remain under the British (and American) influence.

In Greece the British landed their troops in 1944 and in the Civil War that followed they openly backed the Royalists in order to restore the monarchy. When the Civil War ended in 1949 more Greeks were killed than during the resistance against the German occupation. The Greek Communist Party was made illegal and there were thousands of political prisoners. The Greek Governments which were subsequently elected served the interests of the British and the Americans.

During the Greek Civil War (1945-49), the people in Cyprus were equally divided to pro-Royalists and pro-Communists. As the post-war Governments in Greece were purely "puppets" to British and American interests, it was very naive and illogical for the Greek Cypriot nationalists led by the Ethnarchy to try to enlist the support of such Governments. This reluctance of the Greek Governments was made known to the Cypriot nationalist leaders simply because they could not afford to act against the wishes of those who helped to bring them to power.

## BRITISH GOVERNMENTS AND PRIME MINISTERS SINCE 1945

The table below provides a list of the Governments and Prime Ministers who were directly involved with the Cyprus problem since 1945.

Clement Attlee (Labour) 1945 -51
Winston Churchill (Conservative) 1951 - 55
Anthony Eden (Conservative) 1955 - 57
Harold Macmillan (Conservative) 1957 - 63
Douglas Home (Conservative) 1963 - 64
Harold Wilson (Labour) 1964 - 70
Edward Heath (Conservative) 1970 - 74
Harold Wilson (Labour) 1974 - 76
James Callaghan (Labour) 1976 - 79
Margaret Thatcher (Conservative) 1979 - 90
John Major (Conservative) 1990 - 97
Tony Blair (Labour) 1997 -

# PROPOSALS FOR A CONSULTATIVE ASSEMBLY 1947

As the Civil War was still raging in Greece (1945 - 49), on the 9th July 1947 the British Governor **Reginald Fletcher (Lord Winster)** sent invitations to the Ethnarchy (the Cyprus Church) , the Mayors of the five towns, leaders of the Trade Unionists and to various persons in other organisations in order to take part in a *Consultative Assembly* which would make recommendations on the form of a constitution. The Ethnarchy rejected the invitation because they feared that the issue of *Enosis* would be sidestepped by any possible constitutional agreements. The Left, after some hesitation, decided to join the talks.

The talks began on the *1st November 1947*. The meeting was chaired by *Sir Edward Jackson,* a High Court Judge in Cyprus and was attended by the following:

1. *John Clerides*, Mayor of Nicosia.
2. *Ploutis Servas*, Mayor of Limassol.
3. *Adamos Adamantos,* Mayor of Famagusta.
4. *Lysos Santamas*, Mayor of Larnaca.
5. *Polycarpos Nicolopoulos,* Mayor of Morphou.
6. *Andreas Ziartides,* from PEO Trades Union Federation.
7. *Andreas Fantis*, from PEO Trades Union Federation.
8. *Niazi Fadil,* Turkish Mayor of Lefka.
9. *Hassan Shasmas*, Turkish Trade Unionist.
10. *Irfan Hussein*, Turkish Agrarian Union.
11. *Soupi Kenan*, Local Councillor from Larnaca.
12. *Rauf Denktash, Lawyer from Nicosia.*
13. *Said Gaip*, leading member from Nicosia.
14. *Ali Rapid*, leading member from Paphos.

15. *Yiorgos Aradipiotis*, Lawyer from Larnaca.
16. *Michel Houris*, Lawyer from Limassol.
17. *Socrates Evangelides*, Judge from Limassol.
18. *Panayiotis Hadjimichael*, leading member from Vasili village (Famagusta).

The chief purpose of the Consultative Assembly was to discuss constitutional proposals for self-government. Legislative power was to be in the hands of the elected body but the executive power would still be in the hands of the Governor. According to Ploutis Servas, (one of the participants), Sir Edward Jackson had stated that the proposed constitution would have been a temporary one for a period of ten years and after that time the people of Cyprus would be *free to exercise the right of self determination.* (P. Servas: *Kypriako - Efthynes*, p. 129).

The seven left-wing delegates together with Yiorgos Aradipiotis were critical of the proposals and on the 26th November they made counter-proposals regarding the Constitution. The left wing delegates were fully aware that the proposed Constitution was still a Colonial Constitution because Cyprus was still a Crown Colony. It was not an ideal Constitution but they felt that there was room for improvements. The Church leadership and the right wing organisations were campaigning for Enosis now, they were constantly accusing AKEL of co-operating with the Colonial rulers.

A massive rally was held in Nicosia in support of *Self-Government - Enosis.* Cyprus had never previously witnessed such a big rally organised by AKEL and the PEO Trades Union and would not until the return of Makarios from exile. This massive rally was followed by other rallies in the other towns. The organisers  were arrested and tried. The Mayor of Limassol, the Deputy Mayor of Famagusta, Local Councillors from Nicosia and Larnaca and other leading AKEL members were arrested, brought to trial and sentenced to prison for between two to six months with hard labour. One leading AKEL member, Miltiades Christodoulou (later Government Spokesman in the Makarios Government), was sentenced to six months imprisonment by Judge George Vassiliades, who himself was one of the founding members of AKEL. He then left and was appointed by the Colonial authorities  a High Court Judge!

The leadership of AKEL was still hesitant  so the Party decided to send the then General Secretary **Fifis Ioannou** and PEO Trade Unionist leader **Andreas Ziartides** to seek the advice of fraternal parties such as the KKE (the Greek Communist Party), the CPGB (Communist Party of Great Britain) and the Cominform in Bucharest. The KKE, in 1948 was fighting in the Civil War against the British and the Americans. According to Ziartides,  he and Fifis Ioannou had  left Cyprus incognito and travelled to Greece  via Cairo, Paris, Prague and Budapest.

In November 1948 they first met with Markos Vafiades who was  the commander-in-chief of the *Democratic Army* and also Prime Minister of the "government of the mountains". Vafiades advised them to discuss this matter with **Nikos Zachariades**, the leader of KKE. Vafiades himself was purged from his position a few days later. The two Cypriot Communist leaders met with Zachariades, Vladas, Gousias and Ioannides  on the mountains of Northern Greece.  Fifis Ioannou made a presentation from his notes about the British proposal for a Consultative Assembly and wanted to know the views and the advice of the KKE leadership. According to Ziartides, Zachariades made the following remarks:

" *Listen, comrades, you made a mistake. You deviated to the right. You had been discussing with Imperialism the question of a constitution, whilst at the same time we, up here, your Greek brothers 'fought' the British in an armed struggle. It was a mistake. You should not expect to arrive at Enosis via such a colonial constitution. You should go back and correct your mistake.* "

Many years later, Fifis Ioannou writing for the Cypriot newspaper *Apoyevmatini* (21 August 1976) quoted Zachariades as saying:

"*The line for constitutional reform in Cyprus is a version of 'liberalism' . We, here, will march victorious to Athens in one way or another in two months time. Therefore, you there in Cyprus can no longer be talking about self-government as an intermediate stage to the ultimate aim of Enosis. Enosis with Greece should become your immediate aim.*"

According to Fifis Ioannou (in the same newspaper article), Zachariades had advised the Cypriot communists to engage in an armed struggle. What was astonishing was the fact that Andreas Ziartides and Fifis Ioannou gave *two different versions* of what was actually said by Zachariades. Andreas Ziartides insisted that the delegation met with Zachariades only once whereas Fifis Ioannou argued that they had two meetings with the KKE leader! Fifis Ioannou also mentioned that the advice from the British Communist Party (i.e. to accept self-government and then Enosis) was given to them prior to their meeting with Zachariades whereas Ziartides argued that the meeting in London with **Harry Pollitt**, the General Secretary of the British Communist Party, had taken place after the meeting with the KKE leadership. (*See article by Yiorghos Leventis: Self Government - Enosis or Immediate Enosis*: The *Influence of Zachariades on the Shift in AKEL's Strategy. The Cyprus Review, Vol.13. Spring 2001*).

According to Ziartides, Harry Pollitt advised the AKEL leadership to continue with **constitutional arrangements** because he believed that they will eventually lead to self-determination. He advised AKEL to pursue a *"gradualist approach"*.

From 1940 until 1956, Nikos Zachariades was considered as the "Stalin" and the "Messiah" of the Greek communist movement. Zachariades was imprisoned by the Metaxas dictatorship and during the German occupation he was handed over to the Nazis where he was transferred to Germany and kept in a concentration camp. When he was released after the war he led the Greek Communist Party (KKE) in the Civil War against the pro-Monarchists that were backed by the British and the Americans.

During Zachariades' leadership, hundreds of Greek Communists were purged and exterminated, branded as Trotskyists because they dared to speak their mind and opposed his line or views. Those who dared, were branded as *opportunists, enemies of the working class or traitors*. Ploutis Servas mentions in his book *"Efthynes"* that he himself was a victim of verbal abuse by Zachariades who described him as *"an opportunist, as petit bourgeois, haberdasher* and *as chicken-hearted!"* (P. Servas: Efthynes. Vol. 1. p.134). It is with these and even worse "colourful adjectives" that Zachariades used to brand all those who disagreed with him.

In the subsequent vote that followed in the AKEL Central Committee, 12 heeded the Zachariades viewpoint (i.e. to oppose Self government and to struggle for *Enosis* now) and voted against the Consultative Assembly. Only five members voted in favour for Self-government. They were *Ploutis Servas, Adamos Adamantos, Vasos Vasiliou, Miltiades Christodoulou and Costas Partasides*. Some of them were later expelled from AKEL. The talks for a Consultative Assembly collapsed and with it the opportunity

*The author with Ploutis Servas in Nicosia 1997*

of Self-government in 1947 and the right of self determination some ten years later.

Ploutis Servas's willingness to accept *constitutional changes* which would have eventually led to the right of self-determination, was to cause him to loose his position

118

in the party because he was branded by the new leadership of AKEL (Ezekias Papaioannou) as an *"opportunist and willing to co-operate with the imperialists!"*. This was the "standard" Stalinist terminology used in those days. Ploutis Servas who was leader of the K.K.K. (the Cypriot Communist Party) and had helped to create AKEL in 1941, in order to give the party a broader base and a wider appeal, found himself expelled from this party some eleven years later in 1952.

*Adamos Adamantos,* a brilliant left-wing orator and scholar and former Mayor of Famagusta also fell from AKEL's favour because he dared say that *"he was not prepared to even sacrifice his little finger for the cause of "Enosis".* True to his socialist principles Adamantos supported the co-operation and friendship of the Greek and Turkish communities in Cyprus. In the 1953 Municipal Elections in Famagusta, AKEL refused to support Adamantos' candidacy and Andreas Pouyiouros was elected Mayor instead.

## GREEK GOVERNMENTS AND PRIME MINISTERS SINCE 1946

The table below provides a list of the Governments and Prime Ministers who were directly involved with the Cyprus problem since 1946.

Constantinos Tsaldaris (People's Party, 1946 - 50)
Sophocles Venizelos (Liberal, 1950 - 51)
Nikolaos Plastiras (National Progressive Centre Union 1951 -52)
Alexandros Papagos (Greek Rally, 1952 - 55)
Constn Karamanlis (ERE-National Radical Union 1955 - 63)

Georgios Papandreou (Centre Union, 1963 - 65)
Stefanos Stefanopoulos (Centre Union, 1965 - 67)
George Papadopoulos (1967 - 73) Military Dictatorship
Adamantios Androutsopoulos (1973 - 74) Dictatorship
Constantinos Karamanlis (New Democracy, 1974 - 80)
Georgios Rallis (New Democracy, 1980 - 81)
Andreas Papandreou (PASOK - Socialist, 1981 - 1990)
Constantinos Mitsotakis (New Democracy, 1990 - 1993
Andreas Papandreou (PASOK - Socialist, 1993 - 1996)
Costas Simitis (PASOK - Socialist, 1996 -

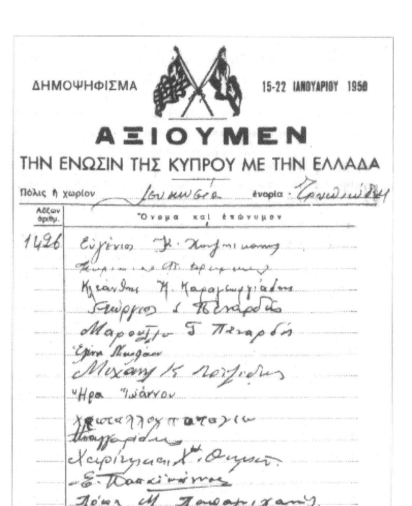

*The Enosis Referendum 15 January 1950*
*(The 12th signature is that of AKEL General Secretary*
*Ezekias Papaioannou)*

# THE "ENOSIS" REFERENDUM
## 15th JANUARY 1950

The British Governor of Cyprus from 1949 to 1954 was *Andrew Wright.* In 1948 *Makarios* became Bishop of Kition at the age of 35. During the same year the Ethnarchy (Church Council) was reconstituted and Makarios was appointed to chair this body which consisted of other religious leaders as well as all the right-wing Mayors and right-wing candidates who failed in the Municipal Elections. No left-wing Mayor was invited to join. It was in fact "*a right-wing and an anti-communist body*".

When the Governor refused to carry out a Plebiscite to decide about the future of Cyprus, Makarios and the Ethnarchy decided to organise their own. The Plebiscite which called for *Enosis* (Union with Greece), was held on *15th January 1950* in all the Greek Churches and was signed by *215,108* people or *95.7%* of those entitled to vote.

## Greek Premier Refuses to Receive Cypriot Delegation and Plebiscite

Soon after the *Enosis* plebiscite was over, a delegation headed by *Bishop Kyprianos* of Kyrenia went to Athens to present the volumes with the signatures of the Greek Cypriots to the Greek Prime Minister *Nikolaos Plastiras*. To the delegation's astonishment the Greek Premier refused to see them and receive the Plebiscite volumes!

Plastiras was still a "hostage" to British and American political and economic interests. One must not forget that the Greek Civil War had recently finished (1949) and that Plastiras owed his new found position as Prime Minister "thanks" to the British and the Americans who had crashed the Communists in the Civil War. The British and the Americans were his new "masters" and he could not displease them....... for the sake of Cyprus!

The disappointed Cypriot Delegation then handed the volumes to **D. Gontikas**, the President of the Greek Parliament. Some time later **George Papandreou** (a former Prime Minister) explained to the then Mayor of Nicosia **Themistocles Dervis** why Greece was unable to help Cyprus. He argued that :

*"Greece is at present able to breathe only because it is supported by one British and one American lung. Therefore it cannot risk (asphyxiation) to suffocate in order to support Cyprus!"*

On the 28th June 1950 **Archbishop Makarios II** died. Makarios, the young Bishop of Kition, was elected as his successor and enthroned as the new **Archbishop Makarios III** in October 1950, at the young age of 37. As we shall see, the new and young Archbishop was to play a crucial part in Cyprus's subsequent history. Sometime later, when Makarios complained to the Greek Premier Plastiras about his reluctance to support *Enosis*, Plastiras told Makarios that:

*"If you had come to my humble dwelling and asked me to fight for Cyprus, I would have gladly done so because I am a soldier. But you have come to the Office of the Prime Minister of Greece and you are asking me to set Greece on fire without being able to help Cyprus. Do keep quiet!"*

123

Makarios however, was neither willing to pay heed to the advice of the Greek Premier, nor was he prepared to "keep quiet".

In 1951 Makarios approached the Liberal Greek Premier **Sophocles Venizelos** (who was the son of the famous statesman Eleftherios Venizelos) and urged him to raise the issue of Cyprus at the United Nations. He even threatened him that if he refused to do so then he would approach the Government of Syria to raise the issue and that he would denounce him publicly to the Greek people. Sophocles Venizelos angrily responded by saying:

*"You can do whatever you want . You may denounce me wherever you like, but Greek Foreign Policy will not be determined by you!"* (This statement was made by Sophocles Venizelos during a debate on Cyprus in the Greek Parliament on 25th April 1956).

As mentioned earlier, the Greek Civil War had recently ended and the Greek governments were subservient to British and American interests. To expect them therefore, to act otherwise, as Makarios had expected them, was simply unrealistic.

## THE "OATH FOR ENOSIS" TAKEN IN ATHENS AND NICOSIA

The Ethnarchy and Makarios in particular tried to convince several Greek Governments to take the issue of Cyprus to the United Nations. All the post-war Greek Governments however, and Greek Foreign policy in particular was greatly influenced and determined by decisions made in London and in Washington.

In June 1952 Makarios went on the Radio and accused both the Greek Government, as well as the Opposition, claiming that they were refusing to raise the issue of Cyprus at the United Nations. Through his travels to London and New York as well as through his increasing contacts in the Non-Aligned countries, he succeeded in adding the issue of the *Right of People to Self Determination* on the UN Agenda.

On the 16th December 1952, the UN General Assembly supported the resolution by 35 votes in favour, 14 against and 11 abstentions. Makarios was now armed with a U.N. Resolution which backed his claim. His real claim, however, was not so much the right of the Cypriot people to self determination and become another Independent state (as it was the case with other colonial states), but it was for *Enosis*, and many people at the United Nations interpreted this as an attempt to "transfer" the Island from the hegemony of one member state (Britain) to that of another member state (Greece).

On the 7th March 1953 Makarios with ten other men met at **Professor Gerasimos Konidaris'** house in Asklepios Street in Athens. Among them were **General Papadopoulos**, **George Stratos** (a former Defence Minister) and the **Loizides** brothers. There, they took an oath and signed this oath confirming their pledge and full support for the cause of *Enosis*. They pledged that they were prepared to give their lives, that they will abide and obey to all orders and adhere to strict and absolute secrecy. **Colonel George Grivas** signed the oath a few days later and on the 13th March 1953 Grivas was entrusted with the leadership of the armed struggle.

Makarios, encouraged by the United Nations Resolution of the 16th December 1952, asked **Andrew Wright**, the British Governor, to carry out a new Plebiscite. As it was to be expected, the Governor refused. Makarios was determined to carry on and on 28th June 1953 addressed a congregation of more than 10,000 people at the Church of **Phaneromeni** in **Nicosia**. In a passionate speech, he asked the crowd to join him in taking the Oath *"to struggle for their national demand, with no retreats or compromises, aiming at one and only demand, that of Enosis and nothing but Enosis."*

In 1953 the Prime Minister in Greece was **Marshal Alexandros Papagos.** After many hesitations, Papagos gave instructions to **Alexis Kyrou**, the Greek Ambassador at the United Nations, to raise the question of Cyprus. Alexis Kyrou raised the issue on the 21st September 1953. His speech however, was full of praise for Britain, he spoke of *"... the great help that Britain gave to Greece at different times and about the close co-operation that existed between the two countries."*

The speech in fact, instead of raising the issue of Cyprus' right to self determination, was so full of praise for Britain that it left most delegates speechless because they were puzzled and wondered after hearing this "eulogy" as to whether Britain was really..... a Colonial power that was treating Cyprus unfairly and unjustly!

# TURKISH GOVERNMENTS AND PRIME MINISTERS SINCE 1950

The table below provides a list of the Governments and Prime Ministers who were directly involved with the Cyprus problem since 1950.

Adnan Menderes (Democratic Party, 1950 - 60)
General Cemal Gursel (Army coup 1960 - 61)
Ismet Inonu (1961 - 65)
Suleiman Demirel (Justice Party, 1965)
Bulent Ecevit (Republican People's Party, Coalition, 1974)
Bulent Ecevit (Republican People's Party, 1978 - 79)
Suleiman Demirel (Justice Party, 1979 - 80)
Kenan Evren (Military Dictatorship 1980 - 83)
Turgut Ozal (Motherland Party, 1983 - 1987)
Mesut Yilmaz (Motherland Party, 1991)
Suleiman Demirel (True Path Party, 1991 - 93)
Tansu Ciller (True Path Party, 1993 - 95)
Mesut Yilmaz (Motherland Party, Coalition 1996)
Bulent Ecevit (Democratic Socialist Party, 1999)

# THE PAPAGOS - EDEN MEETING
# DECEMBER 1953

The Greek Premier, Marshal Papagos  believed that the Cyprus problem could be solved amicably between Britain and Greece, mainly because of the close ties that existed between the two countries.  When Foreign Secretary *Sir Anthony Eden* went to Athens on 22 December 1953, Marshall Papagos went to see him at the British Embassy. According to Protocol, however,  this should have been the other way round, i.e. a visiting Diplomat goes to see the

Prime Minister and not the Prime Minister to visit the foreign Diplomat. British influence in Greece at that time was so strong that "protocol" did not mean anything.

When Papagos eventually raised the issue about the future of Cyprus, Sir Anthony Eden replied bluntly:

*" I shall repeat what I said previously, that is, as far as the British Government is concerned, there is no Cyprus issue for the time being nor is there one for the future. "*

Marshal Papagos felt rather insulted by these remarks and had decided to raise the issue at the United Nations. When it was eventually raised at the UN, the Americans did everything they could to stop a resolution which would support Cyprus' right to self determination. Eventually a resolution proposed by New Zealand was adopted which *"confirmed the reluctance of the United Nations to apply the same right of self determination to Cyprus"*. Strangely enough Greece voted in favour! The Soviet Union and the other socialist countries abstained.

## HOPKINSON'S "NEVER"

**Henry Hopkinson** was Minister for the Colonies in the Churchill Government in 1954. In a debate in the House of Commons on 28th July 1954 Hopkinson had announced a new constitutional plan for internal self government for Cyprus. No change of sovereignty was contemplated and the offer was less liberal than the 1948 offer in that it did not provide for an elected majority. James Griffiths, the former Labour Secretary for the Colonies, asked Hopkinson about the Dominion status of Cyprus and also about the issue of self-determination. Hopkinson gave the following reply:

*"It has always been understood and agreed that there are certain territories in the Commonwealth which, owing to their particular circumstances can **never** expect to be fully independent. I think the right Hon. Gentleman will agree that there are some territories which cannot expect to be that. I am not going as far as that this afternoon, but I have said that the question of the abrogation of British sovereignty cannot arise - that British sovereignty will remain."*

*(House of Commons Debate, Vol. 531, cols 504-6).*

In the same debate, the Labour MPs Lena Jeger, Richard Crossman, Tom Driberg and others challenged the position taken by the Colonial Secretary. Lena Jeger said that she regretted the failure of members over the years to take the question of Enosis seriously and she also referred to the 1950 referendum of the Ethnarchy which had resulted in a 98% in favour of Enosis. She was also critical of Hopkinson's plan of "appointing nominated stooges" instead of being elected by the people. Labour M.P., Richard Crossman described Hopkinson's statement that Cyprus will **never** be granted its freedom as "astonishing" and asked the Cabinet to change its mind and warned of forthcoming problems and bloodshed similar to those of Palestine. He stated: *"May I say that the tragedy of the Middle East, is that there is not a country whose people got their rights from the British without murder."*

Hopkinson's statement had not only infuriated Labour MPs in the House of Commons but most of all the people of Cyprus, who now realised more than ever that an armed struggle was the only way forward to achieve their aim, i.e. the right to self-determination. Richard Crossman's warning

**The author with C.M.Woodhouse at the Houses of Parliament**

was not heeded by the Government of the day.

The British Government in order to forestall the Greek demand for *Enosis* supported the demands of the Turkish Cypriots. Christopher Woodhouse a well known Conservative politician and historian, in his Autobiography entitled *"Something Ventured"* (1982) wrote the following:

*"Harold Macmillan (Foreign Secretary at the time) was urging us to stir up the Turks in order to neutralise the Greek agitation. I wrote a minute in opposition to this tactic. I also asked the Prime Minister's private secretary if I could see Churchill on the subject, but he absolutely refused even to pass on the suggestion, which he clearly regarded as impertinence."*

130

# THE RISE OF TURKISH CYPRIOT NATIONALISM

As the Greek Cypriots were preparing to wage a struggle for *Enosis* the Turkish Cypriots, led by Dr Fazil Kutchuk, (1906 - 1984) argued that Cyprus should be returned to Turkey because it was ruled by Turkey from 1571 until 1878, when it was ceded to Great Britain as a security against Russian threats. Writing in his newspaper **Halkin Sesi** (Voice of the People) on 17th August 1954, Dr Kutchuk made the following arguments opposing *Enosis* and suggested that Cyprus should be returned to Turkey:

*"Turkey was the undisputed owner of Cyprus just before Great Britain took it over on trust. If world events have ended that "trust" during 1914-18 subsequent world events have certainly revived that trust from all moral points of view....*

*If Great Britain is going to consider this Enosis question at all or is going to quit the island she has a legal as well as a moral duty to call Turkey and hand Cyprus back to Turkey, and ask the Turkish government to deal with the Enosis problem which the tolerant and ill-advised British administration has fostered in the island.*

*From a legal as well as moral point of view, Turkey as the initial owner of the island just before the British occupation, has a first option to Cyprus. The matter does not end there. From a worldwide political point of view as well as from geographical and strategical points of view Cyprus must be handed to Turkey if Great Britain is going to quit...."*

Dr Kutchuk and his supporters, seeing the Greek Cypriots

campaigning for *Enosis* and fearing the implementation of such consequences, began campaigning for "a national re-awakening" among the Turkish Cypriot community. They opposed any solution which would lead to the Union of Cyprus with Greece.

In 1957, Dr Kutchuk published a pamphlet entitled *The Cyprus Question : A Permanent Solution.* In this pamphlet he suggested the horizontal partitioning of Cyprus from the town of **Polis Chrysochous** in the West to **Famagusta** in the East. Dr Kutchuk's view was that because Cyprus was previously ruled by Turkey then Cyprus should be returned to Turkey. The Greek Cypriots rejected Dr Kutchuk's "logic" because they argued that if this was to be implemented in the case of Cyprus, then using the same "logic", places such as Constantinople (which was once the capital of the Byzantine Empire) and most coastal towns and villages of Asia Minor, which were previously inhabited by Greeks, should not longer be ruled by Turkey but they should become an integral part of Greek state.

A further criticism from the Greek Cypriot nationalists was the fact that Dr Kutchuk ignored the actual composition of the population of Cyprus which was made up of 80% Greek Cypriots and 20% Turkish Cypriots. The argument was that in any democratic society or in any democratic election, the wishes of the majority are respected.

Dr Kutchuk supported the partition of the island because he believed that the Turkish community will be better protected. The Turkish community however, was spread all over the island, there were many mixed villages so in order to implement Dr Kutchuk's policy of Partition would have meant carrying a policy of **Ethnic Cleansing,** i.e. moving large numbers of Greek Cypriots out of their homes and villages in order to create an area to re-settle those Turkish Cypriots. (This forceful movement of the population was to happen in 1974 when Turkey invaded Cyprus).

Dr Kutchuk and subsequently Denktash, expressing their fears about their future existence, wanted to transfer the colonial administration from British to Turkish hands. It is true that in later years both Greece and Turkey wanted to include Cyprus in their geographical boundaries. They both considered Cyprus as part of their own "family" and both wanted it and nearly went to war against each other. The British Colonial administration was neither willing nor prepared to pass a "Wise Solomon Judgement" and hand over Cyprus to its "real parent"(!). Britain's strategic interests in the Eastern Mediterranean and the Middle East in particular dictated their continued presence in Cyprus. The pleas of the Cypriots for the right of self determination meant nothing to the colonial administrators.

A further criticism against Partition was the fact that Freedom and Democracy had triumphed after the Second World War and people were entitled to exercise the right of self-determination. The Turkish Cypriot leadership believed that the 80% Greek Cypriot majority had no right to rule over the 18% Turkish Cypriot community. For the Greek Cypriot nationalists this attitude of the Turkish Cypriot leadership was unacceptable as they were content to be ruled by the British and raised no objections but they were not prepared to accept "Majority rule" if the British withdrew. They raised the issue of *Partition* only when the Greek Cypriots raised the issue of *Enosis.*

The British Colonial administration who did not wish to

abandon Cyprus especially for strategic reasons, found in the Turkish Cypriot nationalist leadership a staunch supporter in order to deny the Cypriot people the right of self-determination, using the pretext that a substantial minority of the population was against it.

## PREPARATIONS FOR THE "ENOSIS" STRUGGLE

The British Governor of Cyprus from 1954 to 1955 was **Robert Armitage.** On the 25th January 1955 **Socrates Loizides** and 12 of his colleagues arrived in Cyprus from Greece on a small ship called the *"St. George"*, which was loaded with fire-arms and other ammunition. The ship was intercepted by the British and all the crew were arrested. Socrates Loizides carried with him a document, which was a Proclamation by the *National Front for the Liberation of Cyprus (Ethniko Metopo Apeleftherosis Kyprou) EMAK.*

In this proclamation, EMAK stated that:

*" It will not accept Communists in its ranks and AKEL and all left-wing Cypriots were asked to abstain from the struggle"!*

The proclamation said that the participation of Cypriot Communists was not needed because it would damage the cause and that in any case, they had sufficient fighters to carry out successfully the struggle for liberation! This right wing organisation, which in effect wanted to monopolise the national struggle, not only ignored the existence of the Turkish-Cypriot community in the Island but also ignored and excluded all left-wing Cypriots which, if one can judge by the Municipal Election results of the late 1940s, constituted at that time about 40% of the population!

On the 1st April 1955 the EOKA struggle commenced. *Archbishop Makarios* assumed the political leadership and *Colonel George Grivas* was responsible for the military operations. Grivas took the pseudonym *"Dighenis"* after the 11th century Byzantine legendary hero *Vasilios Dighenis Akritas*. Grivas's deputy was *Gregoris Afxentiou*. The first proclamation by EOKA signed by *Grivas - Dighenis* went out to all parts of Cyprus. In this proclamation, Grivas called upon the Cypriots to overthrow the British yoke and reminded them of the ancient Spartan saying that it was their duty to fight and die for their freedom.

## THE EOKA OATH

All members of EOKA had to take the following oath:

*"I swear in the name of the Holy Trinity that:*

*I shall work with all my power for the liberation of Cyprus from the British yoke, sacrificing for this even my life.*

*I shall perform without question all the instructions of the Organisation which may be given to me and I shall not bring any objection, however difficult or dangerous these may be.*

*I shall not abandon the struggle unless I receive instructions from the Leader of the Organisation, and after our aim has been accomplished.*

*I shall never reveal to anyone any secret of our Organisation, neither the names of my chiefs nor those of any other members, even if I am captured and tortured.*

*I shall not reveal any of the instructions which may be given me, even to my fellow combatants.*

*If I disobey this oath I shall be worthy of every punishment as a traitor, and may eternal contempt cover me."*

Acts of sabotage were carried out in Nicosia, Limassol and Larnaca in the early hours of 1st April 1955. The leadership of AKEL at first condemned these acts as irresponsible. Some months later, many left wing people rallied to the cause of *Enosis* and joined the struggle for liberation. Many of them were arrested and imprisoned. The decision of AKEL to back the cause of *Enosis* (union with Greece) alienated the few Turkish members that it had and eventually they left the Party altogether.

## MAKARIOS BUILDS CONTACTS WITH OTHER NATIONAL LEADERS

On the 15th April 1955 Makarios, accompanied by Zenon Rossides, travelled to Bandung in Indonesia in order to attend the First Non-Aligned Conference as an observer. It was there that he met and had talks with Prime Minister Nehru of India, President Nasser of Egypt and other leaders. The purpose of his visit was to establish contacts with former colonial leaders in order to promote the cause of Cyprus.

The British were now becoming suspicious of Makarios

because he was trying to build contacts with leaders from other countries and they feared that he may secure their support, especially at the United Nations.

Meanwhile, EOKA had circulated a leaflet in Turkish in July 1955 assuring the Turkish Cypriot community that their struggle was against British Colonialism and not against them. The Turkish-Cypriot leaders **Dr Fazil Kutchuk** and **Rauf Denktash** and their *"Cyprus is Turkish Party"* were against the idea of Cyprus becoming part of Greece. The Turkish Cypriot leader Rauf Denktash admitted on a Cyprus television interview held on 14th February 2001 that Dr Kutchuk and himself had helped to form T.M.T. as a counterbalance of EOKA, i.e. if the Greek Cypriots wanted *Enosis* (union) with Greece then the Turkish Cypriots also wanted union with Turkey.

The nationalistic antagonism between the two communities eventually helped the colonial power to implement its *"Divide and Rule"* policy. It must be said that the course of Cypriot history would have been very different if the struggle, right from the start, was a joint struggle of all Cypriots, Greeks and Turks, for self-determination and for an independent Cyprus state, i.e. for a common homeland. Sadly, this was not to be, mainly because of the opposing nationalistic aspirations of the leadership of both communities.

# THE TRI-PARTITE CONFERENCE AUG. 1955

In August 1955 the British Government invited the Governments of Greece and Turkey to a **Tri-partite Conference** to be held in London in order to discuss "*Political and Defensive Matters in the eastern Mediterranean, including Cyprus.*" It should be noted here that under the 1923 Treaty of Lausanne, Turkey had renounced all her rights on Cyprus after the Island was annexed by Britain in 1914. In 1925 Cyprus had become a Crown Colony.

Why then, did the British Government want Turkey to be involved in this **Tri-partite Conference**, in order to discuss the future of Cyprus? As subsequent events showed, the intention was to get Turkey involved on the issue of Cyprus and thus create a rift among Greece and Turkey.

The Greek-Cypriots were fighting for *Enosis*. The British were against *Enosis* so the best way to avoid *Enosis* was to get Turkey involved. Sir Anthony Eden's plan was to get Turkey involved and thus not only delay the outcome of a solution but eventually shift the burden of responsibility from British shoulders on to those of Greece and Turkey.

The Greek Government fell into this British "political trap" because, by agreeing to attend this conference and to discuss the future of Cyprus **with Turkey**, it was consenting and giving the latter the right of a say in the matter, when in fact Turkey had renounced such rights at the Treaty of Lausanne in 1923.

Makarios foresaw this happening and together with his colleagues (**Lanitis, Loizides, Rossides, Kranidiotis** and others) went to Athens to see **Stefanopoulos**, the Greek Foreign Minister, and warned him of the dangers.

Although Makarios was against Greece taking part in such a Conference, fearing for Turkey's subsequent involvement on the issue of Cyprus, a communique was issued after their meeting which amazingly indicated Makarios's consent (!) provided that *"in addition to the Tri-Partite Conference, the issue of Cyprus should also be taken to the United Nations"*.

Stefanopoulos must have persuaded Makarios to give his consent for the Tri-partite Conference in return for raising the Cyprus issue at the United Nations. Four days later, when Makarios was speaking at a press conference, he had changed his mind!

The Tri-Partite Conference was held at Lancaster House in London, on the **29th August 1955**. It was attended by the three Foreign Secretaries: **Macmillan, Stefanopoulos and Zorlu.** **Macmillan** stressed the friendship between Britain, Greece and Turkey and the importance of their membership in the NATO alliance. He said that the aim of the Conference was to try to reconcile the "unhappy differences centred on Cyprus which were imperilling the common defence of the three nations in the eastern Mediterranean. He recalled that in 1878, Britain had entered into a defensive alliance with Turkey. He also emphasised the importance of Turkey's position in the front line of Western defence.

The Greek Foreign Minister **Stefanopoulos** welcomed the direct discussions, stressed the importance of the common security of the three countries and recognised that Britain must have a base in Cyprus. He also stated that although the Greek Government  supported the right of the Cypriots to self-determination, it never contemplated the withdrawal of British forces from Cyprus.

The Turkish Foreign Minister **Zorlu** argued that the 1878 Treaty of Alliance with Britain clearly indicated the importance of Cyprus to the defence of Turkey, and  that the fate of the island was the exclusive concern of the British and Turkish Governments. Any demand for a change of status was tantamount to a demand for the\ revision of the 1923 Treaty of Lausanne which would not be restricted to Cyprus, but would raise other complex issues. Turkey, he said, had always treated the Cyprus question as a British domestic issue. The island's  importance for Turkey emanated from the "exigencies of history, geography, economy and military strategy, from the right of existence and security." (See *The Tripartite Conference on the Eastern Mediterranean and Cyprus, Cmd 9594), October 1955.*

It may be said that Makarios's fears were fully  justified. He made a very serious political blunder  in agreeing with Stefanopoulos in the first place because he assumed  that by taking the issue of Cyprus to the United Nations, things would follow a different course. When he  changed his mind (as he often did) it was too late, because  Turkey's interest in Cyprus was re-awakened by the British,  irrespective of the  terms of the 1923 Lausane Treaty. Nikos Kranidiotis who attended the Conference  as an unofficial observer (sent by the Ethnarchy - the Cyprus Church)  confessed many years later  that "*the Tri-Partite Conference was the beginning of  all  the troubles for Cyprus".* ("Nea" Newspaper, 3 August 1978).

## ANTI-GREEK RIOTS IN CONSTANTINOPLE (ISTANBUL)

As the Tri-partite Conference was still going on in London, on the 6th September 1955 the news that an explosion had taken place in the grounds of the Turkish Consulate in Salonica (which used to be Attaturk's house), had led to riots in Istanbul and Smyrna. Two Turks, Hasan Ucar who worked previously at the Consulate and Oktay Engin, a student, were convicted by a Greek court of causing the explosion.

On the night of the 6 - 7 September 1955 the Greek community in Istanbul was terrorised. Some 75 Greek churches were burnt or destroyed, 860 shops were wrecked and looted and over 7,000 houses were damaged. What was astonishing was the fact that the official Turkish view described the riots *"as a Communist plot which aimed against western interests and Greek-Turkish friendship!"*

## SIR JOHN HARDING 1955 - 1957

On the 3rd October 1955, the Government of Sir Anthony Eden replaced Robert Armitage as Governor of Cyprus with a "military man" **Marshal Sir John Harding**. A state of Emergency was declared and about 37,000 British troops patrolled the whole Island. Hundreds of people were arrested and imprisoned or held in detention centres.

The new Governor and Archbishop Makarios had several talks during the first two months of 1956 in an effort to reach an agreement on the self-government of Cyprus.

*Archbishop Makarios and Sir John Harding*

The last talks were held on 29th February 1956 in the presence of Colonial Secretary **Alan Lennox- Boyd**. Makarios had put forward five principles for the proper functioning of self-government and Harding put forward six points. The two sides were very close to a solution because Makarios yielded from his original demand of *'nothing less than Enosis'*. As Makarios was to confess much later (in the Michael Cacoyiannis film **The Long March** in 1974) :

*".... considerable progress was made and that Grivas wrecked this peaceful process which was taking place by carrying bombing activities whilst the talks were being held."*

# MAKARIOS SENT TO EXILE

After the collapse of the talks with Makarios, Harding was determined to crash the EOKA movement and rule the island with *"an iron fist"*. On the 9th March 1956 Makarios was about to board a plane for Athens for further talks with the Greek Government. He was arrested and together with the Bishop of Kyrenia Kyprianos, Papastavros Papagathangelou (who recently died in May 2001 at the age of 90) and Polycarpos Ioannides, they were deported *without trial* to the Seychelles in the Indian Ocean.

*Bishop Kyprianos, Archbishop Makarios, Polycarpos Ioannides and Papastavros Papagathangelou*

News of Makarios's deportation with three other colleagues led to a week-long strike in Cyprus and riots in Greece. The Greek ambassador in London (Vasilis Mostras) was recalled. The deportation was described both unreasonable and foolish. Makarios and his colleagues were to stay in exile for the next 13 months. In the House of Commons some MPs  suggested that Makarios should be released and be allowed to address an all-party meeting of both Houses.

On 9th May 1956 the Greek **Archbishop Dorotheos** addressed a rally of some 10,000 people in Athens about the two impending hangings in Cyprus, of **Michael Karaolis** and **Andreas Demetriou**. The demonstrators then marched  towards the British Embassy in  Athens. The  police tried to disperse the demonstrators and fired indiscriminately, killing seven of them and  injuring about 200 people.  In Nicosia, on 10th May 1956 the British authorities hanged the two young men **Michael Karaolis** and **Andreas Demetriou**. These two hangings were to be followed by three more on the  8th August 1956, those of **Andreas Zakos, Harilaos Michael** and **Iakovos Patatsos.** On 21st September 1956,  there were three more executions: those of **Michael Koutsoftas, Andreas Panyides** and  **Stelios Mavromatis**. The last person to be hanged on 14 March 1957 was **Evagoras Pallikarides**, an 18-year old student from Paphos.

Racial tension between the Greeks and Turks began in 1956. The Turkish Cypriots opposed the Greek Cypriots' struggle for **Enosis.** The entire auxiliary police force who supported the British forces were now made up of Turkish Cypriots.

In the summer of 1956, **Nasser** of Egypt had nationalised the Suez Canal. The British presence in Cyprus was to play an important part, not only during the Suez crisis which followed soon afterwards,  but also for the future of Britain's presence in the region.

# THE 9 YOUNG CYPRIOTS WHO WERE HANGED

**Michael Karaolis**
*10.5. 1956*

**Andreas Demetriou**
*10. 5. 1956*

**Andreas Zakos**
*9. 8. 1956*

**Harilaos Michael**
*9 .8.1956*

**Iakovos Patatsos**
*9.8.1956*

**Stelios Mavromatis**
*22.9. 1956*

**Michael Koutsoftas**
**9. 8. 1956**
**Andreas Panayides**
**22. 9. 1956**
**Evagoras Pallikarides**
**14. 3. 1957**

# THE RADCLIFFE CONSTITUTION

On 12th July 1956 A. Lennox-Boyd, the Colonial Secretary, appointed **Lord Radcliffe** to prepare a set of proposals for a constitution for the self-government of Cyprus. Lord Radcliffe visited Cyprus twice to consult with the people but the Greek Cypriots stressed that Makarios was their legitimate representative. Radcliffe published his recommendations in a White Paper on the 19th December 1956. The main proposals were briefly the following:

1. A Legislative Assembly to consist of a speaker, a deputy speaker and 36 other members.

2. A Chief Minister to act as Head of Government in self-governing matters and to be appointed by the Governor.

3. A Minister of Turkish Cypriot affairs to deal with education and other communal affairs.

4. A Bill passed by the Legislative Assembly will only become law if it is approved and signed by the Governor.

On the same day (19th December 1956) that this White Paper was published, the Foreign Secretary announced in the House of Commons that the other possible solution would be the partition of the Island. The Radcliffe proposals were accepted by the Turkish government and the Turkish Cypriot leadership but were rejected by the Greek government and the Greek Cypriots. Meanwhile Makarios was still in exile in the Seychelles.

## U.N. RESOLUTION 1013 (XI)

On 26th February 1957 the United Nations Political Committee adopted the resolution on Cyprus, prepared by the Indian Foreign Secretary *Krishna Menon* (Resolution 1013 (XI). The resolution stated: *"The solution of the Cyprus problem required an atmosphere of peace and freedom of expression and that a peaceful, democratic and just solution would be found in accordance with the purposes and principles of the Charter of the U.N......"*

During the same month (February 1957) Harding had announced that the days of EOKA were numbered. On the 3rd March 1957, the British forces discovered the hideout of the deputy leader of EOKA *Gregoris Afxentiou* in the mountains of Macheras. Afxentiou ordered his colleagues to come out, but he himself refused to come out and was prepared to die rather than surrender. The British troops employed helicopters to pour petrol over the hideout and Afxentiou was burned alive. The spot where he was killed has now become a shrine of patriotic pilgrimage.

**Gregoris Afxentiou burnt alive on the Macheras Mountains 3 March 1957**

On 14th March 1957 Grivas declared a truce and on 6th April Makarios and his co-exiles were released. They arrived in Athens on 17th April but they were not allowed to return to Cyprus. In fact they had to stay in Greece until after the signing of the Zurich-London agreements of 1959. Soon after his release Makarios wrote to Macmillan on 28th May 1957 reminding him of the February UN Resolution on Cyprus and the truce which commenced on the 14th March. He was now expecting some positive response from the British Government. In the summer of 1957 the British Government initiated private discussions with the Greek and Turkish Governments proposing a round the table conference.

Meanwhile in Cyprus, the policy of repression continued to such an extent that even a British Newspaper, the *Daily Mirror*, described Tory policy in this way:

*"The policy of the British Government in Cyprus is now inhuman. There is no other word for it. A stupid plan of repression that has not succeeded and cannot succeed in the second half of the 20th c."* (17. 6. 1957).

## SIR HUGH FOOT - THE LAST
## BRITISH GOVERNOR 1957 - 1960

In November 1957 Harding retired from service and was replaced by Sir Hugh Foot, who was previously a Colonial Secretary of Cyprus 1943 - 45 and later Governor of Jamaica. (Foot was the brother of Michael Foot who later became the leader of the Labour Party). Foot arrived in Cyprus on the *3rd December 1957.* He was very different from Harding. He tried to implement a different strategy, that of negotiation as against that of confrontation which was pursued by his predecessor. He believed in dialogue and spoke to many leading Cypriots, visited many village cafes and spoke to ordinary people. A month later he returned to London with a set of proposals to end the state of emergency which were accepted by Whitehall.

In January 1958 Foot and Selwyn Lloyd went to Ankara and Athens for talks. Whilst in Athens Foot had a meeting with Makarios for about half an hour.

The **Foot - Macmillan Partnership Plan**, which was worked out in May 1958, was presented to the House of Commons in June. The main points of this plan were the following:

*1. A "partnership" in Government between the two communities in Cyprus and Britain, Greece and Turkey.*

*2. The international status of Cyprus to remain the same for the following seven years.*

*3. The administration of Cyprus to be directed by a Council which will consist of the British Governor, representatives from the Greek and Turkish governments and six Cypriot ministers to be elected, four from the Greek Assembly and two from the Turkish.*

*4. The British Governor (in consultation with the Greek and Turkish Governments) would be responsible for external affairs and matters of defence and security.*

The Plan was put forward to the Greek and Turkish Governments for their consideration. Basically it consisted of Foot's proposals for internal self-government and external rule by Britain, Greece and Turkey. The plan was rejected by all sides.

According to Glafcos Clerides, on the 12th April 1958 Sir Hugh Foot phoned him at about 10.00 p.m. and wanted to see him at the Government House. Clerides went there and the conversation centred on the inter-communal conflict, the senseless looting, burning, killing and the EOKA 'violence'. Sir Hugh Foot told him that Cyprus had to be saved. He then said:

*"I want to get a message to Colonel Grivas. I must meet him and talk face to face to him. I want to persuade him to agree to a cease-fire. I am willing to meet him alone, unarmed and at any place he chooses." (See: G. Clerides: "My Deposition" Vol. 1 pp 58 - 59).*

Clerides at first pretended that he had no contact with Grivas but promised the Governor that he would try through some other contacts, especially those EOKA members whom he defended during their Court hearings. The Governor's message was conveyed to Grivas but his response was negative. He feared that it was a trap.

## EOKA AND T.M.T. OPPOSE GREEK - TURKISH FRIENDSHIP AND CO-EXISTENCE INTER-COMMUNAL VIOLENCE

It was common knowledge that EOKA and TMT struggled for two diametrically opposing causes. EOKA wanted the Union of Cyprus with Greece and TMT wanted Partition. They only had one thing in common: Both were extreme right wing and anti-communist organisations.

Grivas had a pathological hatred against the Communists. Spyros Papageorgiou a former leading EOKA member in his book *"AKEL the other KKE"* refers to a letter sent by Grivas to Makarios at the end of 1957 where Grivas shows his anti-communist hysteria:

*"The Communists must be attacked and be humiliated. The Communists are our opponents whether we like it or not. It is advisable to exterminate them as a political entity so that they may not be able to exert any further influence in our*

*national issue..."* (See: S. Papageorgiou: *"AKEL the other KKE."* pp. 335 - 336).

According to Michael Poumpouris' book *"Meres Dokimasias - Days of Trial"* in the village of Styllos in Famagusta, the British had discovered an EOKA list of names of left wing people which were targeted to be executed because they were Communists and suspected as British collaborators. This list, according to Poumpouris, was found on the 18th December 1957, on the day the British troops had murdered EOKA local leader **Theodosis Hajitheodosiou**. (See: M. Poumpouris: *"Meres Dokimasias" p. 61).*

The programme of Grivas' masked gunmen to exterminate Cypriot Communists had began on the night of 21 January 1958 in the village of Koma tou Yialou when two brothers **Elias** and **Nikos Tofaris** were shot as they were leaving the cafe.

One of the most brutal attacks took place on 23rd May 1958 in Lefkoniko against **Savvas Menikos**. Photis Papaphotis an EOKA District leader, had ordered his arrest and punishment. Menikos was arrested on his return from work as he was on his way to Goufes, his village. He was arrested in Lefkoniko and tied on a eucalyptus tree in the village square outside the church and was stoned to death by a fanatical crowd. He was accused of being a "traitor" and for telling off some children who were shouting "Long Live EOKA!"

Menikos' murder provoked a public outcry and revulsion throughout the island. It provoked such revulsion that the Greek Consul, Angelos Vlachos, wrote to Grivas to complain about Menikos brutal stoning to death. Grivas replied by showing no remorse whatsoever, saying that:

*"The punishment method of Stoning people to death was a genuine Greek tradition and mentioned the example of the death of the Spartan Pausanias."*

Grivas had his "history" facts wrong. Pausanias was not "stoned to death" but was shut in a temple with all entrances blocked, so that he would die of starvation. (See: Angelos Vlachos: *"Mia fora kai ena kairo enas Diplomatis - Once upon a time there was a Diplomat"* Vol. 4. p. 348).

Papaphotis, who had ordered Menikos' arrest and punishment, was to admit many years later that Menikos *was not a traitor*, but he had ordered his arrest and wanted him to be humiliated by the people in the Lefkoniko square and to be told about his "anti-nationalist" behaviour! Papaphotis further claimed that "Menikos could not endure the people's reproaches and insults and died from a heart attack!" Menikos obviously died from the vicious attacks with stones and not from what Papaphotis said. Like Grivas, Papaphotis showed no remorse for giving the order for Menikos' arrest and subsequent torture to death.

The year 1958 was also marked by a number of murders of left-wing Greek Cypriots by the masked men of Grivas. Grivas and EOKA had formed a special section to deal with Greek-Cypriot communists who favoured independence rather than *Enosis.* Those who were murdered were branded as traitors or collaborators. Such people were murdered in the villages of **Lysi, Koma tou Yialou**, **Lefkoniko** and **Milia** as well as in other parts of the island.  A danger of civil war was looming. Makarios was still in Athens and was not allowed by the British to return to Cyprus.  Although he was asked to intervene and condemn these fratricidal killings,  he never condemned them publicly to show that he was against such fratricidal attacks. He simply called for unity!

Today, it is a well known fact  that many innocent people lost their lives at the hands of the EOKA masked gunmen simply because they held left-wing political views. In a small community,  those orphan children sadly carried the "stigma" of  their fathers, who  were branded as  "traitors". Some of them tried to show that their parents were innocent and that they were unjustly executed. They challenged the leaders of the *Association of ex-EOKA servicemen* for evidence but they were constantly refused !

Even some forty years after the EOKA struggle, the leading participants still refuse to admit to their mistakes and publicly rehabilitate those innocent victims who died at their hands. A typical example is the interview given on Cyprus Radio by  Thasos Sophocleous, a  leader of the Association of EOKA Fighters. When he was challenged on the Cyprus Radio to provide the evidence, he gave the following arrogant reply:

*"We have carried out a struggle as we have done and we do not have to give any explanation to anyone!" (RIK - Third Programme, "Proino Dromologio"  16. 6. 98).*

**Rauf Denktash** (born 1924) was the leader of **Volkan** (*Volcano*), an organisation which advocated Partition. Volkan was renamed in late 1957 as  *Turk Mudafaa Teskilati* i.e.  *Turkish Defence Organisation* or *T.M.T.* for short. Like EOKA which boycotted British goods, T.M.T. urged all Turkish Cypriots to boycott Greek goods and threatened them with violence and execution if they co-operated or had any dealings with the Greek Cypriots.

Before the violence which erupted in 1958 many Turkish Cypriot workers joined with Greek Cypriot workers in the May Day celebrations and co-operated with them in the Trade Union movement. The T.M.T. opposed this Greek-Turkish co-operation.

On the 22nd May 1958 the first murder attempt was made on *Ahmed Sadi*, who was in charge of the Turkish office of the PEO Trade Union. He was shot by three Turkish gunmen on his doorstep and seriously wounded.

On the 24th May 1958 another Turkish Cypriot, *Fazil Onder*, chief editor of the weekly newspaper *Inkilapci* was murdered by the T.M.T.

On the 29th May 1958 *Ahmet Yahya*, a committee member of the progressive Turkish Cypriot Athletic Cultural Centre was murdered.

*Ahmet Ibrahim*, a barber from Limassol was executed on 30th June 1958 because he expressed himself in favour of Greek-Turkish co-operation.

Communal violence erupted once again in Cyprus in the summer of 1958. On 7 June a bomb exploded outside the Press Office of the Turkish Consulate in Nicosia. This led to an outrage and communal violence.

During the trial of the *Menderes* government (1960 - 61),

it was confessed that the bomb which exploded outside the Press Office of the Turkish Consulate was planted by Turks. **Aydin Konuralp**, of the Turkish Cypriot weekly **Nacak**, testified that news of a coming massacre by the Greeks was fabricated in order to incite Turkish Cypriots to take action against the Greeks. The testimony was supported by the evidence of **Emin Dirvana** (who later became Turkey's ambassador to Cyprus). Within two months, 56 Greeks and 53 Turks were killed. Numerous Greek and Turkish houses were burnt down and people were forced to move to other parts of the island.

Rauf Denktash was to admit himself many years later, on 26 June 1984 on the ITV channel, that the bomb at the Press Office of the Turkish Consulate was placed by Turks in order to create an atmosphere of tension and so that the views of the Turkish Cypriots may be known. *(ITV Documentary: "End of Empire: Cyprus, Britain's Grim Legacy" 26. 6. 1984).*

On 12th June 1958 about twenty Greeks returned from Nicosia to their village in Kontemenos but complained that the Turks in the mixed village of Skylloura were causing harassment. News of this harassment led about 25 villagers from Kontemenos to go to Skylloura (in two groups) in order to safeguard the freedom of movement. These people were arrested by the British troops and taken to Yerolakos Police Station. They were then driven back to the Turkish village Guenyeli. They were dropped off in the fields and were told to walk the four miles back to their village. Some 200 Turks armed with guns, knives, clubs, axes, and metal bars, had surrounded them and massacred eight Greeks and nine others were seriously wounded.

On 3 July intercommunal disturbances took place in Omorphita (a Nicosia suburb) and Greek families were driven out of their homes. Greek houses were burnt down in Lefka and in Paphos. The Greek Cypriots retaliated by driving Turkish Cypriots out of their homes and burning their houses in various parts of the island. In three months alone, between June and August 1958, this racial violence led to the death of 107 people, 56 Greeks and 51 Turks.

## MAKARIOS AND KUTCHUK ACCEPT INDEPENDENCE

By 1957 Makarios had realised that his political ambition to achieve *Enosis* with Greece had become unrealistic and unachievable, mainly because of Turkey's opposition. The fears expressed by Makarios prior to the August 1955 London Tri-partite Conference (Britain, Greece and Turkey) were now realised. Makarios and the Greek Cypriots had two pillars of opposition: Britain (the colonial power) and Turkey, who suddenly became interested after the Tripartite conference as "defender" of the minority's ethnic interests.

While he was still in Athens, in September 1958, Makarios gave an interview to British M.P., **Barbara Castle**, for the **Daily Herald** newspaper. He told Barbara Castle that he was now prepared to forego *Enosis* and accept Independence for Cyprus. Makarios's change of heart to accept Independence had infuriated Grivas, Bishop Kyprianos of Kyrenia and many other EOKA fighters who advised him to stick to the right of self-determination.

*British Journalist and MP Barbara Castle with Makarios*

On 6th December 1958 *Averof* and *Zorlu* (the Greek and Turkish Foreign Ministers) met at the United Nations and on 18th December (during a NATO meeting), the two ministers met with *Selwyn Lloyd* (the British Foreign Secretary) in Paris for further talks. The Turks were now prepared to drop their claim for partition in favour of independence but insisted that the Turkish Cypriot community should have an equal share in the administration and also a Turkish military force should be stationed on the island. The proposals were communicated to Makarios and Kutchuk. The two Foreign Ministers met again in Paris on 18 and 20 January 1959 and agreed that top level talks (with the Prime Ministers present) should be held in Zurich early in February.

The Zurich and London Agreements in February 1959 brought to an end the four year struggle. From the 1st April 1955 when the EOKA struggle had commenced, to 30th March 1959 when the struggle was over, a total of **509** Greek, Turkish and British people lost their lives and **1258** were wounded.

## THE ZURICH - LONDON AGREEMENTS
## FEBRUARY 1959

On the 11th February 1959 the agreements were initialled by the Greek and Turkish Governments, whereby Cyprus was to become an independent republic with a Greek-Cypriot President and a Turkish-Cypriot Vice-president. It was agreed that there should not be a referendum on these agreements. The two Prime Ministers also agreed to exert their influence on Archbishop Makarios *to proscribe AKEL*, the Communist Party of Cyprus, and also to join the NATO alliance. *Averof* and *Zorlu* then went to London to brief *Selwyn Lloyd* about their agreement. Karamanlis returned to Athens and informed Makarios about the agreements which they had just initialled.

A London Conference was arranged for 17th February 1959. It was held at *Lancaster House* and was attended by the British, Greek and Turkish Premiers (Macmillan, Karamanlis and Menderes) together with their Foreign Secretaries (Selwyn Lloyd, Averof and Zorlu) and by Archbishop Makarios representing the Greek Cypriots and Dr. Kutchuk representing the Turkish Cypriots.

Selwyn Lloyd who chaired the meeting asked Makarios if he accepted the Agreements as they stood. Makarios said that he wanted to have some clarifications on eight particular points, especially those on the "rights of veto". Evangelos Averof, the Greek Foreign Minister then interrupted and said that "**Greece always honours its signature**" (meaning that they already have initialled the Zurich Agreements).

The talks were adjourned for the following day. Karamanlis and Averof arranged a meeting at the Greek Embassy (George Seferis was Ambassador) for the 34 Greek Cypriot representatives who had come to London as advisers to the Archbishop. They exerted as much pressure as they could to get them to accept the Agreements. Averof told the Cypriot representatives that if they did not accept these Agreements, the entire responsibility will be theirs and threatened them with the consequences saying: "*Let the flow of bloodshed be upon you and upon your children!*"

Most of them agreed and urged Makarios to sign. (Strangely enough, some of those who strongly advocated acceptance of the Agreements and exerted pressure on Makarios to sign, e.g. **Dr. Dervis** (ex-Mayor of Nicosia), **Bishop Anthimos** of Kition and others, turned against Makarios a few months later and accused him of betraying the national cause of **Enosis** by signing these Agreements).

The next day, Makarios was pressurised at Lancaster House to state with a "Yes" or a "No" whether he accepts the Agreements. According to the Greek Government delegation, Makarios was already aware of the content of the Agreements because this was communicated to him in Athens and they could not understand why he behaved in

160

that way. The Agreements were duly signed by all parties on the *19th February 1959.*

According to the Cypriot Newspapers (20th May 1959) Makarios issued a statement saying that:

*"He was not pressurised by the Greek government to sign the agreements and that no power in the world could force him to sign an agreement which was contrary to the interests of the Cypriot people."*

**Greek and Turkish Foreign Ministers Averof and Zorlu architects of the Zurich-London Agreements**

Although Makarios had made the above statement, he was to contradict himself sometime later because he never forgave the fact that *he was pressurised* by both the British and Greek governments to sign and this is confirmed by most of the 34 Greek Cypriot Representatives who went to London to offer him their advice. Furthermore, according to **Andreas Fantis** (a former deputy leader of AKEL): *"Makarios had vowed in 1961 to dispose completely of the Zurich - London Agreements within a period of 5 years."* (Phileleftheros: 4.11.1992).

On the 20th February 1959 Makarios issued a proclamation from London addressed to the Cypriot people. He said among other things that:

*"By signing the London agreements, the foundations have been laid of a free republic and a new era of welfare and progress has commenced for the whole Cypriot people".*

In the same proclamation he praised Grivas and the EOKA fighters for their contribution during the four year struggle. He said:

*"Today's agreement indicates the worthiness of their great sacrifices and of their patriotic activity."*

# MAKARIOS RETURNS TO CYPRUS
# 1st MARCH 1959

Makarios was now free to return to Cyprus. According to **Nikos Kranidiotis**, Makarios chose to fly to Cyprus through Rome and not through Athens as he did not wish to make any public statements during his stopover. On the way to Cyprus he asked his aide Nikos Kranidiotis to write the speech he was to deliver when they would arrive in Nicosia. When Makarios looked at the text he told Kranidiotis to give the speech a triumphal tone. When Kranidiotis suggested that the Zurich-London Agreements were not anything like the *"triumph at Marathon"* Makarios insisted that the speech should sound triumphal. *(N. Kranidiotis: Dyskola Chronia pp. 385 -386).*

Makarios arrived on the 1st March 1959 and was accorded more than a hero's welcome. Tens of thousands of people from all over the Island had thronged outside the Archbishop's Palace in Nicosia to see and cheer their exiled leader. The gathering resembled very much that of an imperial Roman reception! Addressing that "electrifying atmosphere", who kept chanting rhythmically the name "Makarios", the Greek Cypriot national leader made a passionate speech and used the same words that were uttered after the victorious Battle of Marathon in 490 B.C. against the Persians. He told the crowd the word **NENIKHKAMEN - i.e. We have won!** In the eyes of the Greek Cypriots Makarios was considered the new "Moses", who led his people out of the "bondage of British colonialism." Some Greek Cypriots were disillusioned because their "Moses" did not succeed to reach their *Promised Land*, i.e. *Enosis* with Greece. He also said among other things the following:

**Makarios returns to Cyprus and is accorded a hero's welcome**

*"We are going to construct a happy society, a society of God!.... Long live the free and independent Cyprus".*

A similar rally was held in the Turkish part of Nicosia which was addressed by Dr Kutchuk who said that:

*"Although the Greeks may control the steering wheel of the state vehicle the Turkish Cypriots are in charge of the brakes."*

This was a reference to the fact that the Turkish Cypriots possessed the right of veto and could stop the Greeks at any time from implementing policies which they did not approve.

The Greek Premier Mr Karamanlis exclaimed soon after signing the treaties: *"This is the happiest day of my life."* The AKEL (Communist Party) warned that the Zurich and London agreements did not correspond with the wishes of the people.

Perhaps the most tragic mistake was the fact that Makarios and Kutchuk having rejected both **Enosis** and **Partition,** and having both accepted **Independence** and agreed to work together in the administration of the new independent Republic, they should have appeared together to address a joint rally of Greek and Turkish Cypriots. They should have shaken hands in front of the people and they should have told both Greek Cypriots and Turkish Cypriots that *"as from now on, they will be working together for the good of their common homeland."* Unfortunately, both leaders were too proud and too nationalistic, they feared that they might be branded as "traitors" of their original cause. Although they accepted Independence as a solution, they still suspected each other. The wounds of the recent inter-communal violence had not healed, but worst of all, as subsequent events showed, they both remained "hostage" to their nationalistic ideals.

# GRIVAS ACCEPTS THE AGREEMENTS AND RETURNS TO GREECE

On 9 March 1959 Grivas issued a proclamation calling on all his EOKA followers to lay down their arms and accept the agreements. A large number of staunch supporters of Grivas and of *Enosis* felt betrayed by the settlement and blamed Makarios for signing these agreements. In the same way many Turkish Cypriots who were staunch supporters of *Partition* also felt betrayed.

On 17 March 1959, Grivas returned to Greece. He was given a national hero's welcome and was awarded a string of honours:

*1. The Greek Government promoted him to a General.*

*2. The Greek Parliament proclaimed him as "Worthy of the Nation".*

*3. King Paul conferred upon him the "Order of Valour".*

*4. The Athens Academy awarded him its Gold Medal.*

*5. The Mayor of Athens presented him with the Key of Freedom of the City of Athens.*

The political prisoners were released in March 1959. **Nikos Sampson** (who was sentenced twice to death) together with his colleagues who were imprisoned in England were also freed. Sampson spent the next few months in Rhodes and Athens. When he returned to Cyprus he was given a hero's welcome. As soon as he returned, he toured a number of towns and villages making speeches and everywhere he went was accorded a hero's welcome.

**Grivas in Athens at the Monument
of the Unknown Soldier**

The newspaper *Phileleftheros* described on the 19.8.1960 how he was welcomed in Tymbou village: *"The streets of the village were decorated with Greek flags, and as soon as he arrived he was showered with flowers"*. Sampson had expected Makarios to appoint him as one of his Ministers but when this did not happen, on 24. 10. 1960 he published the newspaper *Machi* (Combat), which was initially funded by Greek Foreign Minister Averof and Kykko Monastery.

The ink on the Zurich-London Agreements had hardly dried on the paper it was written, when a new organisation was founded by the ex-EOKA fighters on the 1st April 1959. It was called *EDMA* (*Unitary Democratic Front of Re-creation*). Its purpose was stated to be the completion by peaceful means of the work which had been undertaken

**Nikos Sampson with Grivas**

four years earlier. The EDMA was created with the consent of Makarios and the blessing of Grivas. Clerides wrote :

*"Jealousies between the ex-fighters and conflicts of opinion on the issue of Enosis and independence coupled with outside interference by both pro-Grivas and pro-Makarios zealots led to the dissolution of the Front. Before it was dissolved it created pro-Makarios and pro-Grivas groups amongst the ex-fighters". (G. Clerides: My Deposition, Vol. 1. p. 96).*

In the summer of 1959, Grivas accused Makarios of misleading him about the agreements, i.e. that they contained *"verbal commitments"* for which he was not informed. On 30 July Makarios, Karamanlis, Averof and Kutchuk issued a statement denying such accusations. Makarios sent *Yiorkadgis* and *Georghiades* (members of the provisional government) to Athens for talks with Grivas.

Grivas would not be convinced and threatened to *"fight with all his might to frustrate the nationally harmful endeavours to enslave the Cypriot people."*

In an effort to bring about a reconciliation, Makarios met Grivas on the Island of Rhodes from 6 to 9 October 1959. Makarios told Grivas that *"only the Communists and the Turks would benefit from this rift"* and Grivas agreed with him. Grivas, like Makarios, was both ambitious and a megalomaniac. He soon forgot what he had agreed with the Archbishop in Rhodes.

In March 1959 Grivas had promised to retire from politics and was welcomed in Greece as a "national hero" and was awarded many honours by the Greek state. However, he did not keep to his word and by September of the same year, he had made himself so unpopular by his speeches and actions.

Grivas cherished the idea of a **Greater Hellas**, that it was still possible for Greece to become a great country by extending its borders and incorporating other Greek-speaking populations. He had already "forgotten" the terrible consequences of the 1922 Asia Minor disaster, which uprooted nearly one and a half million Greeks from their homes in Asia Minor. During a tour of the Epirus region he made a speech where he stated that *"he visualized a powerful Greece which will include all the enslaved territories such as Epirus and Cyprus."*

On 20 September 1959 he accused the Greek leadership that they were plotting to exterminate him because they suspected him of a conspiracy to overthrow the government. Those in government, who a few months earlier had praised him as a "national hero", were now accusing him of *"either deliberate lying or suffering from a 'persecution' complex!"*

**Makarios and Grivas in Rhodes**
**October 1959**

# PART 4: CYPRUS SINCE INDEPENDENCE

## THE CYPRUS CONSTITUTION

The Constitution of Cyprus was never approved by the people. It was a divisive one which treated the population in *ethnic terms* and not as one Cypriot community. The Greek Cypriots who constituted 80% of the population and the Turkish Cypriots who constituted 18% were to control (according to the constitution), 70% and 30% respectively of the posts in the Civil Service and the police force. It was also provided that there should be separate Municipalities, two army contingents of 950 and 650 soldiers respectively from Greece and Turkey, as well as 99 square miles for the British military bases.

The House of Representatives consisted of 50 Members, 35 were Greeks, and 15 Turks. In fact only 8 of the 15 Turkish Members were able effectively to oppose any Bill supported by 42 M.Ps! The Constitution furthermore provided that the President and the 35 Greek Cypriot MPs., were to be elected by the Greeks and the Vice-President
and the 15 Turkish Cypriot MPs., to be elected by the Turks. Out of the ten Ministries 7 were to be manned by Greeks and 3 by Turks.

In April 1959 Makarios and Kutchuk, even before they were elected as President and Vice-President respectively, set up a "Provisional Government" having appointed their own Ministers.

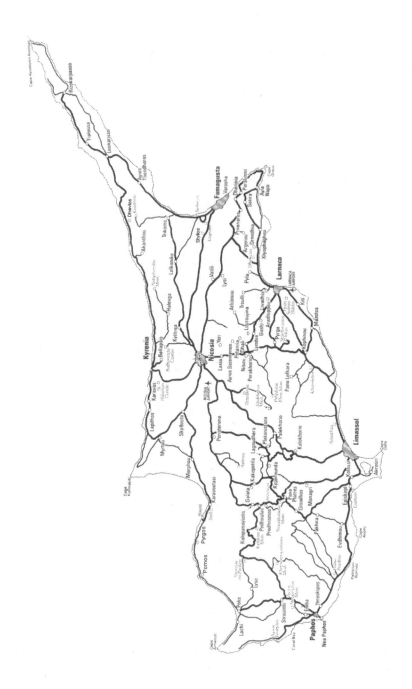

172

The political climate which existed at that time was such that both Makarios and Kutchuk were revered as ethnic leaders of their respective communities. It was those two, after all, who signed the Zurich-London Agreements. In a climate of political fanaticism the slogans all over the island said that Makarios was the *"One and only National Leader".*

The Greek Cypriots held the following Ministries:

1. Foreign Affairs.   2. Interior.   3.Justice.   4. Finance. 5. Communications and Works.   6. Commerce and Industry. 7. Labour and Social Services.

The Turkish Cypriots were in charge of the following Ministries:

1. Defence.   2. Agriculture   and   3. Health.

The Ministers appointed by Makarios were mainly young EOKA men and their inexperience was criticised by   *Dr Themistocles Dervis,*  the former Mayor of Nicosia,   as Makarios's *"Children Orchestra!"*  Perhaps Dr Dervis was offended because he was an experienced politician and was left out of the Cabinet. He too was a staunch supporter of *Enosis* and strangely enough,  when Makarios hesitated at first to sign the Zurich - London Agreements, he said that *" if Makarios does not sign,* (i.e. the agreements) *then he himself would append his signature with all his fingers and toes!!"*

Dr Dervis's subsequent exclusion from the Cabinet immediately turned him against Makarios. The very same man who a little earlier was prepared to append his signature with all his fingers and toes accepting Independence, had now accused Makarios of betraying the cause of *Enosis* ! He had now become a political rival to the Archbishop.

*Archbishop Makarios, Sir Hugh Foot and Dr Kutchuk*
*signing the Treaty of Independence 16. 8. 1960*

# THE FIRST PRESIDENTIAL ELECTIONS
## 13th DECEMBER 1959

The first Presidential elections were held on 13 December 1959. There were two candidates: **Archbishop Makarios** and **John Clerides** (the father of Glafcos Clerides, the President of Cyprus 1998 - 2003). Makarios was until then the "undisputed" leader of the Greek Cypriots, the person who signed on behalf of the Greek Cypriots the Zurich London-Agreements. John Clerides was the leader of the newly formed **Democratic Union**, which consisted of people who antagonised Makarios for betraying *Enosis* and for signing the Zurich London Agreements.

The *Democratic Union* was a rather strange and an "Unholy Alliance" because it was made up of some extreme right wing supporters of *Enosis* who were committed to do away with the Zurich-London Agreements and the Communist party AKEL. The ban on AKEL which was imposed at the beginning of Harding's governorship in 1955 and was not lifted until December 1959, gave little chance to the new *Democratic Union* to organise properly and contest the election.

Extreme right wing people such as Dr. Themistocles Dervis (a former Mayor of Nicosia) and Polycarpos Ioannides were previously political opponents of John Clerides. In fact, Ioannides previously accused John Clerides in a newspaper article as a "traitor" to the cause of *Enosis*. John Clerides was also unpopular with the EOKA supporters because he had previously refused to resign from the Governor's Executive Council. He only resigned when the Governor deported Makarios from Cyprus.

**Glafcos Clerides** states in his Memoirs (*My Deposition*, Vol. 1. pp. 90 - 96) how he acted as a go-between Makarios and his father. He tried to get his father to stand down and to allow Makarios to be elected unopposed in order to avoid a split among Greek-Cypriots. He also advised Makarios to use in the Government the elder statesmen for their experience, in order to help and advise the young ex-EOKA inexperienced Ministers. Makarios was reluctant and also suspicious to use the old politicians, the *"old foxes"*, for fear that they might plot against him and challenge his authority. Such was Makarios's passion for power that he felt that he would not be able to rule "as he pleased", if he had been surrounded by elder statesmen.

The 1955-59 struggle, and Grivas in particular contributed significantly in turning Makarios into a "national legend" among the Greek Cypriots. He had been exiled by the British and this was sufficient enough to turn him into a national hero. The British Colonial policy at the time was to arrest and imprison the national leaders and then negotiate with them later. They knew that these national leaders were anti-Communists and they were prepared to do business with them. They implemented this policy towards Kenyata in Kenya, to Nkrumah in Ghana, to Gandhi in India and many others. This British Colonial practice of first arresting and imprisoning or exiling the national leaders had worked because practically all former British colonies became members of the British Commonwealth and their economies depended considerably on the British economy.

# ΓΙΓΑΝΤΕΣ

ΚΑΡΙΟΝ
ΚΑΙ
ΜΟΝΟΝ
ΚΑΡΙΟΝ

# ΚΑΙ ΝΑΝΟΙ

A 1959 election poster portraying Makarios as a Giant and his opponent John Clerides as a dwarf (above)

A Democratic Union leaflet stating why the people should not vote for Makarios (Haravghi, 13. 12. 1959) (right)

# ΜΑΥΡΟ ΣΤΟΝ ΜΑΚΑΡΙΟ

## ΚΑΙ ΝΑ Ο ΛΟΓΟΣ

ΓΙΑΤΙ ὑπέγραφε χωρὶς τὴ θέληση καὶ τὴν ἔγκριση τοῦ λαοῦ τὶς ἀτιμωτικὲς συμφωνίες Ζυρίχης—Λονδίνου.

ΓΙΑΤΙ ἐπανέφερε στὴν Κύπρο τὴν τουρκικὴ κατοχή.

ΓΙΑΤΙ ἔγινε ἐπίορκος καὶ ἐνταφίασε τοὺς προαιώνιους καὶ ἱεροὺς πόθους τοῦ λαοῦ γιὰ τὴν αὐτοδιάθεση.

ΓΙΑΤΙ ἀπὸ Ἀρχιερέας μεταμορφώθηκε σὲ κομματάρχη.

ΓΙΑΤΙ ἵδρυσε κόμμα, τὸ ὁποῖο συντηρεῖ μὲ ἑκατοντάδες χιλιάδες λίρες, ποὺ προέρχονται οὐσιαστικὰ ἀπὸ τὸν λαὸ καὶ ἔπρεπε νὰ ἐπιστρέφωνται σ' αὐτόν.

ΓΙΑΤΙ κατακουρέλιασε τὸ κύρος τῆς Ἐκκλησίας, ῥίχνοντας τὴν σὲ ἐκλογικὲς διαμάχες.

ΓΙΑΤΙ ἀπὸ κήρυκας τῆς ἀγάπης ποὺ ἔπρεπε νὰ ἦταν, γίνεται κήρυκας τοῦ μίσους καὶ τῆς διχόνοιας.

ΓΙΑΤΙ ἐγκατέστησε στὴν πολιτικὴ καὶ κοινωνικὴ μας ζωὴ τὴν εὐνοιοκρατία.

ΓΙΑΤΙ ὁδηγεῖ τὸν τόπο στὴ φασιστικὴ δικτατορία.

ΓΙΑΤΙ στὸ ὄνομα του διαπράττονται ἀκατονόμαστα αἴσχη.

ΓΙΑΤΙ καταστρέφει τὴν παιδεία μας, μετατρέποντας τὰ σχολεία σὲ προεκλογικὰ κομματικὰ ὄργανα.

ΓΙΑΤΙ ἀρνεῖται νὰ δώσει τὴ γῆ στοὺς ἀγρότες.

ΓΙΑΤΙ ἀρνεῖται νὰ κατοχυρώσει τὰ συνδικαλιστικὰ δικαιώματα.

ΓΙΑΤΙ μᾶς ἔδεσε σὲ καταστροφικὲς στρατιωτικὲς συμμαχίες.

ΓΙΑΤΙ ἀρνεῖται φιλικὲς σχέσεις μὲ ὅλα τὰ κράτη τοῦ κόσμου.

## ΜΑΥΡΟ ΛΟΙΠΟΝ
## ΣΤΟΝ ΜΑΚΑΡΙΟ

Makarios believed himself to be the "New Moses" and the "New Messiah" who would redeem Cyprus of all its problems! He chose to appoint young Ministers in his Government because he would be able to tell them what he wanted them to do. The elder and more experienced statesmen would have challenged Makarios' authority and he did not wish to have that. Only in that way could he feel safe and be the absolute political and religious leader of Cyprus. In 1960, Makarios succeeded in becoming *"both a Henry VIII and a Cardinal Woolsey , a Louis XIII and a Cardinal Richelieu, all dressed in one".*

The **Democratic Union** (an unholy alliance of Communists and right wing people) in a desperate attempt to discredit Makarios called upon the people not to vote for him for the following reasons:

* *Because he signed the Zurich-London Agreements without consulting the people.*

* *Because he brought back to Cyprus the Turkish occupation.*

* *Because he betrayed his oath and buried the eternal and sacred wishes of the people for self-determination.*

* *Because from being a Church leader he had become a Party leader.*

* *He had founded a Party which he maintained by spending hundreds of thousands of pounds, i.e. the people's money.*

* *He had humiliated the reputation of the Church by involving the Church in election clashes.*

*Instead of being a herald of love he had become a herald of hatred and discord.*

*He had introduced in our political and social life the system of favouritism.*

*He leads our country towards a fascist dictatorship.*

*Shameful acts of violence are committed on his behalf.*

*He ruins our educational system by converting schools into pre-election party meetings.*

*He refuses to give the land back to the peasants.*

*He refuses to safeguard Trade Union rights.*

*He has bound us to catastrophic military alliances.*

*He refuses to have friendly relations with all the countries of the world.*
(Haravghi Newspaper 13. 12. 1959).

The Constitution provided that the President must be elected by the Greek Cypriots and the Vice-President by the Turkish Cypriots. In the first presidential contest held on 13 December 1959 there were **238,879** Greek Cypriot registered electors. Makarios won the election by securing **144,501** votes (or 66.82% of the vote) and John Clerides **71,753** votes (or 33.18% of the vote). For John Clerides to secure 33% of the vote against the "legend" called Makarios was very significant. After the defeat of the **Democratic Union**, AKEL left this "unholy" alliance and strangely enough, offered its full support to Makarios, i.e.

to the man they opposed a few weeks earlier! The Vice-President was elected by the Turkish-Cypriots and **Dr. Fazil Kutchuk** was returned unopposed by the Turkish community as the first Vice-President. Cyprus was officially declared an Independent Republic on **16 August 1960** but the **1st October** was made as official date to celebrate Independence Day.

*The President and Vice-President of Cyprus*

At dawn of 16 August 1960 the Union Jack was lowered from the Governor's House, thus ending 82 years of British rule. The Cyprus flag was raised at the Parliament building. The new flag portrayed neutral colours (neither the Greek blue nor the Turkish red) the map of Cyprus in yellow with two green olive branches at the bottom of the map on a white background. The emblem of the Republic was a Dove with an olive twig in its beak. Sadly the flag and the emblem which symbolised peace and co-existence among the two communities remained only symbols of that aspiration. Both communities, instead of putting fanaticism and nationalism aside and working together to build their new common homeland, still raised on every occasion the national symbols of Greece and Cyprus. They were and remained Greek and Turkish first and Cypriot last!

*The Cyprus Flag*

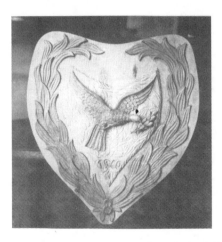

*The emblem of the Cyprus Republic*

**Archbishop Makarios 1960 -1977   Spyros Kyprianou 1977 - 1988**

**George Vassiliou 1988 - 1993**     **Glafcos Clerides 1993 - 2003**

# THE FIRST GENERAL ELECTIONS
## 31st JULY 1960

The first Parliamentary Elections were held on *31st July 1960.* The House of Representatives according to the Zurich-London Agreements consisted of 50 Members: 35 Greek Cypriots and 15 Turkish Cypriots. As there had been no previous Parliamentary elections, there were no organised political parties, apart from AKEL (the Communist Party), to contest the elections. Those who did not support AKEL, i.e. all right-wing Greek Cypriots, came under the umbrella of the Church and this was why the *Patriotic Front* was created just before the elections. The Majority electoral system was adopted and not that of Proportional representation. This system favoured the Patriotic Front which supported Makarios. After losing in the Presidential elections earlier, (December 1959) AKEL left the *Democratic Union* and when the right wing Cypriots were divided into pro-Makarios and pro-Grivas supporters, i.e. to pro-independence and pro-Enosis supporters, AKEL decided to back Makarios.

## *Makarios decides about the allocation of seats and the composition of Parliament !*

In any democratic society the political parties are free to contest as many seats as they wish. In the early years of the new Cyprus Republic this was not the case. Political power was to be shared among the Greek Cypriots according to the wishes of Makarios! Prior to the Parliamentary elections, the AKEL leadership suggested to Makarios that AKEL should contest *six* out of the 35 Parliamentary seats and the Patriotic Front to contest the other *29* seats. Makarios proposed that AKEL should only contest *four* seats. Talks were arranged at Glafcos Clerides's house, between Clerides and Ezekias Papaioannou (the AKEL General Secretary) in the presence of Lefkios Zenon (President of the District Court of Nicosia) and a compromise was reached: AKEL was to contest only *five* seats and the Patriotic Front the other 30. According to the constitution, if a party obtained **six** seats out of the 35, it was in the House as a political group and it was entitled to have a parliamentary spokesman, whereas if it obtained fewer than six seats, its members were there as *individuals*. Clerides later confessed that these were the real reasons why Makarios objected to AKEL contesting *six* seats. Although Makarios had agreed for AKEL to contest *five* seats, there were many others in the Patriotic Front who were against this concession and did not want to see any AKEL members in the new Parliament, claiming that AKEL did not participate in the national struggle!

The outcome of the results was predicted from the start! The **Patriotic Front** which supported Makarios secured the 30 seats and **AKEL** secured the other 5 seats as pre-arranged! The 15 Turkish Cypriot seats were won by the **National Front Party** of Dr. Kutchuk.

In September 1960 Cyprus joined the United Nations as its 99th Member. In February 1961 Cyprus joined the Commonwealth and in May of that year became a Member-state of the Council of Europe.

*President Makarios and Vice President Dr Kutchuk inspect the arrival of the 650 strong Turkish Force in Cyprus (as envisaged by the Zurich- London Agreements). This photo was published many times in the nationalist newspaper "Patris" accusing Makarios as being responsible for bringing Turkey into Cyprus*

## THE NON-ALIGNED MOVEMENT

Ever since he assumed power, Makarios decided that Cyprus should be associated with the Non-Aligned Movement. Contrary to he wishes of the USA, Britain, Greece and Turkey, who wanted Makarios to associate Cyprus with the NATO alliance, he believed that Cyprus should remain neutral and not become the "puppet state" of either the West or the East. In the 1950s he had already developed friendly relations with Prime Minister Nehru of India, President Nasser of Egypt and President Tito of

Yugoslavia. Now that he was formally in power as a Head of State he visited some of these countries which helped Cyprus during the United Nations debates.

During the years 1961 and '62 Makarios made a number of international visits. He visited Egypt where he had talks with

*Makarios with Presidents Nasser of Egypt and Tito of Yugoslavia in 1961*

President Nasser. In 1961 he took part at the Non-aligned Conference held in Belgrade. In January 1962 he made a state visit to the USA where he was welcomed by President Kennedy. During the same year he made a state visit to Turkey where he was welcomed by President Gursel and Prime Minister Inonu.

*Makarios with President Gursel and Prime Minister Inonu in Ankara 1962*

## MISTRUST RIGHT FROM THE START
## GREEK AND TURKISH SECRET PLANS

At the beginning of this work it was stated that the leadership of the two ethnic communities on the island strove for two different goals. The Greek Cypriots wanted **Union** with Greece and the Turkish Cypriots demanded **Partition**. The leadership of both sides were nurtured in these ideals and neither side was sincere when they appended their signature on the Zurich-London Agreements. Makarios did not hide his ambition and on the 1st April 1960 in a speech commemorating the first anniversary of the EOKA struggle he stated that **"the**

*Zurich-London Agreements were a springboard for further victories."* The Turkish leadership did not hide either their real ambitions, that their ultimate goal was Partition.

During the inter-communal conflict which erupted in December 1963 the Greek-Cypriot security officers confiscated a document from the safe of Vice-President Dr Fazil Kutchuk. This document was prepared by a militant organisation of Turkish Cypriots and stated that the Zurich-London agreements were accepted as an interim temporary measure in order that the rights of Turkey with regard to Cyprus would receive international recognition. It also stated that the agreements would provide time for the Turkish Cypriots to prepare themselves better and to profit by the blunders of the Greek Cypriots, who would decide to abrogate the agreements.

**The Turkish Plan** which was dated 14th September 1963 was found in Dr Kutchuk's safe and was signed by himself as Vice-President and by Rauf Denktash as President of the Turkish Communal Chamber. This plan stated among other things the following: *"In the event of the Greeks abolishing the constitution officially, the Turkish community, taking its destinies in its own hands, should go ahead with the establishment of a Turkish Republic.....The Turkish Vice-President will be accepted as President of the Republic of the Turkish community.... Our mother country will recognise immediately the Government to be formed...."*

**Polycarpos Yiorkadgis**, the Minister of the Interior was behind the Greek Cypriot militant organisation which prepared **The Akritas Plan**, which was named after his

EOKA code name. Makarios knew of this organisation and its strength, arms and its training. From the conversations that Clerides had with Makarios, the latter had planned to gradually abolish the Zurich - London agreements and the *excessive rights* given to the Turkish community. He believed that the proposed 13 points for amending the constitution were only the first step. He also disclosed to Clerides that if the Turkish community resorted to force to prevent unilateral amendments the security forces would maintain law and order, and if they proved inadequate for the task, then the paramilitary organisation *Akritas,* recruited by Yiorkadgis (the Minister of the Interior) would be called upon to assist them. (*G. Clerides: Cyprus - My Deposition, Vol. 1. pp. 209 - 210*)

There was a climate of suspicion and mistrust on both sides right from the very beginning, which led to the creation of para-military organisations and the accumulation of arms.

## THE MAKARIOS PROPOSALS TO AMEND THE CONSTITUTION

It has been mentioned earlier that both the President and the Vice-President possessed the right of veto. This was also true of the Members of the House of Representatives. Only *eight* out of the 15 Turkish Cypriot deputies were able to veto any bill proposed by the other 42 deputies!

In February 1961 the Turkish deputies expressing their disagreement with the proposed tax laws used their right of veto. This in effect meant that the government could not collect income tax and customs duties. When the Turkish Cypriot deputies proposed in December 1962 an extension of the municipal laws for one year as from 1st January 1963 this was opposed by the Greek Cypriot members. The matter was referred to the Cyprus Constitutional Court which was chaired by **Dr Ernest Fortshoff** a German Professor, who ruled that both moves were illegal.

The non-existence of a *Municipalities Law*, an *Income Tax Law* and a *Customs Law* in 1963 was drifting the two communities apart. In August 1963 Makarios informed Dr Kutchuk that he planned to revise certain provisions of the Constitution. Dr Kutchuk responded on 22 August 1963 warning the President against any revision because *"it would not be binding on the Turkish community."*

Makarios was determined to amend the Constitution and he had informed the Greek Government of his intentions. The Greek Government had advised him *against such plans* because the Turkish Government and the Turkish Cypriots will resist any changes. Evangelos Averof in his book *A Story of Lost Opportunities* states that he wrote to Makarios on 19th April 1963 warning him of the dangers that might result from such a course, both for Cyprus and Greece. The then President of the House of Representatives Glafcos Clerides, also advised Makarios that it was premature to make such changes.

Meanwhile, in Greece and Turkey there were Government changes. In Greece, Karamanlis resigned after an eight year rule, on 11 June 1963, when King Paul and Queen Frederica refused his advice not to make the Royal visit to London. In Turkey, Menderes was deposed in May 1960 by an army revolt led by Lt. General Jemal Gursel. There were attempted coups in 1962 and 1963 and Inonu's civilian government resigned on 2 December 1963.

When Clerides realised that Makarios was adamant, he advised him to wait at least after the February 1964 General Elections in Greece.

Makarios had made up his mind and would not listen to anyone. He also sought the views of Sir Arthur Clark, the British High Commissioner, who had advised him to limit the scope of the proposals. On the 30th November 1963, Makarios handed 13 proposals to the Vice-President for discussion and sent copies to the British, Greek and Turkish governments (the three Guarantors). As it was to be expected, the Ankara Government and Dr Kutchuk rejected them at once.

The thirteen proposals of Makarios for revising the Constitution (written on 30th November 1963) were briefly as follows:-

*1. The right of Veto of the President and the Vice-President of the Republic to be abandoned.*

*2. The Vice-President of the Republic to deputise for the President of the Republic in case of his temporary absence or incapacity to perform his duties.*

*3. The Greek President of the House of Representatives and the Turkish Vice-President to be elected by the House as a whole and not as at present the President by the Greek members and the Vice-President by the Turkish members of the House.*

*4. The Vice-President of the House of Representatives to deputise for the President of the House in case of his temporary absence or incapacity to perform his duties.*

*5. The Constitutional provisions regarding separate majorities for the enactment of certain laws by the House of Representatives to be abolished.*

*6. Unified Municipalities to be established.*

*7. The administration of Justice to be unified.*

*8. The division of the Security Forces into Police and Gendarmerie to be abolished.*

*9. The numerical strength of the Security Forces and of the Defence Forces to be determined by Law.*

*10. The proportion of the participation of Greek and Turkish Cypriots in the composition of the Public Service and the Forces of the Republic to be modified in proportion to the ratio of population of Greek and Turkish Cypriots.*

*11. The number of the members of the Public Service Commission to be reduced from ten to five.*

*12. All decisions of the Public Service Commission to be taken by simple majority.*

*13. The Greek Communal Chamber to be abolished.*

# INTER-COMMUNAL VIOLENCE, THE *"GREEN LINE"* AND THE LONDON CONFERENCE

Makarios' proposals were rejected. The three Foreign Ministers of Cyprus, Greece and Turkey met in Paris on 20 December to try and resolve the deadlock. While negotaitions were taking place in Paris, violence erupted in Nicosia. In the early hours of 21 December, a Greek Cypriot police patrol car driving along Hermes Street in the old town of Nicosia stopped a car for routine check but shots were fired and one of the policemen was wounded. The policemen returned the fire and a young Turk was killed and a Turkish woman seriously wounded and died on her way to the hospital. Violence soon spread in the Omorphita area, in the Nicosia-Kyrenia road and a Turk was shot at passing through the village of Deftera. Makarios and Kutchuk appealed to the public for calm. Both the Greek and Turkish Governments urged Makarios and Kutchuk respectively to exert their influence to stop the violence. On 23 Deember Turkish extremists forced the inhabitants of the Armenian quarter of Nicosia to leave their houses. Greek Cypriot extremists led by Nikos Sampson took reprisals against the Turkish Cypriots in Omorphita.

On 27 December 1963 **Major General Peter Young** and the Greek and Turkish commanders agreed to establish a joint peace-keeping force. On 28 December Duncan Sandys, Secretary of State for the Colonies arrived in Cyprus and suggested a conference to be held in London on 15 January 1964 to discuss the furture government of Cyprus. On the 30 December 1963 a **Green Line** was drawn on a map to separate the Greek from the Turkish quarter of Nicosia. The *Green Line* which was guarded by the British troops cut straight across the suburbs of

*"The Green Line" divides Nicosia - the only divided capital in Europe*

**Omorphita** and **Neapolis**. The Greek areas of **Kermia, Ayios Kasianos** and **Ayios Iakovos** were left behind Turkish lines.

The London Conference took place at Marlborough House on 15 January 1964 and talks went on until the early days of February.. It was attended by the Greek and Turkish Foreign Ministers (Palamas and Erkin), by Clerides and Denktash and was chaired by **Duncan Sandys**, the British Colonial Secretary. The Conference could not suggest a settlement. Duncan Sandys stated that they could not play permanently the role of the police and proposed that the Constitution remains as it stands with its existing terms of reference regarding the guarantees, to maintain the *Green*

194

*Line* and to bring to the island, for a temporary period, a peace-keeping force from the NATO alliance. This idea was rejected by Makarios and Khruschev, the Soviet leader, wrote on 7 February a letter of protest to the governments of Britain, USA, France, Greece and Turkey against a NATO force because he described it as "a crude encroachment of the sovereignty, independence and freedom of the Republic of Cyprus".

## CYPRUS AND THE UNITED NATIONS

The table below provides a list of the General Secretaries of the United Nations since 1961, all involved with the Cyprus problem.

U Thant (Burmese diplomat, 1962 - 71) Special UN Representative: (a) Sakari Tuomioja (b) Galo Plaza (c ) Osorio Tafall.

Dr Kurt Waldheim (Austrian statesman, 1972 - 1981) - Special UN Representative: Javier Perez de Cuellar

Javier Perez de Cuellar (Peruvian diplomat, 1982 - 1992) Special UN Representative: Oscar Camilion.

Boutros Boutros-Ghali (Egyptian diplomat, 1992 - 1996) Special UN Representative: Joe Clark.

Kofi Annan (1996 to the present) - Special UN Representative: Alvaro de Soto

# AMERICAN AND NATO PROPOSALS

A few days later, on the 31st January 1964, the British proposals for a Peace-Keeping Force in Cyprus (which were made at the London Conference) were presented as joint proposals from the British and U.S. Governments. The main terms were briefly the following:

*1. A peace-keeping force to be established in Cyprus made from member-states of NATO.*

*2. The Governments of Greece, Turkey, Britain and the USA to support the formation of this peace-keeping force.*

*3. The Governments of Greece and Turkey to undertake the obligation not to exercise the right of unilateral intervention (according to Article of 4 of the Agreements) for a period of three months.*

*4. The governments of Greece and Turkey to undertake to restrain the Greek and Turkish Cypriot communities from any hostilities.*

*5. The three Guarantor powers together with the USA to ask Archbishop Makarios and Dr Kutchuk (a) to accept a Peace-keeping Force and (b) to give assurances that they will restrain their respective communities from any hostilities.*

*6. The interested parties agree to accept a **Mediator** in order to solve their differences in a spirit of mutual compromise. The mediator will be selected by mutual agreement among the Guarantor powers, with the consent of Archbishop Makarios and Dr Kutchuk and to come from* *a member state of NATO, excluding the USA or one of the three Guarantor powers.*

It was later added to the above proposals that the NATO Peace-keeping Force will not be under direct NATO command but under British command and that its strength should not be less than 10,000.

The proposals were rejected by the Cyprus Government. Although the Greek Government accepted them, they asked for some clarification, suggesting that they should be accepted by the Cyprus Government and that the reference in the text should be about the President and the Vice-President of the Republic rather than mentioning Archbishop Makarios and Dr. Kutchuk by name.

The United States Government, fearful of Soviet influence in the area, sent **George Ball**, Acting Secretary of State to Athens, Ankara and Nicosia in February 1964 to persuade these governments to accept the plan. The Greek and Turkish governments accepted it but Makarios refused to comply.

One may say that It was rather strange because Makarios' original aim was to achieve **Enosis** with Greece, which would have meant that Cyprus would have been automatically part of NATO since Greece was already a NATO member. Yet Makarios, as President, now resisted any attempt to turn Cyprus into a NATO base and in this he had the full support of the USSR. **Khrushchev,** the Soviet leader, had a sent a letter of protest on the 7th February 1964 to the heads of government of the USA, Britain, Greece, Turkey and France against the NATO proposals because in the Soviet Union's view: *"they constitute a* *crude encroachment on the sovereignty, independence and freedom of the Republic of Cyprus."*

George Ball never forgave Makarios for his refusal to accept the plan and five years later, in 1969 at a Brooklyn Institution Conference he described Makarios as : *"that son of a bitch who will have to be killed before anything happens in Cyprus."*

**US Under-Secretary of State George Ball with Makarios February 1964. He later described Makarios "as a son of a bitch"**

# THE GRIVAS "CONFERENCE" IN ATHENS

When Grivas left Cyprus for Athens in March 1959, he had promised that he will stay away from politics. He did not keep to his word. The earlier praise and the honours which were bestowed upon him by the Greek Government made him think and feel that he was destined for higher things. He saw himself as the "military Messiah", the "redeemer" and "creator" of a **Greater Hellas** which would incorporate all Greek-speaking people from Northern Epirus, to Cyprus and Asia Minor. His political dreams however were shattered when he tried his luck at the Greek polls. The Greek people who knew his past history during and after the second world war and his paramilitary organisation known as *"X",* rejected him at the polls by the biggest of margins in 1961. His power and influence in Greek politics proved to be very insignificant to say the least.

Having tried and failed in Greece, he now turned his attention to Cyprus once more because this was "fertile" ground. Soon after the inter-communal clashes in Cyprus, he invited to Athens some 150 of his supporters, some of whom were Members of the Cyprus Parliament. Grivas's "Conference" took place on the 25th January 1964 and the purpose was to set up an organisation to fight for *Enosis.*

He had already forgotten the declarations which he made back in 1959 when he called upon all EOKA members to work together with Archbishop Makarios in the new Republic. Grivas now argued that *Enosis* was the only real solution to the Cyprus problem. He accused Makarios as a *"tyrant"* and as an *"oppressor"* and because of his policies *"communism had made great strides".* The final declaration of the Conference had "appointed" Grivas as the

"Representative" of all Greek Cypriots in negotiations with the Greek Government over the National issue of Cyprus. The declaration also stated that it would maintain the friendly relations between Greece and Turkey and of the NATO alliance.

# GEORGE PAPANDREOU COMES TO POWER IN GREECE

In the Greek General Elections held on 3rd November 1963 *George Papandreou*, leader of the *Union of the Centre* defeated the Conservative Party of Constantinos Karamanlis - the *National Radical Union (ERE)* . The Conservative era of Karamanlis which lasted for eight years (1955 - 1963) was now over.  On 16 February 1964 Papandreou was re-elected by an even bigger majority. Everyone believed that Papandreou would follow more liberal policies and  that he would work closer with Makarios.

In April 1964 Makarios went to visit Papandreou in Athens. It was then that Papandreou promised him military support. By mid-summer some 10,000 Greek officers and soldiers were already on the island.

The purpose of the presence of Greek forces in Cyprus was said to be to prevent a possible invasion from Turkey. Some others argued that Papandreou was suspicious of Makarios and wanted to keep a watchful eye on him because he began "flirting" with the Soviet Union and the Eastern bloc. Whatever the reasons, this was a very foolish decision because both George Papandreou and Makarios

*Makarios with George Papandreou in Athens, April 1964*

ignored completely the fact that Cyprus was *a sovereign
independent Republic* and that any decision to station an
army contingent (apart from that which was specified in the
1959 Agreements) was both *illegal and unconstitutional.*
(As we shall see later, Turkey gave an ultimatum to Greece
demanding the immediate withdrawal of this Greek
Division during the *Kophinou* events in 1967).

The Cyprus Government, rather than accept NATO forces
on its territory, sought the assistance of the United Nations
and on 4 March 1964 a Security Council *Resolution No.
186* unanimously recommended the establishment of a
U.N. Peace-keeping force in Cyprus. The UNFICYP has
been in Cyprus ever since 1964. On 27th March 1964, U
Thant the Secretary General of the UN, appointed *Sakari
Severi Tuomioja* as the first Mediator.

In March and April 1964 heavy fighting broke out among Greek Cypriots and Turkish Cypriots (especially around St Hilarion Castle) and Turkey threatened repeatedly to invade.

On 12 June 1964 with the consent of the Greek Government, Grivas arrived secretly in Cyprus. His visit was to remain secret and that it would not last for more than a week. Grivas however, did not return back to Athens as originally agreed but stayed in Cyprus and sometime later took over the command of the National Guard.

At the suggestion of Grivas, conscription was introduced in June 1964. This was another violation of the Agreements and the Constitution because there was no reference to a Cyprus army. (In fact, he stayed in Cyprus for more than three years and only returned to Athens after the **Kophinou fiasco** in November 1967). Speaking on the Radio a few days after his arrival, Grivas stated that the purpose of his visit was aimed at three things:

*1. To preach unity and reconciliation among the Greek Cypriots.*

*2. To exert his influence for peaceful co-existence with the Turks.*

*3. To contribute and help the Governments of Greece and Turkey so that a just solution may be found and that Cypriots should be able to exercise the right of self-determination.*

As the inter-communal violence escalated Turkey again threatened to invade but **President Lyndon Johnson** wrote to **Ismet Inonu**, the Turkish Prime Minister, advising him against taking such drastic action.

The Greek Prime Minister George Papandreou declared in an interview on 27 June 1964 that *"Grivas's presence in Cyprus is exceptionally useful because it contributes to the stability of peace!"* In fact the contrary was true. Grivas's arrival and role was suspicious not only to the Turkish Cypriots and the Ankara Government but also to those Greek Cypriots who had accepted Independence as the final solution.

Grivas' arrival was welcomed by those Greek Cypriots who considered him as the champion of **Enosis** and who felt betrayed by Makarios's policies. Subsequently Grivas was appointed to be in charge of the Greek forces on the island. His arrival in June was also seen as one way of keeping a check on Makarios's dealings with the USSR and the Eastern bloc countries (because Grivas was a well known anti-communist).

At a meeting held between Papandreou, Makarios, Grivas, Petros Garoufalias (the Greek Minister of Defence) and Polycarpos Yiorkadgis, held at Kastri in Athens (George Papandreou's residence) the Cypriot Minister of Interior and Defence, **Polycarpos Yiorkadgis**, argued that he should be in charge of all the Greek forces in Cyprus. His Greek counterpart, **Petros Garoufalias**, reacted angrily saying that so long as he is the Minister of Defence *"all the Greek troops will be answerable to him"*.

Garoufalias also reminded the Cypriot Minister of the Zurich-London Agreements which specifically state that the post of Minister of Defence in Cyprus is supposed to be held by a Turkish Cypriot and that he is only meant to be a Minister of the Interior. What the Greek Minister paradoxically "failed" to say was that both the Greek and Turkish Governments were constantly violating the Zurich-London Agreements and the Cyprus Constitution  by stationing illegally thousands of soldiers on the territory of an independent republic!

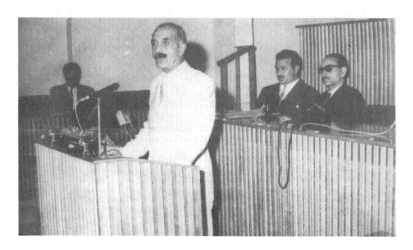

*Grivas addresses the Cyprus Parliament*

## THE ACHESON PLAN
## July and August 1964

In June 1964 both George Papandreou and Ismet Inonu visited separately, President Johnson at the White House. Johnson was exerting pressure on the Greek Government to come to terms with Turkey over Cyprus and suggested to meet at Camp David in order to try and reach a settlement.  Papandreou was warned by George Ball and Robert McNamara that *"if Turkey attacked Cyprus and possibly Greece, the USA would be unwilling to  lift a*

*George Papandreou with President Johnson June 1964*

*finger."* Papandreou gave in to American pressure and accepted Dean Acheson to work closely with the U.N. official mediator Tuomioja in Geneva. Makarios was ignored. As subsequent events showed, Acheson was appointed to play the part of a new "super-mediator" and Tuomioja would act as his "advisor".

**Dean Acheson** who was a former Secretary of State (1949 - 53) and also an adviser to Kennedy and Johnson was asked to be a US mediator on Cyprus. Acheson prepared two draft plans for a solution. On 28 July 1964 Acheson submitted a "final" draft of his plan which consisted 15 provisions for a settlement. These were briefly the following:

*1. Cyprus to be immediately united with Greece.*

*2. A Greek General Administrator (Minister) for Cyprus to be appointed by the Greek Government.*

*Ismet Inonu with President Johnson June 1964*

*3. Turkey to have a military base on a lease basis for a period of 50 years in the Karpasia area and should not exceed 4.5% of the total area of Cyprus. (It was proposed the area from the village of Komi Kebir to the Cape of Apostolos Andreas). (Originally Acheson proposed a Turkish sovereign base but later changed it to a 50 years lease).*

*4. The existing six district areas (Nicosia, Limassol, Famagusta, Larnaca, Paphos and Kyrenia) should not be increased to more than eight. The Greek Government to appoint Turkish District Officers in two of these districts.*

*5. An Adviser on Moslem matters to be appointed who would work closely with the Greek Minister (Administrator)*

*6. The Turks of Cyprus should be recognised as a minority similar to the Turkish minority in Thrace.*

7. A United Nations Representative to be permanently resident in Cyprus in order to monitor the implementation of the minority regime and agreements.

8. Greece and Turkey to have the right of individual appeals concerning Human Rights.

9. Greek sovereignty will include Karpasia even if the area is on a lease basis to Turkey.

10. To exclude the main villages in Karpasia and the Monastery of St. Andreas from the area under a Turkish lease basis.

11. A joint military (defence) command to be set between Greece and Turkey with an American representative.

12. The joint Greek-Turkish command will not be restricted on military matters but also on political and tourist matters.

13. The joint military command will meet regularly in order to join their efforts for the common benefit of the two countries.

14. Turkey undertakes to receive back all the expelled Greek people from Constantinople and other Turkish cities and to recognise their right as minorities similar to the status of the Turks in Thrace.

15. Turkey undertakes to respect the rights of the population of the Islands of Imbros and Tenedos

Papandreou was so enthusiastic about the *Acheson Plan* and commented that it was *"like being offered a block of flats and I give one flat on a 50 year lease".* On 21 August

1964 **Ioannis Sossides,** the Director of the Diplomatic Office, was sent to Geneva to inform Acheson that he (Papandreou) accepts the Plan and that he was exerting his influence on Makarios to do likewise. In his message to Acheson, Papandreou wrote:

*"Our National Defence Minister Mr Garoufalias has been sent to Cyprus on a "double" mission: to postpone a Cyprus deal with Moscow and find out Makarios's views on the (Acheson) Plan. Mr. Garoufalias succeeded in preventing Mr Kyprianou's (Foreign Minister) visit to Moscow and also Makarios's visit to Cairo in order to meet President Nasser. Archbishop Makarios rejects the proposal of offering an area for bases to either NATO or Turkey.*

*We would have preferred of course to achieve Enosis without any exchanges. This would be right since the Turkish minority will have the full protection under the Greek administration and will enjoy the same protection as the Muslim minority in Thrace.*

*Greece is prepared to support the idea of a Turkish base even if the Archbishop disagrees on this, provided that the area of the base is more or less similar to the existing British bases (i.e. 99 square miles).* (L. G.Papadopoulos: *Keimena 1959 - 1974, pp. 180 - 2*).

George Papandreou and Grivas had accepted the Acheson Plan. Papandreou advised acceptance of the Plan because he wanted to achieve *Enosis* and was prepared to make concessions to Turkey. Makarios on the other hand wanted "unfettered" independence and rejected it. Two years later on 27 October 1966 in a speech at Samel College in North Carolina, Acheson admitted that *"Partition was the best solution for Cyprus"*.

# TURKEY BOMBS CYPRUS AUGUST 1964
## MANSOURA - KOKKINA CLASHES

Turkey was supplying arms by sea to the Turkish-Cypriot stronghold of **Mansoura** and **Kokkina** on the north-west coast of the Island. The Greek-Cypriot National Guard led by Grivas decided to put an end to this supply route. They feared that if the Turks were properly equipped and armed they might be able to cut off the western road from Xeros to Paphos.

On 8 August 1964 Grivas and the Makarios Government, without consulting George Papandreou and the Athens Government, gave orders to the National Guard to go ahead and the Turks were pushed out of Mansoura and Ayios Theodoros and retreated into Kokkina village.

The Turkish Government retaliated immediately by sending 30 jets on the same afternoon and 64 more jets on the following day and bombed the area of **Tillyria** with napalm bombs. A number or people were killed or wounded and many houses destroyed. The Greek Prime Minister George Papandreou was furious and sent the following message to both Makarios and Grivas:

*"We express our deepest sorrow that our agreements are of no use. What we agree is one thing and what you do is another and most adverse consequences result..."*

On 9 August 1964 Makarios sent a telegram to N.S. Khruschev, the Soviet leader, asking him for urgent Soviet support. Khruschev responded on the same day informing Makarios that he had sent a telegram to Turkey's Prime

Minister Inonu urging him to stop immediately all military action against the Republic of Cyprus. Khruschev also sent a telegram to the UN Secretary General urging him to take all the necessary measures to settle the Cyprus problem. (See Khruschev's telegram to Makarios 9. 8. 1964 in L. G. Papadopoulos: *To Kypriako Zitima, Keimena 1959- 1974, p. 171).*

The Security Council of the United Nations passed a resolution (No.193) on 9 August calling for a cease-fire. When Rauf Denktash had left for Turkey, he was banned from returning to Cyprus as he was involved in the December 1963 inter-communal troubles. At the same time the government of Cyprus appealed to the USSR and Egypt for military support to help protect the independence of the Republic. Six days later, on 15 August 1964, the Soviet Government announced that *" it will help Cyprus to defend its freedom and independence if a foreign armed invasion of the island took place."* (See above *Keimena,* p.173).

As the United States were very concerned about any possible Soviet influence in the region, it revised the Acheson plan aimed at safeguarding the south-eastern flank of NATO. On 20 August Acheson proposed *Enosis* in return for a NATO base on the island under Turkish command. Makarios believed that the plan would lead to a *Double Enosis* and rejected it. The Greek king tried to influence the Government to accept the plan. The Turkish government, although it was willing to accept the first Acheson plan and called for further negotiations, it was not prepared to accept the revised plan.

In August 1964 Johnson summoned **Alexandros Matsas**

the Greek Ambassador in Washington to discuss the Acheson Plan. When the Ambassador told Johnson that no Greek Government or Parliament had the right to give a Greek island to another country, (he was referring to the Greek island of Castellorizo), Johnson reacted angrily using vulgar language:

*"Then listen to me Mr Ambassador: You can fuck your Parliament and your Constitution. America is like an elephant and Cyprus is like a flea. If these two fleas (i.e. the Greek Cypriots and Turkish Cypriots) continue to annoy the elephant then the elephant is likely to crash them with his trunk!"*

On 29 August 1964 George Papandreou addressed a letter to Makarios criticising him for taking action without consulting the Greek Government. He accused Makarios of violating their (Papandreou - Makarios) agreement twice and cited the examples of the attack on Mansoura (Tillyria) and the threats concerning the replacement of the existing Turkish Force in Cyprus (which was agreed under the Zurich-London Agreements).

Papandreou had warned Makarios that no decisions were to be taken by Cyprus, which might lead to direct or indirect clashes, without the prior consultation and consent of the Greek Government. Papandreou also told Makarios that if he was able to speak from a position of strength, this was due to the Greek military presence on the Island. Makarios was further reminded that the Greek army in Cyprus was not there to fight for an "unfettered independence" as often propagated by Makarios but for *Enosis*.

Makarios was therefore expected to adapt to these "new realities" because he had been accustomed to taking decisions on his own without consulting anyone. Papandreou emphasised that the responsibility for the future of Hellenism rested with the Greek Government and not with Government in Nicosia. He concluded his letter with the hope that Cyprus will be united with Greece.

Makarios had met Papandreou later and discussed with him the content of his letter. Some six months later, on 21 February 1965 , Makarios replied to Papandreou's letter where he re-iterates that in the event of an unexpected Turkish attack, the Greek and Cypriot Parliaments will declare Enosis. He wrote:

*"I would also like to add, that even if Cypriot Hellenism was confronted with the unlikely event to struggle without the support of Greece, the aim of the struggle will still be Enosis and not the "unfettered Independence." .... We've always had Enosis as our only slogan in all our struggles... Enosis was also our previous aim but in order not to lead our Mother country into adventures, we were forced by the Greek Government to accept a temporary solution...."*
*(*See: L. G. Papadopoulos: Keimena 1959-1974, p. 189).

One can see from the above two letters that both Papandreou and Makarios were not "committed" to Independence and the Zurich-London Agreements and their main aim was to implement *Enosis.*

On 12 September 1964 a trade delegation headed by Mr Araouzos, Minister of Commerce, went to Moscow. On 30 September, Spyros Kyprianou, the Foreign Minister, signed on behalf of the Cyprus government an agreement to purchase arms from the Soviet Union.

The Soviet arms were to be supplied through Egypt. The

American Administration which exercised so much influence on the Greek Government insisted that they should use their influence on Makarios to stop these arms. When eventually the Soviet missiles were loaded on a ship and were on their way from Alexandria to Cyprus the interference and objection from the Greek Government was so powerful that the ship was instructed to return back to Egypt.

This political "flirt" of Makarios with the Soviet Union had infuriated the pro-American Greek Prime Minister George Papandreou. Soon after the rejection of the **Acheson Plan** Papandreou tried to "revenge" Makarios for not being "politically obedient" to Athens, by establishing closer relations with General Grivas. Papandreou's Government is said to have donated £12,000 to **Socrates Eliades** (a close friend of Grivas) in order to publish in Cyprus the pro-Enosis newspaper called **Patris** (Fatherland). This newspaper published in its first issue messages of greetings from George Papandreou and George Grivas. Papandreou's message concluded with the remark that we are **united for Enosis**.

On 5 October 1964 Andreas Papandreou (the son of the Greek Premier) in an interview to the French newspaper **Le Monde,** revealed that the Americans were trying to impose a solution of partition for Cyprus. This interview provoked a stormy reaction from the pro-American circles in Greece and Andreas Papandreou who was a Minister of Co-ordination, tendered his resignation. Makarios grasped this opportunity to co-operate with the "rebel" son Andreas Papandreou, since the father, George Papandreou, was now on the side of Grivas.

In October 1964 Andreas Papandreou was invited to Nicosia as an official guest of the Cyprus Government. His brief stay in Cyprus was used by Grivas in his Report to *P. Garoufalias*, the Greek Minister of Defence, that Andreas was the ring leader of an organisation in the army called *Aspida* (Shield). Andreas Papandreou described this as a Grivas-Garoufalias fabrication in order to bring down the Papandreou Government. (*M. Drousiotis: From the National Front to EOKA B. (in Greek) p. 33*).

## THE GALO PLAZA REPORT

The Finnish mediator Tuomioja died in September 1964. On 16 September 1964 *U Thant*, the UN Secretary-General, appointed *Galo Plaza* a former president of Ecuador, as the new U.N. mediator for Cyprus. Galo Plaza was expected to try and resolve the three different and conflicting viewpoints:

*1. The Greek-Cypriots' insistence on independence.*
*2. The Turkish insistence on Partition.*
*3. The Greek Government's preference for Enosis.*

After many months of studying the Cyprus problem and speaking to all interested parties, on 26th March 1965, Galo Plaza presented his *Report on Cyprus* to the Secretary General and recommended among other things the following:

*1. Talks should start among the Greeks and Turks of Cyprus because the solution of the problem must be an agreed solution by the parties concerned.*

*2. Return to the Zurich-London agreements is neither*

214

*possible nor desirable.*

*3. Unfettered independence, majority rule, with internationally guaranteed human and minority rights, was the best solution, provided the Government of Cyprus undertook a self imposed, unilateral undertaking, that in the interest of peace, the right of self determination would not be exercised and the independence of Cyprus would be maintained.*

Makarios welcomed the Galo Plaza Report, especially the recommendation of talks among the two communities. The Greek government was also supportive. The Turkish government and the Cypriot Vice-President were cautious and critical of certain parts of the Report.

## RUSSIANS PROPOSE A FEDERAL SOLUTION

In January 1965, the Soviet Foreign Minister Andrei Gromyko spoke in favour of a federal solution of the Cyprus problem. (*New York Times 22 January 1965*) . A federal solution was anathema to the Greek Cypriot leadership because it was interpreted as another form of partition. Gromyko's proposal had provoked an anti-communist uproar and hysteria from all right wing circles in Cyprus. What was strange about Gromyko's proposal was the fact that a few days previously, he had met in Europe with Ezekias Papaioannou, the AKEL General Secretary and this issue was never raised among the two fraternal parties. AKEL was therefore astonished by Gromyko's comments on federation and in order to salvage its own prestige among the Greek Cypriot people issued a statement condemning Gromyko's declaration. The irony of this is that some years after the Turkish invasion of 1974, the Greek Cypriot leadership (including AKEL) not only were prepared to accept a *Federal solution* (which they so vehemently rejected previously) but they were prepared to accept something worse than a Federal solution, i.e. a Bi-zonal and Bi-communal Federation!

## GREEK AND TURKISH CYPRIOTS WHO BELIEVED IN CO-EXISTENCE

The nationalist leadership of both communities had encouraged "ethnic fanaticism" on both sides. The majority of the ordinary people in both communities believed in friendship and peaceful co-existence. The Greek left wing party AKEL and the Trade Union PEO as well as many progressive Turkish Cypriot people campaigned for this inter-communal friendship and co-existence.

A shining example of this bi-communal friendship, understanding and co-operation was the Turkish Cypriot **Dr Ihsan Ali** (1904 - 1978), who was a medical practitioner in Paphos. Dr Ihsan Ali was for a time a personal adviser to Archbishop Makarios and he often wrote letters to the Turkish Prime Minister Inonu stressing the importance of the peaceful co-existence of the two communities in the island. His co-operation with the Greek Cypriots, especially with Makarios, was considered by the Turkish right wing nationalists as a betrayal to their cause of *Partition*.

On 11 April 1965 **Dervish Ali Kavazoglou**, a Turkish Cypriot member of the Central Committee of AKEL, and

*Costas Mishaoulis*, a Greek Cypriot Trade Unionist were ambushed and murdered in their car on the Nicosia - Larnaca road by the Turkish organisation T.M.T.

Kavazoglou and Mishaoulis were great supporters of Greek and Turkish friendship and strong believers of the communities co-existence. The extreme nationalists however on both sides did not want the two communities to co-exist and would brand them as "traitors"! The names of Kavazoglou and Mishaoulis as well as that of Dr Ihsan Ali were to become symbols of Greek and Turkish Cypriot friendship.

*Kavazoglou and Mishaoulis murdered in 1965. They believed in Greek-Turkish friendship and co-operation*

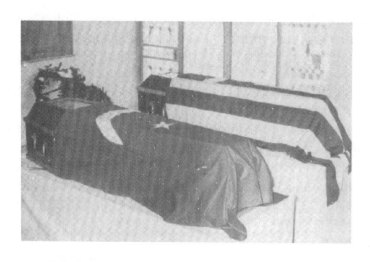

*Kavazoglou and Mishaoulis - Comrades in life, comrades in death*

# THE MEETING AT THE PALACE IN ATHENS

On 7th May 1965 (in the evening)  King Constantine chaired a meeting at the Palace which was attended by the following: Prime Minister George Papandreou, the former Prime Ministers K. Pipinelis and P. Kanelopoulos, Foreign Minister S. Kostopoulos, Defence Minister P. Garoufalias, President Makarios, Foreign Minister Spyros Kyprianou and Defence Minister P. Yiorkadgis.

At this meeting both the Greek Government and the Cyprus Government were acting unconstitutionally in the sense that they were not respecting the Zurich-London Agreements and the Cyprus Constitution which led to the establishment of the Cyprus Republic as an independent state. Makarios, the President of the supposedly  independent Republic was re-iterating that his main aim was to achieve *Enosis* but without making any territorial concessions to Turkey. The only concessions that he was prepared to make were to increase Minority rights to the Turkish community. Makarios was asked whether he would consider leasing a base to Turkey for about 30 years. (*Pavlos Petrides: George Papandreou and the Cyprus Problem, Documents 1954 - 1965, pp. 351 - 376*).

## STEFANOPOULOS REPLACES PAPANDREOU

On 15 July 1965 George Papandreou stepped down as Prime Minister because he had disagreed with King Constantine. Papandreou wanted to replace Petros Garoufalias as Minister of Defence and wanted the portfolio of Defence for himself but the King refused.

In September 1965 Stefanopoulos became Prime Minister of Greece. His relations with Makarios were far from cordial. On 9 March 1966 Stefanopoulos, like his predecessor, made a further blunder by showing complete disregard to the Agreements and the Constitution of Cyprus. He had appointed General Grivas as **Supreme Commander** of all Forces in the island, i.e. of the Greek Division and the National Guard of Cyprus. Makarios objected to Grivas having the National Guard under his command and in retaliation he decided to arm his supporters (known as Auxiliary Forces).

In 1966 through the secret mediation of King Constantine and Lord Mountbatten and then through further secret talks between the Stefanopoulos Government and Harold Wilson's Government, an understanding was reached whereby the British Government was prepared to consider the possibility of offering the British base at Dhekelia to Turkey if the latter agreed to Cyprus uniting with Greece.

The Greek and Turkish Foreign Ministers met in Paris on the 17th December 1966 to discuss this proposal. A few days later the Stefanopoulos government resigned and this was the end of the matter. A caretaker government was formed under Paraskevopoulos which lasted until the 3rd April 1967.

## THE MILITARY DICTATORSHIP IN GREECE

On 4 April 1967 Panayiotis Kanelopoulos formed a caretaker government which was to last until **28 May 1967** when General elections were scheduled to be held. Instead, on **21 April 1967**, some Greek army officers headed by **George Papadopoulos, Nikolaos Makarezos** and **Stylianos Pattakos** staged a coup and imposed a dictatorship. Political parties and Trade Unions were banned and thousands of people were arrested. Press censorship was imposed and progressive books and literature and some theatrical productions were banned. The music and songs of Mikis Theodorakis were also made illegal!

The Colonels used the excuse that *"Greece was in danger from the Communists!* Many people believe that the American CIA was behind the military coup, hence the immediate recognition of this regime by the US administration.

In Cyprus, protests against the military junta were organised by the Socialist Party of EDEK. The Government of Makarios however, *did not condemn* the military coup and the overthrow of Democracy in Greece. Makarios saw it *"as another change of government "(!)* and described the rule of the Junta in these words:

*"For Cyprus, every Government in Greece is the National Government of the Mother country!"*

Makarios and the Cyprus Government were leading the people politically downhill! By its very own actions, the House of Representatives provided all the evidence that Denktash and the Turkish Cypriot side needed to promote their own propaganda on partition: *"that the Greek Cypriots were not prepared to live and work in an Independent Republic but were always working towards implementing Enosis."* On 26 June 1967 the House of Representatives acted "illegally" by passing a resolution which in effect called for its own closure because it stated the following:

*"The House of Representatives interpreting the eternal wishes of Hellenism of Cyprus declares that it will continue the struggle for Enosis with the Mother Country that it will continue to promote the unity and co-operation among the Greek Cypriot people and the people of the Greek Motherland for the success of our National Struggle !*

On 9 August 1967 one of the ring-leaders of the military junta **George Papadopoulos**, in his capacity as Minister to the President visited Cyprus. Papadopoulos was welcomed by Makarios and at a state banquet given in his honour. All the political parties were represented including the Communist Party AKEL. The only political Party which refused to attend was the Socialist Party of EDEK. The EDEK leader Dr Vassos Lyssarides refused to attend and sit at the same table and "honour" one of the dictators and oppressors of the Greek people.

*Greek dictator George Papadopoulos visits Cyprus*
*August 1967*

## THE EVROS SUMMIT FIASCO
## SEPTEMBER 1967

**Evros** is the river which separates Greece from Turkey. It was near this border at the Turkish village of *Kesan* and at the Greek town of *Alexandroupolis* that the Junta Premier **Constantinos Kolias** and the Turkish Premier **Suleiman Demirel** agreed to have a summit to discuss Cyprus on the 9th and 10th September 1967. As there was complete censorship by the Junta hardly any information divulged from the Greek side.

According to the Turkish Ambassador in Athens who

attended the summit, the Stefanopoulos Government was prepared to negotiate a settlement for *Enosis* in exchange for a Turkish military base in Cyprus on a *lease* basis. Kolias informed his delegation that he was prepared to make such a base a *sovereign* Turkish base. When the Turkish side rejected the proposal, Papadopoulos turned to Kolias and said *"Let's leave, they are not in the mood of negotiating!" (S.Papageorgiou: From the Zurich Agreements to the Attila Line (in Greek) Vol. 3. pp. 180 - 181).*

**Greek Junta leaders meet Turkish Premier Demirel**

The Turkish newspaper **Hurriet** wrote on  11 September 1967 quoting  Demirel as saying to the Greek delegation the following:

*"Do you still insist on Enosis? If this is the case why are we meeting here?  Turkey has declared in the past and still declares that in such an event (Enosis) this will lead to a Turkish-Greek war... If the Greek Premier talks about a subject  which we have not accepted and do not intend to*

*accept and that he will not come forward with another proposal, then in such a case why are we meeting and what subject are we discussing?"*

According to **K. P. Panayiotakos**, who later served as the Junta's Ambassador in Nicosia (5 December 1970 until 28 January 1972) and later became Deputy Foreign Minister, he blamed Makarios (!) for the failure of the Greek-Turkish summit at Evros, because he was against the territorial concessions and the installation of a NATO base that the Junta was prepared to make. According to Panayiotakos, Makarios asked the Soviet Ambassador in Nicosia to urge the Soviet Government to intercede and oppose such an agreement because it would violate the territorial integrity of the Republic of Cyprus. Demirel was due to visit the Soviet Union at that time. *(K.P. Panayiotakos: At the First Defence Line (in Greek), 4th edition pp. 35-37).*

## DENKTASH RETURNS SECRETLY AND IS ARRESTED

Rauf Denktash had left Cyprus in 1964 and the Government issued a statement that if he returned to Cyprus he would be arrested and prosecuted for criminal offences due to his involvement in the December 1963 inter-communal troubles. He was not banned from entering the Republic because this would have been contrary to Article 14 of the Constitution. On 31 October 1967 he arrived secretly in Cyprus on a fishing boat but was arrested on the north-eastern coast. He was confined to the Nicosia military camp and Clerides stated that he was instructed by Makarios to visit and question him. He told Clerides that if the Cypriots declared Enosis, Turkey would intervene. Clerides also suggested to Makarios that Denktash should be transferred to police custody.

*Rauf Denktash when he was arrested in 1967*

According to Clerides, some extremists thought that it might be a good thing if Denktash was shot while "trying to escape". Clerides contacted both Makarios and Grivas stressing to both of them the consequences of such a foolish action and both agreed that it would harm the Government's image abroad. (*G. Clerides: My Deposition, Vol. 2, p. 204*).

The Turkish Government demanded his immediate release and the Greek Junta exerted pressure on Makarios to release him. If he was prosecuted and convicted he would have been a political prisoner and he would have become a national hero in the eyes of all Turkish Cypriots. It was decided not to prosecute him and Denktash was eventually released and left for Turkey on 12 November 1967.

# THE KOPHINOU CLASHES
## November 1967

In the town of Larnaca, **Artemis Avenue**, separated the Greek from the Turkish neighbourhood. In 1967 the Greek Cypriot police increased their patrol of the area. This was seen as harassment by the Turkish military authorities who insisted that these police patrols should stop. If they did not, they threatened that the police patrols at Kophinou would be terminated. Negotiations took place but no agreement was reached.

**Kophinou** was a Turkish Cypriot village situated half-way along the main road which connected Nicosia and Limassol and also Limassol - Larnaca. **Ayios Theodoros** was a mixed village situated about three to four miles south of Kophinou. A short distance away on high ground was the Turkish Cypriot village of **Mari**. After the 1963 inter-communal troubles, Kophinou was defended by armed Turkish fighters and Greek Cypriot police patrols visited Ayios Theodoros at regular intervals. When the police patrols were prevented from entering Ayios Theodoros, the Greek Cypriot Defence Council thought that the Turks were planning to create another Turkish enclave that would eventually cut off communications between Nicosia and Limassol and Limassol Larnaca.

The Defence Council met on 31 October 1967 and decided that the freedom of movement for police patrols along the Kophinou - Ayios Theodoros road should be restored. As the Council was debating what action to take, news reached them that Denktash had arrived secretly in Cyprus and had been arrested. A final decision on Kophinou was postponed.

*Grivas at the Kophinou operations 1967*

It should be remembered that George Papandreou was furious with both Makarios and Grivas in 1964 for not being consulted with in regard to the **Mansoura-Kokkina** operation. On this occasion, General Grivas made sure that the Junta was consulted and that he had their full support. The Junta gave Grivas and Makarios the "go ahead" with the **Kophinou operation**.

The code name of the Kophinou - Ayios Theodoros operation was called *"Feast."* Strong units of the National Guard surrounded the villages of Kophinou, Ayios Theodoros and Mari on the 13th, 14th and 15th November. In the clashes that followed 24 Turkish Cypriots and 2 Greek Cypriots were killed.

The Greek Ministry of Foreign Affairs sent an urgent message to Makarios at midnight on the 15th November to stop the operation and move out of Kophinou at once. On the 17th November the Turkish Government sent an ultimatum to the Greek Junta threatening with invasion, if the following demands were not met:

*1. General Grivas should be recalled immediately.*

*2. All 10,000 Greek troops stationed in Cyprus since 1964 should be removed within 45 days.*

*3. An indemnity should be paid to Turkish Cypriots killed and damages for their destroyed properties.*

*4. The Greek Cypriot National Guard should be disbanded.*

*5. Pressure on the Turkish Cypriot community should cease.*

President Johnson sent his envoy, **Cyrus Vance**, to try to negotiate with all sides and avoid a war among two members of NATO, as this would seriously weaken the south-eastern flank of the NATO Alliance. An agreement was eventually reached on the 26th November 1967. The Greek Junta and the Cyprus Government gave way and a Greek-Turkish war was averted. Grivas was flown back to Athens on 19 November 1967. The withdrawal of the Greek army Division began on 8 December.

Some time later, George Papandreou boasted that he had sent the Greek army Division in 1964 in order to defend Cyprus and that the Junta withdrew it in 1967 after the Kophinou incidents. As subsequent events showed, Papandreou's decision to send the Greek Division to

Cyprus was very unwise to say the least because he was acting contrary to the Cyprus Agreements, the Treaty of Alliance and the Cyprus constitution.

The subsequent military events at Kophinou orchestrated by both Makarios and Grivas and backed by the military Junta in Greece were even more foolish. Grivas felt very bitter because he was recalled by the Junta. He felt betrayed and supported the royalist counter coup staged by ex-king Constantine against the Colonels in December 1967 . This royalist coup ended in failure and Constantine ended first in Rome and then in London.

Makarios was a staunch royalist. His interest to restore the monarchy in Greece was so great that he even went to Rome to find and persuade the exiled Constantine, to "patch up" his differences with the dictators. Makarios in essence wanted to maintain cordial relations with whichever Government was in power in Greece, including the military Junta because as he argued "that was the Government of the mother-country".

Makarios was the "Statesman of all Seasons". He would befriend whoever was in power and would disregard anyone who was no longer powerful or influential. A typical example of this attitude was shown towards **Andreas Papandreou**. When George Papandreou (Andreas' father) was in power, Makarios befriended Andreas Papandreou. When the Junta came to power and Andreas Papandreou and **George Plytas** (a former Mayor of Athens) went to Cyprus and asked to see Makarios, he refused to meet them because he did not wish to displease those who were in power in Athens, i.e. the Junta.

# THE 1968 PRESIDENTIAL ELECTION
## *Makarios v Evdokas*
## *Makarios's "feasible" v The "desirable" solution*

According to the Constitution, the term of office for both the President and for Parliament was for five years. Since Cyprus became independent in 1960, the next Presidential and Parliamentary elections should have been held in 1965. The intercommunal unrest was used as an excuse to postpone the Presidential elections until 1968 and the Parliamentary elections until 1970 and the necessary legislation was introduced for this purpose.

It was at this time that Makarios came up with the idea of a *"feasible"* as against the *"desirable"* solution to the Cyprus problem. The "desirable" solution was of course Union with Greece but it was not, according to Makarios, "feasible" at that time. His statements about the "desirable" and "feasible" solutions were interpreted as an abandonment of Enosis and infuriated the pro-Grivas supporters. The Greek Cypriots were now openly divided into **pro-Enosists** (pro-Grivas) and to **pro-Makarios** supporters.

AKEL, the Communist Party of Cyprus endorsed this new policy of Makarios at its 12th Congress held in Nicosia in March 1970. In a Resolution sent to Makarios, AKEL stated the following:

*"AKEL has unreservedly supported your decision for a change in the Cyprus policy toward a feasible Cyprus solution within the present Cyprus and international conditions. Your patriotic decision, approved by the patriotic majority of the people, is an important service to Cyprus and its cause...."* (Haravghi, 8 March 1970).

(About nine years later, on 19 April 1977, Makarios confessed in the **Agon** Newspaper that *"the struggle for Enosis has brought only disasters for Cyprus."* Tragically, one may add, it took Makarios so many years to realise this and so many lives were lost both for this particular cause, as well as afterwards, when Cyprus became Independent, with all the intercommunal violence).

The Presidential elections were held on 28 February 1968 and there were only two candidates: Archbishop Makarios and **Dr Takis Evdokas** a well known psychiatrist. Makarios was supported by the vast majority of the population including AKEL, the Communist Party. Dr Evdokas was supported by the pro-Grivas supporters and three Bishops (Anthimos, Kyprianos and Yennadios). Makarios polled 220,911 votes or 95.45% and Dr Evdokas polled 12,577 or 3.7% of the total votes.

*Dr. Takis Evdokas pelted with yoghurt during an election campaign*

# THE INTER-COMMUNAL TALKS

A ray of hope appeared when **U Thant**, the Secretary-General of the UN, proposed that inter-communal talks should commence in order to try and resolve the deadlock. He appointed **Osorio Tafall** as his special envoy on Cyprus. The first preliminary talks were held in Beirut from 3 - 5 June 1968. **Glafcos Clerides**, as President of the House of Representatives represented the Greek Cypriots and **Rauf Denktash**, who was now allowed to travel freely to Cyprus and in his capacity as President of the Turkish Communal Chamber, represented the Turkish Cypriots. The formal opening of the talks were held on 24 June 1968 at the Ledra Palace Hotel in Nicosia. The inter-communal talks were greeted by all sides as a step in the right direction.

During the first phase of the talks, which lasted from 24 June until 28 August, the Turkish Cypriots made considerable concessions in that they were prepared to accept the following amendments to the Constitution:

*1. Reduction of Turkish Cypriot representation in the House of Representatives from 30 % to 20%.*

*2. The abolition of the veto powers of the Vice-President.*

*3. Abolition of the separate majorities of the Greek and Turkish members of the House.*

*4. The abolition of the Army of the Republic.*

*5. Reduction of the membership of the Turkish Cypriots in the Public Service Commission, Civil Service and Police* from 30% to 20%.

6. Unification of the lower Courts by abolishing the provision that Greeks and Turks had to be tried by Greek and Turkish judges respectively.

7. The President and Vice-President of the House of Representatives to be elected by both the Greek and Turkish members of the House and not separately.

**Glafcos Clerides and Rauf Denktash with Osorio Tafall**

The Turkish Cypriots were prepared to make the above concessions on condition that the Greek Cypriots would accept the following:

1. The Local government authorities to be elected and not appointed as was the practice.

2. Greek and Turkish villages to be grouped together for the

*purpose of local administration.*

The Turkish side also provided a list of other provisions and additional powers relating to the functions of local authorities, such as Public Health, Local Welfare services etc., which all seemed fair and reasonable. The proposal to elect and not to appoint local government officials was certainly more democratic.

Makarios however was not content with the concessions. According to Clerides, Makarios also insisted that the post of the Vice-President should be abolished. Denktash was prepared to consider this proposal provided the Greek Cypriot side accepted the provisions of Local Government. Makarios was adamant and would not accept the grouping of Greek and Turkish villages and also insisted that local government should be under the control of the Ministry of the Interior. (*G. Clerides: My Deposition, vol. 2. p.247*). He wanted to have in other words, absolute control on everything!

Dr Kutchuk and Mr Orek went to Ankara for consultations with the Turkish Government. On 29 August 1968 at the inter-communal talks Mr Denktash stated that "the Turkish side had decided to insist that the office of the Turkish Vice-President should not be abolished."

# THE ASSASSINATION ATTEMPT ON
# COLONEL PAPADOPOULOS

On 13 August 1968 an assassination attempt was made to blow up the Greek dictator George Papadopoulos. **Alexandros Panagoulis** was arrested and after an investigation, the Junta report stated that Panagoulis had deserted from the Greek army, that he went to Cyprus and was sheltered by the socialist leader Dr Vasos Lyssarides (who was the personal doctor of Makarios), that he was issued by Polycarpos Yiorkadgis with a Cypriot passport in the name of Marios Andreou and that Yiorkadgis had two secret meetings with him in Athens and that explosives were sent to the Cyprus Embassy in Athens through the diplomatic bag which were handed to Panagoulis.

Papadopoulos, the Greek dictator was furious with the report and considered Yiorkadgis as an accomplice in the assassination attempt. He demanded from Makarios that Yiorkadgis should be asked to resign and if he should refuse, then he should be dismissed from the Ministry of Interior and Defence. Yiorkadgis confessed to Clerides that Panagoulis asked for political asylum in Cyprus but it was on the advice of Makarios that Panagoulis was given a Cypriot passport on condition that he left the island. The investigation report was published on 20 October and Yiorkadgis resigned on 1 November 1968.

Papadopoulos's suspicions for Makarios grew even more and relations between the two governments had taken a turn for the worse. Yiorkadgis, who was a former EOKA fighter, was disappointed with Makarios because he had not spoken up for him. His departure from the Ministry of the Interior deprived Makarios of all essential information because Yiorkadgis had numerous links and contacts in all parts of the island. He was also in close contact with many EOKA supporters.

*Alexandros Panagoulis in Court*

# THE FORMATION OF NEW POLITICAL PARTIES

The oldest political party in the island was **AKEL** the *Progressive Working Party of Labour* (i.e. the Communist Party). AKEL was founded in 1941 and it had replaced the K.K.K., i.e. the Communist Party of Cyprus which was founded in 1926. AKEL's leader from 1949 to 1988 was **Ezekias Papaioannou**. In 1968 the **DEK** Party (Democratic National Party) was founded in order to challenge Makarios in the 1968 Presidential elections. It was led by the well known psychiatrist **Dr Takis Evdokas**. This was an ultra-nationalist party, which embraced all the supporters of Grivas who still believed in the struggle for Enosis.

Early in 1969 new political parties were formed. In February 1969 the "*Unified Party*" was formed by three former EOKA members: *Glafcos Clerides,* (who was President of the House of Representatives), *Polycarpos Yiorkadgis* (who was a former Minister of the Interior) and *Tasos Papadopoulos* (who was Minister of Labour). This was a right wing party, the party of the Makarios establishment, the "ruling class" and represented the interests of the middle classes and the EOKA supporters. If a comparison could be made, this *Unified Party* was something similar to the British Conservative Party. *Glafcos Clerides* assumed the leadership.

The other new party was the Socialist Party of **EDEK**, the *Unified Democratic Union of Cyprus*, which was led by **Dr Vassos Lyssarides**. Dr Lyssarides was one of the "*gang of four*" who were expelled from AKEL (the Communist Party) in 1952 after disagreeing with the "official party policy." The other three expelled were the former General Secretary of AKEL Ploutis Servas, Christofis Economides and George Cacoyiannis. The EDEK was a Social Democratic Party (something similar to the British Labour Party). The leader of EDEK was also the personal physician of Makarios.

Two other parties were also formed: The **Progressive Party** was led by Nikos Sampson a newspaper publisher and a former EOKA member. The other party was called **Progressive Array** and although it was led by Dr Odysseas Ioannides, who was appointed Mayor of Nicosia by Makarios, the real force behind this Party was **Andreas Azinas**, the Director of the Co-Operative movement and close associate of Makarios. Dr Ioannides also relied on the support of **PEK**, the right wing agrarian organisation.

*Yiorkadgis and Clerides*

## THE FORMATION OF THE " ETHNIKO METOPO" - NATIONAL FRONT

In the 1960's and early 1970's Cyprus was going through what Greece went through soon after the 1821 War of Independence. Many of those who fought during the EOKA struggle were rewarded by various positions in the government. There were many others who were left out. A section of these people who were obviously disappointed at being left out, now claimed that they had not struggled for "Independence" but for *Enosis*. They were neither happy nor content with "Independence". They believed that the formation of the **Unified Party** represented the views of the new Makarios establishment. They also disagreed with the inter-communal negotiations because they considered such talks to be leading to "a national sell out".

The man behind this **Ethniko Metopo** (National Front) was

***Christakis Tryfonides***, an ex-EOKA Area Commander. According to Clerides, Tryfonides called on Makarios and outlined to him the objectives of this "secret" organisation and that he assumed the leadership of this organisation with the knowledge and consent of Makarios. *(G. Clerides: My Deposition, Vol. 2, p. 321).*

The *National Front*, according to Spyros Papageorgiou, consisted of supporters of the Greek Junta, Yiorkadgis, Sampson and even some supporters of Makarios. The supporters of Grivas had strict instructions from their leader to abstain. This was the time when the EOKA B' was secretly being organised and members were enlisted, arms and ammunition gathered and hideouts prepared. (*Spyros Papageorgiou: From the Zurich Agreements to the Attila Line, Vol. 3. p. 224).*

This extreme right wing and anti-communist organisation, the **Ethniko Metopo** was launched in March 1969. They issued a Declaration stating their aims. They issued proclamations expressing their anti-communist views and also the view that their goal was not independence but Union with Greece. Many had suspected that Grivas and the military Junta in Greece were behind this *National Front*. The main objective of this *Ethnikon Metopon* was to force Makarios to pursue the *Enosis* line and if he still refused to comply then to overthrow him and his regime, which (in their view) was already drifting towards making Independence as the permanent solution.

Their first target, where they planted a bomb, were the offices of the left wing trade union organisation **PEO** *(Pan-Cypriot Federation of Labour)* in Famagusta. In some villages and towns, they wrote on the buildings of some left wing organisations   slogans such as: *"Death to the Communists"* and *"Long Live Pattakos"*. (Pattakos was one of the leaders of the Military Junta in Greece). They also attempted to terrorise newspapers and the Cyprus Radio and Television and demanded the immediate dismissal of a number of employees because they had either left wing views or had at one time  belonged to the left wing party of AKEL.

Such threats were sent to **Phileleftheros** for employing Christakis Katsambas, to **Agon** for employing Diomedes Galanos, to **Machi** for employing  Fifis Ioannou and to **RIK** (Cyprus Radio and Television) for employing Andreas Kyriakou as editor of the News programme and the television producer Tasos Elias because his "crime" was that he had studied and graduated in Communist Czechoslovakia!  In August 1969 Miltiades Christodoulou, the Director of the Government Public Information Office, was shot and wounded, because he happened to be  a leading member of AKEL some twenty years previously!

As it was to be expected, the terrorist  attacks on police stations and other establishments, as well as against many other Greek Cypriots, created difficulties and suspicions at the inter-communal talks and prompted the Turkish Cypriot newspaper "**Halkin Sesi**" to comment  on the 23rd August 1969 as follows: *"If those who are in power are unable to implement the laws against these illegal organisations and are unable to exert their influence and power, how can such a Government (authority) inspire confidence among the Turkish Cypriots?*

Rauf Denktash also raised the issue of the terrorist acts of the "National Front" at the inter-communal talks on the 25th

August. Although on the 28th August 1969 the Council of Ministers proscribed the "National Front" as an illegal organisation it continued its terrorist activities propagating *Enosis* and also helped to torpedo the course of the inter-communal talks.

## THE DOUBLE ROLE OF THE GREEK JUNTA

The American CIA saw Makarios as the main obstacle to any settlement of the Cyprus problem. They used the Greek Junta not only to "keep an eye on him", especially with his dealings with the Soviet Union, but if possible, to overthrow him. The Greek Junta's policy towards Cyprus aimed at giving to the outside world the impression that they were co-operating with Makarios in search for a solution through the inter-communal talks. Internally, however, they were backing EOKA B' both financially and militarily and those Unionists who wanted to implement *Enosis* at whatever the cost - even Double Enosis.

On 17 January 1970 Makarios visited Athens and had talks with the Greek Junta government. The Junta expressed "concern" at the lack of progress at the inter-communal talks and they blamed the Greek Cypriot side for the stalemate because they were not prepared to make concessions on the issue of Local Government. On his return to Nicosia, Makarios briefed Clerides about his Athens visit : that the talks must (a) continue, (b) move at a faster rate, (c) flexibility to be shown and (d) they must not fail. Yet, according to Clerides, Makarios told him that *"he should not move from our existing positions!"*

Clerides tried to explain to Makarios that the Turks were hardening their position because they could see the local situation amongst the Greek Cypriots was deteriorating and that due to massive financial support from Turkey, they were overcoming their urgent economic problems. He advised Makarios of two options:

*1. The Turkish side to agree to the reduction of its participation in the Council of Ministers, the House of Representatives, the Police, the Civil Service from 30% to 20%. The separate majorities to be abolished in return for the Government undertaking the costs of both Greek and Turkish education, the Constitutional provision for separate municipalities to be implemented, and local government to remain in the form it was at the time. There was also a possibility that the Turkish side would agree in this deal to give up the veto Powers of the Vice-President.*

*2. To agree to a wider measure of local government, accepting grouping of villages for purposes of local government, and central government authorities at district level, in return for all the concessions Denktash offered on the executive, legislative, judiciary, the Civil Service and Police. (G. Clerides: My Deposition, Vol.2. pp. 358 - 359).*

Both options were rejected by Makarios. His instructions were to insist on all the concessions already made by the Turkish side and to demand in addition:

*(a) The abolition of the office of the Vice-President.*

*(b) The acceptance by the Turkish side of common electoral rolls.*

*(c ) To offer in return local government at village level only.*

Clerides was to confess later that an opportunity to reach agreement with the Turkish side on the basis of a considerable improvement of the Zurich agreements was lost due to the obstinacy and intransigence of Makarios.

# THE ASSASSINATION ATTEMPT ON MAKARIOS

On 8 March 1970 Makarios was about to fly with the Presidential helicopter to *Macheras Monastery* in order to officiate at the Memorial service of Gregoris Afxentiou. Afxentiou was the deputy leader of EOKA and a national hero. He was burnt alive in his guerrilla hideout on the Macheras mountains by the British forces in March 1957.

Makarios was previously advised to limit his visits and appearances to public places and functions because there was information that his life was in danger from those working for the Greek Military Junta in Cyprus. Makarios ignored such warnings because he believed that *"Greece was like a Mother to Cyprus and that a Mother will never harm her child!"* He never realised that the Junta in Athens was never "*a natural mother*", i.e. a democratically elected Government and as such *"lacked not only maternal but any human feelings!"* because it suppressed, tortured and humiliated its very own people. Such a tyrannical *"step mother"* would never hesitate for a moment to implement the same dictatorial practices to her *"....distant step-children"* in Cyprus!

Makarios believed that on the day of Afxentiou's *Memorial Service,* only fools would think of blackening such an heroic anniversary for Hellenism! Makarios was naive, in a sense, because he considered all Greek Governments in the same way. He often boasted that he had already survived 13 Greek Governments and no Government in Athens would ever attempt to overthrow him! At first he believed the military dictators in Athens would be no different, simply because they were also Greek! Makarios played his cards wrong. He could have become the champion of all the people in Greece and Cyprus if he had spoken against the Junta from the very first day they came to power. He would have had all the democratic people of Greece behind him. He chose instead to co-operate with the butchers of the Greek people, not realising that he himself would be the next victim on their agenda.

Prior to his visit to the Macheras Monastery, he was fully aware of an Order 4026 which came from the General Army Staff of the National Guard and did not pay any heed. As soon as the helicopter took off, it was fired upon by machine gun and although the pilot Major Zacharias Papadoyiannis, was wounded in the abdomen, he managed to land it safely near the Archbishopric. Makarios escaped alive. An investigation had commenced to find the culprits. Six people were arrested and accused of conspiring with Polycarpos Yiorkadgis and with persons unknown, between the 1st September 1969 and 8th March 1970 to kill the President the Republic. Four of them were sentenced to 8 years imprisonment and the other two who were found guilty of conspiring with Yiorkadgis were sentenced to 14 years imprisonment.

Although Makarios knew that the National Guard was implicated in the plot, he issued a statement saying that this was not so. Later, those who were accused for the assassination attempt were pardoned by Makarios and confessed that **Captain Papapostolou**, the Greek

Commander of the Cyprus Commando Force was implicated in this plot. Five years later, Makarios confessed in an interview to Vasos Vassiliou of the Athens newspaper **Vradyni** that the National Guard was implicated in the assassination attempt!

# THE ASSASSINATION OF YIORKADGIS

For Makarios, the prime suspect at the time was his former Minister of the Interior, **Polycarpos Yiorkadgis**. He gave instructions for his immediate arrest but the new Minister of the Interior and the Chief of Police hesitated to carry out the arrest! On 13 March 1970 Yiorkadgis was summoned to court and was accused that after a search at his apartment, two pistols had been found. He was only fined. Yiorkadgis tried to leave Cyprus and boarded a plane for Beirut but at the last minute he was taken off the plane. His political career was now at an end.

According to **Patatakos** (a police officer), Yiorkadgis communicated with **Captain Papapostolou** and arranged a secret meeting with him at Tymbou (a village to the east of Nicosia). Later he told Patatakos that he wanted to find out more about the coup that some officers were planning. He gave Patatakos an envelope and asked him to hide it in Aglangia (a Nicosia suburb) because it contained details about the plan for the military coup.

On Sunday evening, 15 March 1970, Yiorkadgis arranged to meet Captain Papapostolou outside the village of Mia Millia, near Nicosia. Later, according to Patatakos's statement to the coroner, he drove with Yiorkadgis outside Mia Millia village and when Yiorkadgis spotted the stationary car he was expecting, he ordered Patatakos to wait outside. This was about 200 metres away. Yiorkadgis drove on his own to the stationary car and then machine gun shots were heard. The stationary car then sped towards Kythrea. Patatakos ran to the car, its engine was still on but Yiorkadgis was already dead.

Patatakos then returned to Nicosia and together with Clerides went to see Makarios in order to  tell him what had happened.  They also told him about the plot for the military coup and Clerides and Patatakos went to Aglangia to fetch the hidden  envelope with the plan. During the same evening Makarios summoned the Greek Ambassador, who admitted no knowledge of any plot.

No one was arrested for Yiorkadgis's murder. Some of the newspapers on the next day after his murder wrote that *"he was executed because he knew too much !"* Even to this day some 30 years later, his assassination  is still shrouded in some mystery. According to Clerides, the fact that Papapostolou, at the time of the murder of Yiorkadgis, was somewhere else proves only that he did not fire the shots, which killed Yiorkadgis. The fact that  no arrests were made led some people to  suspect  that  Makarios himself was possibly behind this assassination.

**Polycarpos Yiorkadgis**

# THE 1970 PARLIAMENTARY ELECTIONS

The first Parliamentary elections were held in 1960. According to the Constitution, Parliamentary elections should take place every five years. Thus the next elections should have taken place in 1965. The House of Representatives could not extend its own term of office beyond the period that it was elected to serve. This was contrary to the Constitution. Makarios, however, as President, decided to prolong the life of this Parliament until 1970, i.e. for five years after the expiry of its term of office!

The elections were held on the 5th July 1970. The Progressive Party of **Nikos Sampson** and the Progressive Array of **Dr. Odysseas Ioannides** merged just before the elections. With the exception of the pro-Grivas party, the DEK led by **Dr Takis Evdokas**, all the other parties supported the policies of Makarios. Although AKEL could contest for all the 35 Parliamentary seats, its leadership decided to contest only 9 seats.

The electoral system used for this election was the "*Majority system*" which favoured the parties that worked closely with Makarios. As it can be seen from the table below, the left-wing party AKEL polled over *38% of the vote* but managed to elect only *9 MPs!* The Unified Party (which was closest to Makarios) which polled just over *24% elected 15 M.Ps!* The Progressive Party of Nikos Sampson which polled only *17%* (i.e. less than half of the votes of AKEL) managed to elect *7 M.Ps!* The parties that contested the elections and the results were the following:

| Party | No.of votes | Percentage | Seats |
|-------|-------------|------------|-------|
| AKEL | 79, 665 | 38.28 | 9 |
| Unified Party | 51, 111 | 24.35 | 15 |
| Progressive | 35, 782 | 17.00 | 7 |
| EDEK | 26, 906 | 12.34 | 2 |
| DEK | 16, 655 | 8.03 | 0 |
| Independents | --- | --- | 2 |

(Note: The two independent candidates were elected as if they were members of the major parties).

General Grivas had denounced these elections before they were held. He issued the following proclamation in Athens, which was addressed to the Greek people of Cyprus:

*"Greek people of Cyprus! You are not living in a Democracy but under a Dictatorship, because those who are rightfully entitled to speak about Cyprus are kept far away from their Homeland..... The elections will be held without a real opponent since the leader of the armed struggle, the one who expelled the British, the real and unyielding exponent of Enosis, the one who is entitled to speak is kept as an exile in Greece and he is deprived of returning to his own Homeland...." (Spyros Papageorgiou: From the Zurich Agreements to the Attila Line. (in Greek) Vol. 3 p. 241).*

# MAKARIOS VERSUS PAPADOPOULOS

The Junta in Athens never trusted Makarios from the beginning, especially because the latter had associated Cyprus with the non-aligned movement. Makarios's good relations with the Soviet Union and the Eastern bloc had infuriated them even more. They expected from him not only obedience but total submission. They believed that all major decisions which were of national importance should be taken by Athens, not by Nicosia. Athens was considered as the "*National Centre*" and was expected to be seen as such by Makarios and therefore, all major decisions rested with the National Centre.

During the years 1970 - 71 the relations between Makarios and the Greek dictator George Papadopoulos took a turn for the worse. The two leaders exchanged a number of letters expressing each other's mistrust. Their main difference was *"who should have the right of say on Cyprus - i.e. should it be the Government in Greece or the Government in Cyprus."*

Papadopoulos argued that since the question of Cyprus was a national issue and concerned the whole of Hellenism, then the Athens government should have the upper hand and not the Cyprus government. Makarios on the other hand, was of the view that since Cyprus was still an independent state, then his government had every right to make the necessary decisions. The dictator in Athens would not take lessons from Makarios and warned him that if the government of Athens did not take the big decisions then *"he does not wish to involve Greece in military adventures for the sake of Cyprus."*

Makarios feared that he would be accused of drifting away from the national aspiration of *Enosis*. On 14 March 1971 in the village of Yialousa, he made a passionate speech about the "*Greekness*" of Cyprus, ignoring the fact that he was still speaking as the President of an independent republic since 1960: "*Cyprus is Greek. Cyprus has been Greek since the dawn of history and will remain Greek. We have inherited Cyprus as Greek and indivisible. We shall preserve (Cyprus) as Greek and indivisible. And as such we shall surrender Cyprus to Greece!*"

All the above arguments and comments between Papadopoulos and Makarios were taking place while the inter-communal talks were also taking place...... in order to get the Turks to agree to a *constitutional settlement and preserve the Independence and Sovereignty of the Republic of Cyprus !!*

The Turkish government as well as the Turkish Cypriot leadership were both witnessing and seriously considering all these nationalistic outbursts of the Junta leaders and Makarios. They were assessing the situation accordingly, and claimed that the Greek Cypriot side was neither genuine nor sincere in what they were negotiating with them.

The Greek Junta was also critical of Makarios for not reaching an agreement with the Turkish Cypriots because at the inter-communal talks the Turks had agreed on most of his 13 points which he had proposed back in 1963. They accused him of delaying tactics and **for insisting on the abolition of the post of the Vice-President**.

The fanatic anti-communist Greek dictator George Papadopoulos was even more furious with Makarios because he had paid a state visit to the Soviet Union between 2 - 9 June 1971.

## GRIVAS RETURNS SECRETLY TO CYPRUS AND FORMS "EOKA B"

One may remember that Grivas left Cyprus for Athens in November 1967 after the **Kophinou village fiasco.** Strangely enough, Grivas considered himself as an "exile" in the very same country for which he fought to unite Cyprus with! He kept in touch however with many of his EOKA supporters in Cyprus. He was furious and disillusioned with both the Junta leadership and Makarios. He was furious because he was not allowed to return to Cyprus in order to *"complete his mission"*, i.e. to unite Cyprus with Greece. He considered both the Junta leaders and Makarios as *"destroyers of the national aspirations".* He felt that if the Junta and Makarios would not struggle for *Enosis* anymore then he would.

He contacted his old friend **Andreas Potamianos** and asked him to arrange his secret passage to Cyprus as he had done in the past. Potamianos however was reluctant this time and was not prepared to take the responsibility and blame from both the Greek and Cyprus Governments. Potamianos reminded Grivas that earlier they had at their disposal a whole Greek division of 10,000 men and they could not do anything. He asked Grivas, how on earth he would be able to change things on his own? Grivas simply replied: *"I know what I am doing."*

Grivas's boat stopped in Rhodes so that **Stavros Stavrou**

(code named **Syros**), an officer in the Greek army, may join him but because of some suspicious moves at the port the boat sailed away. Syros (Stavrou) arrived in Cyprus by air. Grivas eventually arrived near Pissouri on the evening of **31st August 1971** and was collected by Lefteris Papadopoulos, Costas Papastavrou and Stelios Stylianou and went into hiding in Limassol. It was later revealed that his hideout was in the house of Diana Mavros in Limassol.

In September 1971 Grivas launched the new underground organisation the **EOKA B'** and in January 1972 its political wing, the **ESEA** (*Epitropi Syntonismou Enotikou Agona - Co-ordinating Committee for the Enosis Struggle)* was formed. The chairman of this Committee was the High Court Judge **G. Vassiliades**, the Deputy was the psychiatrist **Dr Takis Evdokas** and the Secretary was **Photis Papaphotis**.

The real aims of **EOKA B'** and **ESEA** were to openly oppose the "pro-independence" line of the Cyprus Government, to overthrow Makarios and proclaim *Enosis*. Other leading members of this ESEA - "political wing" of the EOKA B' were: Dr. Takis Aristides, Socrates Eliades, Spyros Papageorgiou, K. Saveriades, K. Spanos, G.S. Drousiotis, A. Papadakis, A. Karaolis, Stavros Stavrou Syros and K. Kyriakou.

Why did Grivas and his supporters form the EOKA B' ? If they wanted to challenge Makarios and his Government why did they not challenge them in elections? The answer is simple: they could never get elected by the people. *People who cannot win at the ballot box resort to the use of bullets.* Grivas and his supporters did not believe in the democratic process, because if they did, they should have had the decency to challenge Makarios in the Presidential elections. They should have had the decency to stand for Parliament. Grivas and his supporters are to blame for creating the image during the 1955-59 struggle that "Makarios was the only National Leader." When Makarios the "Only National Leader" chose not to follow Grivas's policies, the old General and his EOKA B' organisation resorted to similar methods of violence that he used against the British.

Grivas was a staunch royalist and wanted the return of King Constantine back to Greece. Both the EOKA B' and the ESEA leadership believed that *Enosis* could be achieved if one really wanted it and if one really believed in this goal. They felt that Makarios betrayed the cause of *Enosis*. They were however, very naive, in the sense that they thought that Turkey would not react and would not oppose such a move!

Grivas' arrival in Cyprus in September 1971 and his subsequent adventurous mission was to lead the Greek Cypriots to a new fratricidal bloodbath. The Junta on the other hand did nothing to stop him or bring him back to Athens. He was a well known anti-communist and they knew it. They too were anti-communist. He now despised and antagonised Makarios and they knew it. They too wanted Makarios to disappear from the political stage because they considered him as a "stumbling block" to their designs and decisions.

# THE PALAMAS - OLCAY AGREEMENT

The Greek Foreign Minister **Xanthopoulos Palamas** and **Olcay**, the Turkish Foreign Minister had reached a broad agreement whereby:

(a) Cyprus was an independent sovereign state in the contexts of the Zurich and London agreements. The Treaties of Guarantee and Alliance were valid and would be restated.

(b) Turkey had no territorial claims on Cyprus.

(c ) Agreed amendments to make the constitution more workable were possible. The Turkish side would accept to give up some of the constitutional rights it derived from the Zurich agreements in return for the Greek side accepting separate autonomy of the communities in local government. The adjustment of communal rights must preserve the partnership principle of the two communities and the unitary character of the Republic.

## THE GREEK JUNTA WANTS THE REMOVAL OF BOTH MAKARIOS AND GRIVAS

Makarios's secret decision to import arms from Czechoslovakia for a second time (the first time was in 1966), had infuriated the Greek Junta as well as Grivas. The Junta was furious with Makarios's action because Palamas, the Junta's Foreign Minister, had just reached a broad agreement for a solution to the problem with the Turkish Foreign Minister.

Makarios twice rejected the proposal of the Junta that the arms should be handed to the National Guard (which was under the control of mainland Greek officers). The whole purpose of purchasing the arms was to defend himself and the Cyprus Government from the very "Greek officers of the Junta." **K. Panayiotakos**, the Under Secretary to the Foreign Minister of Greece, on the 11th February 1972 delivered the Junta's Note to the Cyprus Government asking that the imported arms should be under the custody of the U.N. Peace-keeping Force. The Note also spoke of the need to form a Government of National Unity in Cyprus.

Panayiotakos also delivered a verbal message from the Junta saying that:

*"It was the wish of the Greek Government that he should resign from the office of President and that he should retire from the political life of Cyprus."*

A similar message was to be delivered to General Grivas and that he would be asked to return to Greece. Thus the Junta wanted to kill two birds with the same stone, i.e. to get rid of Makarios and Grivas on the one hand and also to form a Government of "national unity", a government which in essence would be obedient and answerable to the interests of the Junta.

Meanwhile, rumours had already spread that the Greek Junta was about to stage a coup to oust Makarios. Previously, Makarios had been so confident and claimed that *"no Government from the Mother country would ever harm her own child!"* The Greek Junta however was neither a Government elected by the people nor did it represent the interests of the people of the "Mother country". The Junta's instincts were far from "maternal", they were more pro- CIA and pro- American instincts. Makarios now realised that the Colonels "meant business" and feared not only for his political but also for his physical existence.

It was this real fear that prompted Makarios to summon Clerides on 14 February 1972. He urged him to contact Mr Popper, the American Ambassador, immediately, because he told Clerides that there will be a coup in the early hours of the 15th February. Clerides was to ask the American Ambassador to contact urgently the American President to intercede and stop the Greek Colonels from such an act. Henry Tasca, the American Ambassador in Athens was contacted and in turn he contacted the Junta Prime Minister Colonel Papadopoulos, who assured him that the Greek forces stationed in Cyprus would not overthrow Makarios and his Government.

On 15 February 1972 a massive rally took place in Nicosia in support of Makarios. The newspapers wrote that Makarios is protected by the "People's Shield" and that Makarios "derives his strength from the people". (Phileleftheros, 16.2.72).

A month later, on 14 March 1972, Makarios sent a letter to Papadopoulos as a reply to the Note from the Junta. In this letter, Makarios stated the following:

1. He agreed to place the imported arms under the control and custody of the UN Peace-Keeping Force.

2. He was willing to consider the suggestion to form a Government of National Unity though he thought it was unconstitutional.

*3. He reported that some Greek officers were involved in activities against the Cyprus Government.*

Papadopoulos replied to the Makarios's letter saying that he was not satisfied on the second point and that (Makarios) must accept that Athens, being the "National Centre", must have the final say on the Cyprus problem. Prior to this exchange of letters, the Athens Junta was also plotting Makarios's downfall using another method: They found three "discontented" Cypriot Bishops who were prepared to do their "dirty" work!

The Turkish Government was aware of the Junta's plans to remove Makarios. Panayiotakos (who was the Greek Ambassador in Nicosia) on 25 February 1972 met Ilter Turkmen the Turkish Ambassador in Athens and told him that during his service in Nicosia the Greek Government was in constant contact with the three Bishops who wanted Makarios removed from power. He also expressed the hope that the activities of the three Bishops with the support of the Church in Greece would help to bring about his removal. (*Encyclopaedia of the History of Cyprus, Vol. 14. p. 182*).

# THE CONFLICT IN THE CHURCH AND THE ROLE OF THE JUNTA

**Kyprianos**, the Bishop of Kyrenia, **Anthimos,** Bishop of Kition and **Yennadios,** Bishop of Paphos were staunch supporters of *Enosis.* The Greek Junta turned to these three Bishops in order to try to oust Makarios. It must be said that Bishop Kyprianos was a co-exile with Makarios in 1956 and had antagonised him since 1950, when Makarios was elected as Archbishop because he wanted to be the new Archbishop. As for Anthimos, he was the *Acting Archbishop* when Makarios was in exile and was one of the many who had advised Makarios to sign the Zurich-London Agreements. Now he joined forces with the other two Bishops to dethrone him.

*The three Bishops who wanted to oust Makarios: Anthimos of Kition, Kyprianos of Kyrenia and Yennadios ofPaphos*

In 1972, that is 12 years after Makarios had been President, the three Bishops had argued that according to Church rules, Makarios could not hold two positions, i.e. he could not be both an Archbishop and a President of a state at the same time. They demanded therefore, that if he wished to remain head of the Church then he should resign from his position as President. What was strange about this demand was the fact that Makarios had already been President of Cyprus for the past 12 years and the Bishops had not come up with this kind of request, that his ecclesiastical position was in conflict with his political office!

What was even more strange was the fact that two of the Bishops, Anthimos and Yennadios, actively campaigned for Makarios's re-election in the 1968 Presidential elections! It was rather strange therefore that the three bishops all of a sudden remembered the Holy Scriptures and the rules of the Church, whilst these Church rules did not apply for the previous 12 years and now all of a sudden had to be implemented!

On 2 March 1972 a stormy Church Synod was held in Nicosia. About 70 priests from Paphos had gathered outside the Archbishopric, opposing the views of their Bishop Yennadios and expressed their support for Makarios. On the other "camp" the *pro-Enosis* **Patris** newspaper, had urged the three Bishops not to back down and to insist on Makarios' resignation. The newspaper stated that Makarios had to decide and make a choice whether he wishes to remain: *a Caesar or a Pope, Michael Mouskos* (his lay name) or *Makarios* (his Church name), *a President of a Republic or an Archbishop of an Orthodox Church, an Ethnarch or an Estate Agent, a Merchant or a Hotelier?* (*Patris:* 2nd March 1972).

The three Bishops insisted on Makarios resignation. Makarios was furious at the meeting but promised to respond to their request. He sent a letter to the three

Bishops on **19 March 1972** where he stated the reasons why he should continue as President:

*(1) The struggle of Cypriot Hellenism is a struggle of national survival and also a struggle of survival of the Orthodox Christian faith.*

*(2) If I were to resign the Presidency in the present conditions it may not be possible to hold elections and elect a president. In such a case there will be no Government which will have international recognition. Instead of a Government there will be a Greek Cypriot leadership and administration similar to the Turkish Cypriot.*

*(3) The demand of the Holy Synod for my resignation in critical times will be considered as contempt of the people and will provoke bitter feelings among the faithful with unpleasant consequences for the Church.*

*4. In conclusion I say that although I do not agree with your recommendation for the reasons that I have outlined, if however you insist on your recommendation, I would consider it my obligation to accept it, since there would be no other option for me. I would never wish a division in the Church or the creation of an uproar. Possibly the uproar may not be avoided but for this I would not be held responsible.*

Makarios was too ambitious and never wanted to resign. He argued that his position as President was imperative because of the national issue. He considered himself as **"irreplaceable"**. Back in the 1950's all church walls were painted with the slogan "*Makarios and only Makarios*" "*Makarios is the Only Leader*". Makarios felt that he was the "*New Cypriot Moses*" who was destined to deliver his Greek Cypriot people first out of the "*British Colonial Bondage*" and then lead them to the.... "*Land of Milk and Honey*" which was "*Mother Hellas*".

The Archbishop of Athens and all Greece **Ieronymos** (who was himself appointed by the Junta), in an attempt to "lure" him away from political power, wrote to Makarios suggesting that: "*He is destined for higher things in the Church and that he could be made Ecumenical Patriarch*".

## MAKARIOS MEETS GRIVAS
## 26th MARCH 1972

Makarios was unpopular with both the Greek Junta and the extreme right wing supporters of *Enosis*. Although he was popular with the vast majority of the Greek Cypriot people and had the full backing of the left-wing party AKEL he still feared for both his position and life. In a desperate attempt to come out of his "political isolation" from the Junta and the pro-Enosis supporters, he sought the alliance of General Grivas. He wrote a letter to Grivas asking for a meeting. He asked for Grivas's co-operation to oppose successfully the imposition of an unacceptable solution. **Dr Marios Tritoftides** acted as the intermediary and their meeting took place on the 26th March. Makarios' attempt to get Grivas' support had back-fired because the terms that Grivas had set for Makarios were almost identical to those of the Junta. Grivas sent a letter to Dr Tritoftides on 17 April 1972 where he states what was discussed at the meeting. Grivas's conditions were the following:

*1. The Archbishop must resign from the office of President and must retire from politics.*

*2. Elections to be announced, with a candidate of mutual trust for President.*

*3. He himself (i.e. Grivas) will not mix in politics, but would co-operate fully.*

*4. Co-operation also to be sought with the Ethnarchic Church.*

*5. Reconstitution of the Government to take place in the shortest possible time by giving the main ministries of Foreign Affairs, Interior, Defence and Education to persons of mutual trust, so as to defuse the internal situation.*

*6. The President who would be elected would put forward as the solution of the problem the exercise of the right of self-determination.*

By making these demands, Grivas was expressing the same demands of the Junta in Athens. An exchange of letters followed between Makarios and Grivas. According to Grivas, Makarios had tried to trick him and to use him against the Greek Junta. Grivas accused Makarios that he had given him verbal assurances that what they discussed at their meeting on 26th March 1972 would be implemented in stages. On 4 May 1972 Makarios wrote to Grivas stating the following:

*"The struggle of the people of Cyprus under the present circumstances and conditions, is rather a defensive one and our defence has been, up to now successful. We defend ourselves and refuse to accept a solution which will fetter our national future. Enosis is a purpose of life and a compass for national orientation. Enosis, however, is not achievable if in the first instance, the danger of an*

*undesirable solution is not made distant or removed. I would not hesitate to change the policy according to your proposal if the Greek Government agreed... A struggle for Enosis without the participation of Greece would possibly lead to unpleasant results. On the policy of direct Enosis we must walk side by side with Greece. The view that if we make Enosis our target, Greece by necessity will follow lacks certainty. I cannot say that this would happen. If the Greek Government, after calculating the possibilities and other factors, adopts a negative attitude, the consequences would be a setback for the cause of Enosis. Furthermore I do not exclude the possibility that the danger of double Enosis could be avoided, even if we are determined to resist it...."* Indeed, such "down to earth" thoughts never crossed Makarios's mind when, together with Grivas, they led 1955-59 struggle for **Enosis and Only Enosis** and anyone who spoke otherwise was branded as a traitor!

Makarios continued in his reply calling upon Grivas to support him:

*".. I am not struggling to preserve political office, but for the national survival of the Greek Cypriot people whose future is facing serious dangers, and I would wish us to be allies in this struggle".* (Glafcos Clerides: My Deposition. Vol. 3. pp. 148 - 149).

In an angry response on 16 May 1972 Grivas wrote to Makarios:

*"....You justify your retraction from the verbal promise that you agreed with my views and that you would implement them in stages, by the argument that, your reservations and fears have increased in the light of recent developments and new facts. You are, however, speaking to "Dighenis",*

263

*of whom you ask support and co-operation, and not just anybody, and yet you feel no need to describe, clearly and in detail, these recent developments and new facts in the light of which you have retracted.*

*You ask for my co-operation in preventing serious dangers, without naming these dangers and their origin. You must consider me very naive, if you believe that I would follow you blindly, especially when your "navigation" of the Cyprus problem has changed direction so many times without my consent, especially during the time of the EOKA struggle..."*

*"...You have undermined every effort directed towards the Enosis solution of the Cyprus problem, and your political initiatives have succeeded in derailing the Cyprus problem from the correct road of Self-Determination - Enosis. Trying to achieve the "feasible", i.e. sailing into the unknown, you have thrown Cyprus into international disrespect, so that no country any longer trusts us....." (G. Clerides: My Deposition. Vol. 3. pp. 151 - 153).*

The feud between Grivas and Makarios and their respective supporters was to continue until the death of Grivas in January 1974 and until the military coup of 15th July 1974, staged by EOKA B' and supported by the Greek Junta when Makarios was ousted from power.

# GREEK JUNTA INSISTS ON CYPRUS GOVERNMENT RESHUFFLE

For the Greek Junta, Makarios was the equivalent of John the Baptist. They wanted his head in a platter! They wanted him to step down but when they realised that he would not oblige, they tried to purge some of his close associates. Some of his Ministers became the sacrificial lambs. The Junta considered any Cypriot Minister who expressed the slightest disagreement with their views as an "enemy". Mr Zafiriou, the Charge d'affaires at the Greek Embassy in Nicosia had told Clerides that the Greek Government wanted the immediate removal of the following:

1. *Spyros Kyprianou,* Minister of Foreign Affairs.
2. *Frixos Petrides*, Minister of Education.
3. *Epaminondas Komodromos*, Minister of the Interior.
4. *Miltiades Christodoulou,* Director of the Public Information Office.
5. *George Tombazos,* Director of the Cyprus Information Service.
6. *Lellos Demetriades*, Mayor of Nicosia.

Makarios agreed to "appease" the Junta and on 4 May 1972 at a Ministerial Council, he informed his Ministers that he planned to reshuffle the Cabinet in the middle of June. He explained that this was the wish of the Athens Government. **Spyros Kyprianou** resigned the next day (5 May) and issued a statement explaining why he was not willing to stay on until the date of the proposed reshuffle.

Makarios went ahead with the reshuffle (as dictated by Athens) on 16 June 1972. **John Christophides** was appointed as the new Minister for Foreign Affairs. **George**

*Ioannides* was appointed as Minister of Interior and *Andreas Kouros* was appointed as Minister of Education.

## PROPOSAL FOR BROADENING THE COMPOSITION OF THE INTERCOMMUNAL TALKS - JUNE 1972

In September 1971, the Greek Deputy Foreign Minister Palamas made a proposal that the intercommunal talks in Cyprus be broadened to include constitutional experts from Greece and Turkey. U Thant , the UN Secretary General adopted the Greek proposal that the talks should be broadened and suggested that his Special Representative in Cyprus, Mr Osorio-Taffal should also attend the talks. This proposal was rejected by Makarios.

When the new Secretary-General Dr. Kurt Waldheim took over, he reasserted the proposal regarding the broadening of the talks. Makarios in the end consented on the resumption of the talks.

On the 8th June 1972 Dr Kurt Waldheim made an opening speech about the intercommunal talks at the Ledra Palace Hotel in Nicosia. The actual talks took place from 4th July to 1st September. They were held alternatively at the office of Glafcos Clerides in the House of Representatives or at the office of Rauf Denktash. Two legal experts, the Greek Judge Dekleris and the Turkish Professor Aldikacti also took part in the talks.

# MAKARIOS UNWILLING TO COMPROMISE ON A SOLUTION

On 8 December 1972 there was the last meeting of the intercommunal talks for that year. Professor Aldikacti (the Turkish legal adviser) had announced that the Government of Turkey was prepared to sign an agreement which excluded both Enosis and Partition. Mr Dekleris, the Greek legal adviser would not agree on this issue because he did not wish to see the Greek side officially rejecting Enosis.

Four days later, on 12 December 1972, Clerides had a meeting with Makarios. At this meeting Makarios was still adamant not to give in on the issue of Local Government for the Turkish Cypriots. Clerides was to confess later, that this was a fatal mistake on the part of Makarios. Clerides argued that:

*"The uncompromising attitude of Makarios persisted despite the fact the Turkish Cypriot side had accepted all the 13 points proposed by him for constitutional amendments in 1963, and even went beyond them.* **Makarios would not yield further on the issue of local government** *despite the fact that the Turkish Cypriot side had*

*(a) abandoned its demand for the grouping of villages in order to form separate Greek Cypriot and Turkish Cypriot areas of local government;*

*(b) accepted that the House of Representatives would enact legislation on local government matters, and the Communal Chambers would only enact regulations on the basis and within the limits of laws enacted by the House of*

*Representatives;*

*(c )    accepted    that administrative control would be exercised on behalf of the Government by a Civil Servant and a final agreement had been reached on the powers and functions to be exercised by the local government authorities."*
*(G. Clerides: My Deposition. Vol. 3. pp. 204 - 205).*

Clerides further argued that Makarios not only ignored his advice to compromise (on the issue of Local Government) but also ignored the advice of the Greek Junta Government and of the Representative of the Secretary-General. He went on to state that:

*"The decision of Makarios of 12th December 1972 not to compromise, after the concessions of the Turkish side had made, sealed his fate and that of Cyprus. The die was cast and the worst followed."*
(G. Clerides. ibid, p. 206).

Clerides admitted that he had made a blunder in not speaking publicly and informing the Cypriot people about the proposed agreement with the Turkish side. He felt that if he had spoken out then he would have been accused by both the supporters of Makarios and Grivas and also that his views would have been used for propaganda purposes by the Turkish side. The political stubbornness and unwillingness of Makarios to compromise and the attempts of Grivas to torpedo these talks were interpreted by the Turkish side as an unwillingness to co-exist with the Turkish Cypriots in an independent Cyprus.

The political short-sightedness of the Greek Cypriot leadership were to lead eventually to tragic consequences.

In the late 1950s Makarios and Grivas were turned into "legends of Hellenism" and Clerides associated himself with both of them. It was not easy for him to turn suddenly against his *"nationalist gurus"*. He is therefore partly to blame for not speaking out. He chose to remain silent perhaps because he feared the consequences of being branded by all sides as a "traitor" to the national cause. Although he admits in his *Deposition* ( Vol. 3. p. 207) that he had made a mistake in not speaking out publicly at that time, unfortunately, he made this confession and admission far too late and after the tragic events that followed.

The decision of the three Bishops (Yennadios, Kyprianos and Anthimos) to issue a proclamation on the 9th October 1972 demanding a return to the policy of *Enosis* and stating that they would oppose any solution other than *Enosis* revealed their true intentions. Earlier, they had denounced Makarios for not stepping down as President because they argued, his position was contrary to his ecclesiastical duties. Now they were behaving in exactly the same way, *i.e. they forgot all about their own* "ecclesiastical duties" and were now struggling to implement what Makarios failed to implement, *Enosis.*

This split among the pro-Makarios and the pro-Enosis supporters prompted Denktash to state that:

*"The pro-Enosist propaganda has never ceased. It created the crisis of the years 1963 to 1967. Greek Forces landed in Cyprus. The Enosists were always preparing for action...."*

The Cyprus Government tried to argue that declarations by third parties, which had no official capacity, bore no relation to the talks. The damage however was done. Denktash did not state either that many people on his side were also drifting towards the policy of partition. The activities and behaviour of both leaderships simply indicated that there was no mutual trust.

# THE 1973 PRESIDENTIAL ELECTIONS

Makarios's term of office was due to expire in February 1973. Earlier in January, he had sent his new Foreign Minister, John Christophides, to Athens, in order to try and "warm" the already cold relations which existed between the Greek Junta and the Cyprus Government.

Meanwhile, Grivas's EOKA B' terrorist organisation escalated their violence and attacks on police stations and other public buildings. The three Bishops insisted on Makarios's resignation from the Presidency. In this climate of uncertainty, Makarios had a choice: either to go to the polls and renew his mandate, or introduce legislation to extend his term of office for another year.

Denktash also warned that if Makarios went to the polls, then he would seek an election and stand as President of the Turkish Cypriot Administration. Some of Makarios' close advisers recommended that he stand for re-election because he would secure over 90% of the vote. This would indicate the strength of his popularity and thus isolate the small minority who were his enemies.

Clerides, who was the President of the House of Representatives and the chief negotiator in the intercommunal talks, advised a policy of caution. He advised Makarios against an election and to extend his term of office for a further year. Clerides had feared that if Makarios went to the polls then Denktash would also go the polls, that he would be re-elected and then he would return more demanding to the negotiating table.

Makarios chose to go the polls. As there was no candidate to oppose him he was returned unopposed for a further period of five years. Denktash also went to the polls and was re-elected.

## MAKARIOS, CLERIDES AND LYSSARIDES INTERVIEWED

In March 1973, the present writer met President Makarios, Clerides who was President of the House of Representatives and chief negotiator in the inter-communal talks and Dr Lyssarides who was leader of the EDEK Socialist Party. Some of Makarios recent public statements on *Enosis* were often contradictory so during my conversation with him, I asked him how was it possible for a President of an independent Republic to make such pro-Enosis statements which gave the impression to the outside world that he was not genuinely committed to *Independence.*

Makarios tried to justify the course of political action he was taking. He distinguished between the *"desirable"* and the *"feasible"* solution, saying that *Enosis* was of course the *desirable* solution but it was not *feasible* because of Turkey's objections. The question at stake was what was the point of making public statements about the "desirability" of a solution if in actual fact it was not feasible or implementable?

*The author with President Makarios in March 1973*

Our conversation also concentrated on the possibility of establishing a University in Cyprus (as there was no University at that time 1973). Makarios was against the idea and his argument was the existing national problem, the problem over which language to use, what to do with a large number of graduates etc. He also believed that students should preferably continue for their higher education in Greece.

During my conversation with Glafcos Clerides, who at that time was President of the House of Representative, leader of the *Unified Party* and chief negotiator in the inter-communal talks, I asked for his views on the subject of Enosis. His response was as follows:

*"The overwhelming majority of the Cypriot people prefers Enosis and no one can hide this fact. But the question is not what I want but what I can have at a specific time. If*

*someone is a statesman, he should be able to distinguish between what he wishes and what he is able to have under the circumstances. Perhaps the United States wanted to win in the Vietnam war but when this could not happen they were forced to compromise with reality.*

I also asked him about the progress of the inter-communal talks and what he considered as the "ideal" solution:

*"I do not share the general impression that the inter-communal talks from 1968 - 1971 had led to a deadlock because although they did not lead to a final solution, they have helped to solve many problems such as issues on the executive, legislative and judicial powers. What remains to be solved, from the constitutional point of view is the issue of local administration. The main great difficulties are of an international nature, the rights of the Guarantor powers.*

*The most ideal solution, from the point of view of being the most realistic, is that of a unified, independent, sovereign state. In this state we have to offer the Turkish Cypriots representation and we must recognise to them a degree of local administration but not to an extent where they will constitute a state within a state." (Greek Review: Summer 1973).*

Dr Vasos Lyssarides was the leader of the EDEK Socialist Party and the personal physician of President Makarios. As he was a close supporter of Makarios and he himself was against the Junta, I asked him for his Party's views on the relations between the Cyprus Government and the Junta Government in Greece. He said:

**The author with Glafcos Clerides, March 1973**

"We believe that the democratic freedoms must be restored in Greece because they constitute a necessity for the Greek people and a necessity for human beings. Today is not an age for dictatorial regimes. It also constitutes a necessity for the national interests of Greece because with such a regime it is natural not to be respected at all in Europe; it also constitutes a necessity for Cyprus."

On the subject of Enosis he commented:

"We believe that if it was possible to exercise the right of self-determination the result would have been Enosis (union with Greece). What makes it impossible for the time being is not the lack of interest of the Cypriots for Enosis but the well known prevailing conditions."

I also asked him whether, as a Socialist leader, perhaps it would have made more sense to see all Cypriots as Cypriots and not in terms of majorities and minorities. He commented as follows:

*"Of course we see all Cypriots as equal. If the Turkish community accepted this course we would be willing to make concessions in the fields of education, religion etc, but such concessions should not lead to interrupting the functioning of the state or to partition." (Greek Review, Summer 1973).*

**The author with Dr Vassos Lyssarides, March 1973**

# THE BISHOPS DEFROCK MAKARIOS AND MAKARIOS DEFROCKS THE BISHOPS

When Makarios decided to seek re-election in February 1973, the three Bishops ( Anthimos, Kyprianos and Yennadios) called on a Church Synod in order to defrock Makarios. They were first encouraged by the Greek Junta, but later, when Makarios patched up his differences with the military regime in Athens, the Junta tried to restrain the Bishops. They now had the full backing of Grivas and the EOKA B' organisation.

After Makarios' re-election as President for another five year term, the three Bishops requested Makarios to call a Synod to determine the issue of the incompatibility of his political with his ecclesiastic role and position. Makarios knew their intentions and refused to call a meeting of the Synod. The three Bishops then called a Synod in Limassol and summoned him to appear before them. Makarios refused to attend because he claimed the meeting was constituted without authority. The Bishops then tried and convicted Makarios in his absence. Makarios was defrocked and reduced to the rank of a lay person. He was to be known by his original name as **Michael Mouskos**.

Makarios retaliated by calling a **Larger and Supreme Synod**. He invited two Patriarchs, four Archbishops and eight Bishops from Orthodox Churches outside Cyprus in order to constitute this enlarged Synod. This Synod was called on **14th July 1973** and annulled the decision of the three Cypriot Bishops, found them guilty and defrocked them. The three Bishops were stripped of their positions and were not allowed to exercise their ecclesiastical duties.

# ESCALATION OF VIOLENCE BY EOKA B'

The Church conflict and the attempt to defrock Makarios and then Makarios' defrocking of the three Bishops had terrible consequences both within the Church and the people. The escalation of violence from Grivas and his EOKA B' organisation had increased on a massive scale. The Greek Cypriots were divided into **pro-Grivas,** who wanted **Enosis** now, and into **pro-Makarios** supporters, who accepted Independence for now but **Enosis** remained their main and long term aspiration.

The Turkish Cypriot leadership made considerable capital out of these divisions. A typical example of this is the letter which Denktash addressed to the President of the Non-Aligned Summit Conference in Algiers in 1973, which he sent through the UN Secretary - General. In this letter, Denktash quoted extracts from an interview that Makarios gave to the Greek newspaper **Acropolis**, in order to show that the Greek Cypriots were not interested to co-exist with the Turkish Cypriots in an independent republic and therefore they were neither genuine nor sincere in what they were discussing and negotiating at the inter-communal talks. In this interview Makarios said among other things the following:

*"I cannot say that I am nationally satisfied with the development and course of the Cyprus question so far. I would be nationally satisfied, and so would all Greeks, only if the Cyprus problem were solved through Union of Cyprus with Greece...."*

*" Enosis, regardless of whether it can be realised or not, will always be the national aspiration of the Greek Cypriots*

*and a spiritual creed which cannot be renounced either through a referendum or in any other way...."*

In April 1973 Clerides had asked Makarios to relieve him of his position as negotiator and that he also proposed to resign as President of the House of Representatives. He had reminded Makarios of the two "stumbling blocks" which still existed and the essential decisions which had to be made:

*1. The barring of Enosis and Partition by constitutional and treaty provisions.*

*2. The extent of the local autonomy to be given to the Turkish Cypriots.*

Makarios persuaded Clerides to stay on and the Greek Junta made a public statement on 20 April 1973 declaring its support for the intercommunal talks. Makarios then sent Clerides to Athens in May 1973 for talks on the above two crucial decisions and also to urge the Greek Government to condemn EOKA B' and to recall Grivas back to Athens. Clerides had talks with Mr Kavalieratos, the Greek Deputy Foreign Minister.

On the issue of *Enosis* and *Partition*, the Athens regime rejected any agreement first between Greece and Turkey prohibiting *Enosis* and *Partition*. On the issue of local government, Clerides was told that the Greek Cypriot side should show more flexibility. On the subject of Grivas, he was told that (Grivas) did not have the support of the Greek Government and that those Greek officers who supported him or his EOKA B' were acting on their own initiative and they should be "reported" to the *National Centre* (!).

When Clerides briefed Makarios about his talks in Athens, Makarios raised his arms and commented:

*"You see, Glafcos, these hands, they can cut them off, but **I will not sign again any Constitution excluding Enosis**, unless Greece and Turkey sign first a protocol by which Greece would agree with Turkey not to accept Enosis and Turkey would agree with Greece not to accept Partition."* (G. Clerides: My Deposition, Vol. 3. p. 270).

In July and August 1973 violence had escalated again. On 24 July, the armed men of EOKA B' had abducted **Christos Vakis**, the Minister of Justice and also planned to abduct George Ioannides, the Minister of the Interior. A month later, on 24 August the Greek dictator George Papadopoulos in a radio broadcast appealed to all armed groups and to Grivas in particular to disband his EOKA B' organisation. Grivas responded by giving orders for the release of the abducted Minister of Justice. Three days later on 27th August 1973 Grivas sent a lengthy letter to George Papadopoulos saying among other things:

*1. His message (i.e. Papadopoulos's) did not say anything about the person who is responsible for the current situation (i.e. Makarios).*

*2. That the message was conveyed through RIK (i.e. the Cyprus Radio Station) which reflected the views of the Cyprus President.*

*3. That he (Grivas) was offended by the Radio message because it was not addressed to any ordinary person but to someone who had been a Greek Army officer since 1916 and who fought in two world wars.*

*4. That in the armed groups of the Cyprus Government there were communists involved and asked how is it that in Greece the communists are considered dangerous and enemies and in Cyprus are considered as " allies?"*

*5. Papadopoulos had asked for the dissolution of all armed groups but his organisation (i.e. EOKA B') was not an armed group but a national organisation made up of fighters of the same heroic EOKA.*

*6. The whole issue is not whether we accept what you (Papadopoulos) are saying but whether you accept our reasonable proposals for the **democratisation** of Cyprus and the return to normality.*

(The whole text of Grivas's letter is to be found in Spyros Papageorgiou: *Makarios- A March through Fire*, pp. 203-206). What was extra-ordinary and amazing in Grivas's letter was the fact that he was talking about **democratisation** to Colonel Papadopoulos, a man who in April 1967 had demolished with the army tanks the democratic institutions in Greece! Grivas himself with his EOKA B' was trying to do exactly the same in Cyprus, that is to overthrow the Cyprus Government by force and impose in Cyprus a similar regime to that of the Junta in Greece! If he genuinely believed in the **democratic process**, then the only proper thing to do was to stand as a candidate at the Presidential elections and challenge Makarios or any other leader at the ballot box.

Some time later Grivas accused the Greek Junta that they were plotting to arrest or murder him and accused them of sending four army officers from Greece for this specific purpose, that is to carry out his arrest or execution. Grivas, the man who was behind the abduction of the Cypriot Minister of Justice and threatened with his execution if his demands were not met, the man who conspired to exterminate Makarios for not agreeing with his policies, was now accusing others about conspiracy and plotting on his own life!

On 20 November 1973 Grivas issued a proclamation and challenged Makarios to choose between **Peace and War**, saying that EOKA B' was ready for either choice. A month later, on 19 December 1973, Grivas issued a further proclamation which he addressed to *"The Greek People and the Cyprus Parliament."* In this Proclamation he had accused Makarios as:

*"a sycophant.... who pollutes the high position of a President...... who betrayed his Oath for Enosis.... a usurper of state money....a man who encourages Civil War...... who disobeys the Holy Canons and leads the Church to a schism....."*

The other target of his criticism was Glafcos Clerides, the President of the House of Representatives whom he considered as:

*"a pitiful man who acts as the agent of others ...., who has become a Leader of a party with no supporters....... This man who has been denied by his own father and mother.... Whose mother came to see me in 1964 and asked me to try and bring him back to the right course....."*

Grivas also asked: *"What did they (i.e. Makarios and Clerides) do when Enosis supporters were arrested and tortured by the Police, reminding them of the similar treatment they received during Harding's Colonial times ?*

*What did the President do when explosives were used at a Church in Limassol so that Enosis supporters may not be able to worship there?*

According to Ploutis Servas, Clerides was on Grivas's target list because he was the one next in line of the Presidency, "especially since Clerides threatened to introduce a Resolution in the House of Representatives which would have characterised Grivas as a murderer. To the EOKA B' supporters, Clerides was seen as a traitor because he negotiated the future of an independent Cyprus with Denktash" *(Ploutis Servas: Efthynes, Vol. 3. p. 318).*

## POLITICAL CHANGES IN GREECE

Between the months of July and November 1973 three important events took place in Greece:

*1. Abolition of the Monarchy.* On 27 July 1973 Colonel Papadopoulos through a referendum abolished the Monarchy in Greece and declared the country a Republic and himself as the new President. He appointed Spyros Markezinis as his new Prime Minister, who was sworn in on the 1st October.

*2. The Polytechnic uprising.* On 17 November 1973 the students of the Athens Polytechnic rose up against the dictators and demanded Freedom and Democracy. The dictators sent their tanks and crashed the uprising killing and injuring a number of young people.

*3. The overthrow of Papadopoulos.* Both George Papadopoulos, the new "President" and Spyros

Markezinis, the new "Prime Minister" were to have a short term in office because a week after the Polytechnic uprising they were both ousted by **Brigadier Demetrios Ioannides.**

On 25 November 1973 a new government under **Adamantios Androutsopoulos** was formed but real power lay in the hands of Ioannides who master-minded everything behind the scenes. **General Phaedon Gizikis** assumed the Presidency.

# THE "CYPRUS SEMINAR" IN ROME
# NOVEMBER 1973

Soon after the Athens Polytechnic uprising between 19 - 23 November 1973 a Seminar on Cyprus was held in Rome. This was kept secret until 1975 when Clerides spoke about this Seminar. The Athens satyrical newspaper *Pontiki* revealed for the first time in 1979 that **Evangelos Averof**, the former Foreign Minister of Greece also took part. The Seminar was organised by the *Centre of Mediterranean Studies* which was associated with the *American Universities Field Staff*. The main speakers were **Glafcos Clerides** and **Rauf Denktash**.

The invitations to attend this seminar were sent by Dr Baine, the Director of the Centre. This Seminar was attended by Cyrus Vance (a former US Secretary of State for Foreign Affairs), Philips Talbot, former USA Ambassador to Greece, Michael Stewart, former British Ambassador to Greece, from Turkey Professor Aitin Yialmasin substituted Professor Nihat Erim (former Prime Minister of Turkey), Greek Ambassador Demetrios Bitsios and also former Greek Foreign Minister Evangelos Averof.

It was at this Seminar that **Cyrus Vance** warned that:

" *If the Cyprus problem is not solved and a new crisis arose between Greece and Turkey, the USA would not intervene to prevent an armed conflict between them.*"

**Michael Stewart**, the British Ambassador also stated that: "*Turkey was more valuable to the USA than Greece, and Greece more valuable than Cyprus and expressed his doubts if the USA would intervene again to stop Turkey from taking military action against Cyprus.*"

At the Seminar it was made clear that there were some differences to be ironed out between the Greek Cypriots and Turkish Cypriots. At that stage **Evangelos Averof** suggested that three independent constitutional experts should be appointed to mediate in order to resolve the existing deadlock.

According to Michael Ignatiou, the expenses of the *Rome Seminar* were funded by the Shah of Persia, through Dr Baine and the Centre of the Mediterranean Studies via an Iranian state petrol company. *(M. Ignatiou: The Seminar of Rome, pp 35-36).*

# THE DEATH OF GENERAL GRIVAS

On 27 January 1974 General George Grivas died at the age of 76. He died in the house of Marios Christodoulides in Limassol, which he used as his hide-out. Grivas was born in Trikomo in 1898. Although Grivas used all legal and illegal means to overthrow the Makarios regime, the Cyprus Government declared three days of national mourning during which time his body lay in state. On 28 January 1974 Makarios declared a general amnesty to all those EOKA B' activists who were sentenced and serving terms of imprisonment for acts against the state and issued the following statement:

*"The death of General George Grivas-Dighenis has moved Cypriot Hellenism deeply. The General has given valuable services to Cyprus and to the entire nation. On many occasions I disagreed with the General on the method and handling of the Cyprus issue. I deeply regret that during the last two years I was continuously in disagreement with the General because of the acts and activities, to which he was misled. I do not, however, in the least overlook his tremendous contribution to the liberation struggle of Cyprus Hellenism, which gave him an outstanding position in history. The Greeks of Cyprus will always honour the memory of General George Grivas-Dighenis."*

The Cyprus House of Representatives held a special solemn meeting on 29 January and Glafcos Clerides as President of the House praised the work of General Grivas. On 31 January 1974 the House of Representatives passed unanimously the following Resolution (the AKEL Members of the House abstained):

*"The House of Representatives having gathered today, Thursday the 31st January 1974, at an extraordinary solemn meeting in order to pay tribute and to honour the departed Leader of EOKA, General George Grivas-Dighenis, and having recalled the services which the departed national hero has rendered for the liberation of his motherland, by its resolution declares the departed hero **"Worthy Son of his motherland, Cyprus".***

Grivas *was* until his death, the leader of EOKA B', the leader who organised attacks on police stations and other public buildings, the leader who wanted to overthrow the Cyprus Government, yet Makarios and the House of Representatives were *eulogising* the man who tried to overthrow them! If this is not some kind of *Political Masochism* on the part of Makarios and the right wing dominated House of Representatives, one wonders what is!

**Grivas died in January 1974**

Greek flags flew at half mast in all the Government Ministries. The widow of Grivas wanted her husband to be buried in Athens and Makarios had agreed with her. **Demetrios Ioannides**, however, the "invisible" Greek dictator insisted that Grivas should be buried in Cyprus. He was buried in Limassol and the funeral service was conducted by the three defrocked Bishops. A little later, one of the main high streets of Nicosia was named **Grivas Dighenis Avenue** in honour of his name!

## THE PROSCRIPTION OF EOKA B'

Major George Karousos assumed the leadership of EOKA B' immediately after the death of Grivas. Karousos was prepared to respond positively to Makarios' Amnesty call. The hardliners however would not agree with him. On the 30th January 1974 (even before Grivas was buried), **Kikis Constantinou** the EOKA B' Famagusta area leader, and his men raided the Famagusta National Guard barracks and captured a large quantity of ammunition. On the same day, **Lefteris Papadopoulos** (the Limassol area leader) published an article in a pro-Grivas newspaper stating that:

*"EOKA B' will neither give up nor surrender a single bullet. Whoever wants to take our bullets let them come and collect them from the barrels of our guns...."*

According to Spyros Papageorgiou (who was himself a staunch Grivas supporter and was known by the code name of **Cerberus - Kerveros**), the closest colleagues of Grivas were often at loggerheads and quarrelled amongst themselves for the succession of the old General. (The reader may be interested to know that Cerberus in Greek mythology was a three-headed dog who protected the entrance to the Underworld).

In Papageorgiou's view, *Lefteris Papadopoulos* who was identified by various code names such as *Theseus, Toxotis, Myron* and *Keravnos* had the absolute confidence of Grivas.

Major George Karousos succeeded Grivas for a few days but was recalled to Athens by the dictator Ioannides. In February 1974 the leadership of EOKA B' was assumed by **Lefteris Papadopoulos.** Ioannides, the Junta leader was kept fully informed about developments in Cyprus by both Lefteris Papadopoulos (through his frequent reports) and Nikos Sampson (through his frequent visits to Athens). EOKA B' was directed and financed from Athens at the rate of **one million pounds a year.**

When the amnesty measures proposed by Makarios were rejected on the 25th April 1974, EOKA B' was declared an illegal organisation.

On 19 June 1974 a massive rally was organised in Nicosia which was addressed by Makarios. He described EOKA B' as "**a criminal syndicate**", and blamed its founder and leader (Grivas) that he had bequeathed Cyprus "**a national scourge**". Strangely enough, some five months earlier (in January 1974), when Grivas died, Makarios was full of praise for the same man he now described as the organiser of this **national scourge.** Paradoxically, it was the very same person (Grivas) who, back in the 1950's, had forcibly imposed on all parties and on all the Greek Cypriots the view that "**Makarios was the one and only National Leader!**"

# INTERRUPTION OF INTER-COMMUNAL TALKS

In September 1973 Kavalieratos, the Greek Deputy Foreign Minister, advised Clerides to slow down the pace of the inter-communal talks in view of the Parliamentary elections in Turkey scheduled for 14th October 1973. The Socialist Party of Mr Bulent Ecevit had won that election and Ecevit became Prime Minister. The inter-communal talks were further slowed down because Denktash wanted to have consultations with the new Turkish Government.

On 26th March 1974, Denktash had talks in Ankara with Prime Minister Ecevit, the Foreign Minister Gunes and Defence Minister Hasan Ishik. After these talks, Ecevit made a statement saying:

*"The Turkish Government will exert every effort to secure a peaceful and lasting solution to the problem within the framework of an independent and **federal state**. On this issue there is no reason for people of goodwill to have any suspicion about our intentions."*

This was the first time that the Turkish Government introduced the term "**federal state**" and its reference alone had infuriated both Makarios and Clerides. Clerides told Denktash during their meeting on the 3rd April 1974 that he would refuse to meet him for any further talks until this reference is clarified. Makarios commented that the reference undermines the inter-communal talks, but after a compromise agreement backed by the Secretary-General, the talks were resumed in June 1974.

# MAKARIOS' LETTER TO GENERAL GHIZIKIS

The escalation of violence by EOKA B' was actively supported and funded by the pro-Ioannides Greek officers in Cyprus. They used their posts in the National Guard to make pro-Enosis propaganda and blamed Makarios for following a policy of independence in order to cling to power. It was common knowledge that Greek officers serving in the National Guard were assisting EOKA B' to obtain, by staged thefts, arms from camps in which they served or were in command. Cadet officers were carefully selected from anti-Makarios, anti-independence and pro-Enosis enlisted soldiers.

On 2 July 1974 Makarios sent his letter to General Ghizikis, the Junta President of Greece. The letter was published in the newspapers on the 7th July. In this letter, Makarios said among other things the following:

*1. The National Guard, which is officered and controlled by Greek officers, was from the start the main supplier of both men and materials to "EOKA B", the members of which euphemistically called themselves "Enosists" and the "Enosist Array".*

*2. The root of the evil is too deep and reaches as far as Athens..... Evidence of the guilt of the circles of the military regime can be found in documents which were found recently in the possession of leading "EOKA B" persons. It is from the National Centre that money was sent plentifully for the needs of the organisation.*

*3. In the effort to dissolve the state of Cyprus great is the* responsibility of the Greek Government. The Cyprus state can only be dissolved in the case of Enosis. Since, however, Enosis is not feasible it is imperative to strengthen the statehood of Cyprus. The Greek Government in its entire stance regarding the issue of the National Guard is practising an abrogative policy on the Cyprus state.

4. The National Guard which is officered by Greek officers, will be restructured on a new basis. I have shortened the period of service in order to reduce the ceiling of the National Guard and the extent of the evil. .... I would request that the Greek officers serving in the national Guard be recalled. Their continued service and command in the national Guard would be damaging to the relations between Athens and Nicosia.

5. I do not wish to interrupt my co-operation with the Greek Government. It must, however, be kept in mind that I am not an appointed commissioner nor a locum tenens of the Greek Government in Cyprus, but an elected leader of a large section of Hellenism and I demand analogous behaviour towards me from the National Centre.

6. The contents of this letter are not secret. With hearty wishes. Makarios of Cyprus.

On 5 July 1974 Makarios sent **Haris Vovides,** Director of the Office of the President to London and Paris in order to meet the exiled king Constantine and former Premier Karamanlis in order to seek their support, asking them to make public statements. He had also sent them a copy of the letter he had addressed to General Ghizikis.

# PART 5: CYPRUS SINCE 1974

## THE MILITARY COUP OF 15 JULY 1974

Makarios never received a reply to his letter of 2nd July, which he addressed to General **Phaedon Ghizikis**, the Junta President of Greece. The Greek dictator **Demetrios Ioannides,** together with **General Bonanos** Commander-in-Chief of the Greek armed forces, **General Galatsanos** the chief of the Army and some other military officers had prepared "a different reply" for Makarios. They instructed **Georghitsis** and **Papadakis** who were the Chiefs of the Greek armed contingent and supreme command in Cyprus, to carry out the plans of the military coup.

At about 8.20 a.m. on Monday 15 July 1974, tanks and army vehicles surrounded the Presidential Palace in Nicosia. At that time Makarios was meeting a group of Greek school children from Cairo who had come to Cyprus on a visit.

The Presidential Guard on duty was overcome but Makarios managed to escape from the rear part of the Presidential Palace. He was first driven by a passing van to Palechori village, then to Kykko Monastery and then to Paphos. The Presidential Palace was shelled and set on fire. The Cyprus Radio came under the control of armed forces and at 10.45 they broadcast the following statement:

*"Greek Cypriot people. The tragic situation during the last months in Cyprus was leading directly to civil war. The provoked disorder in the bosom of the Church, and the danger appearing that the armed forces would come under the control of anarchist and criminal elements, with*

*consequences which cannot be calculated for the future of Cyprus, led the armed forces to the decision to remove those responsible for the anomaly i.e. the President of the Republic and its Government, who have usurped the authority of Government for a long time, without the free will of the people of Cyprus and who make every permissible and non-permissible effort to retain the personal regime which they created. The armed forces will appoint a temporary Government of National Unity.*

The statement also mentioned that the inter-communal talks will continue and that impartial elections were to be held within a year. The Radio broadcast kept repeating that **Makarios was dead**.

Makarios, however, was still alive. He had moved to Paphos and on the same afternoon (15th July) through a local broadcasting station in Paphos sent the following message to the Cypriot people:

*"Greek Cypriot people. The voice which you hear is known to you. You know who is speaking to you. I am Makarios. I am he whom you elected to be your leader. I am with you a co-fighter and standard bearer in the common struggle. The coup of the junta has failed. I was the target. And since I am alive the junta in Cyprus shall not pass.*

*The people of Cyprus do not bear coups and dictators. The junta has used tanks and armoured cars to carry out the coup. But the resistance of the Presidential Guard stopped the tanks and the armoured cars. The only achievement of the junta was to occupy the Cyprus Broadcasting station in order to broadcast falsehoods and speak about a change of Government.*

**The Presidential Palace in flames**

*Greek people of Cyprus, the junta has decided to ruin Cyprus, to partition it, but it will not achieve it. Offer resistance in every way to the junta. Do not be afraid, make clear your position and your decision to resist, to struggle. All of you enlist in the legal forces of the state. The junta must not pass and will not pass. Now the struggle is holy and victory ours.*

*Long live freedom, long live the Greek Cypriot people, long live the nation."*

# INTERNATIONAL REACTION TO THE COUP

The military coup provoked international reaction. The Soviet Union condemned the coup and Greece's intervention as violating the independence and territorial integrity of the Republic of Cyprus. Both the USSR and the USA ordered their navies to sail towards the Eastern Mediterranean. Both super-powers were suspicious of each other: The USSR suspected the US for wanting to turn Cyprus into another NATO base. The US Government equally suspected the USSR of trying to extend its influence in the region. The US Government believed that their fears were justified because Makarios had associated Cyprus for a number of years with the Non-Aligned countries movement.

The military coup was also discussed by NATO at an extra-ordinary meeting on 17 July. The Turkish delegate launched an attack on Greece and the Sampson government. Although the Greek delegate tried to defend the Junta's position, the NATO Council decision was that *Greece must withdraw the Greek officers from Cyprus and Makarios must return to the island*.

NATO wanted to avoid a conflict between two member states (Greece and Turkey) because it would have meant a weakening of the Eastern flank of NATO. They feared that this would have been detrimental to the NATO alliance and beneficial to their opponents, the Soviet Union.

# NIKOS SAMPSON APPOINTED AS THE "COUP PRESIDENT"

*Nikos Sampson* was an active EOKA member in the 1955-59 struggle against the British colonial rule and was sentenced to death twice in 1957. He escaped execution following the release from exile of Archbishop Makarios in 1959 and was released from jail in Britain following the general amnesty proclaimed with the declaration of independence. He was later a publisher of two newspapers, the daily *"Machi"* (Combat) and the weekly "*Tharros*" (Courage). He was a staunch supporter of Enosis and took part in the Greek-Turkish inter-communal clashes at the Omorphita district in Nicosia in December 1963. When Grivas organised the EOKA B' organisation, Sampson was one of its leading members. He was a fanatical anti-communist. After the fall of Colonel Papadopoulos in Greece he kept close contact and briefed the Junta leader Demetrios Ioannides on a regular basis.

When Makarios was overthrown, *Major General Georghitsis* looked for a "candidate" to be appointed as "President" of the Republic! Michalakis Triantafyllides, the President of the Supreme Court was the first on his list but he was abroad. Nikos Sampson was eventually recruited and was sworn in as "President" at 3.00 p.m. on 15 July by the defrocked Bishop Yennadios, who was now "appointed" as the new Archbishop. Sampson formed a pseudo-government with EOKA B' activists. Demis Demetriou was appointed Foreign Minister. Many Cyprus Ambassadors were replaced.

***Nikos Sampson 1935 - 2001***
***Military coup "President" 15 - 23 July 1974***

A reign of terror had commenced. Thousands of pro-Makarios and left-wing people were arrested and interrogated. Many were killed and others tortured and imprisoned. Even football clubs and left-wing trade unions and organisations were attacked and vandalised.

The Athens daily newspaper TA NEA revealed that many Greek Cypriots were killed and buried in mass graves. The Greek Cypriot priest Papatsestos, who was in charge of the Nicosia Greek Orthodox cemetery, admitted when interviewed by the newspaper that he himself had buried 127 bodies during the coup and was forced to bury another 77 bodies in mass graves. This revelation in TA NEA was later reproduced in the Greek Cypriot newspapers on 27 February 1976. There was resistance to the coup at the Archbishopric, in Kaimakli, Limassol, Paphos, Morphou, Solea and Marathasa. During the coup 504 people were killed and hundreds wounded.

# MAKARIOS IN LONDON AND AT THE UNITED NATIONS

Makarios was flown by a helicopter from Paphos to the British Base at Akrotiri. From there he flew on a RAF plane first to Malta and from there to London. He arrived in London on 17 July. Makarios believed that Britain, as one of the three Guarantors of the Independence of Cyprus, had a legal as well as a moral duty to respond and honour its Treaty obligations. He had talks at 10 Downing Street with Prime Minister **Harold Wilson** and also with the Foreign Secretary **James Callaghan**. The British Government had assured Makarios of the following:

*1. They recognised him as the legal President of Cyprus.*
*2. They advised him to take the issue to the United Nations*
*3. They turned down his request to intervene to restore constitutional order.*

After his talks with Wilson and Callaghan, Makarios flew from London to New York and on 19 July addressed the Security Council, where he accused the Greek military Junta for the coup against him and the Cyprus Government. He said among other things the following:

*"What has been happening in Cyprus since last Monday morning (15th July) is a real tragedy. The military regime of Greece has callously violated the independence of Cyprus. Without trace of respect for the democratic rights of the Cypriot people, without trace of respect for the independence and sovereignty of the Republic of Cyprus, the Greek junta has extended its dictatorship to Cyprus....*

*The people of Cyprus had for a long time the feeling that a coup by the Greek junta was brewing, and this feeling became more intense during the recent weeks when the terrorist organisation "EOKA B", directed from Athens had renewed its wave of violence. I knew all along that, that illegal organisation had its roots and supply resources in Athens.*

*The coup caused much bloodshed and took a great toll of human lives. It was faced with the determined resistance of the legal security forces and the resistance of the Greek people of Cyprus. I can say with certainty that the resistance and the reaction of the Greek Cypriot people against the conspirators will not end until there is a restoration of their freedom and democratic rights. The Cypriot people will never bow to dictatorship, even though for the moment the brutal force of the armoured cars and tanks may have prevailed.*

*After the coup the agents of the Greek regime in Cyprus appointed a well known gun-man, Nikos Sampson, as President who in turn appointed as ministers known elements and supporters of the terrorist organisation "EOKA B".*

*As I have already stated, the events in Cyprus do not constitute an internal matter of the Greeks of Cyprus. The Turks of Cyprus are also affected. The coup of the Greek Junta is an invasion, and from its consequences the whole people of Cyprus suffers, both Greeks and Turks.*

*The United nations has a peace-keeping force stationed in Cyprus..... I have no doubt that the Security Council will put an end to the invasion and restore the violated independence of Cyprus and the democratic rights of the Cypriot people."*

Then, Panayiotakos, the Ambassador of the Greek Junta (who also served in Nicosia) replied to Makarios's accusations, stating that the military coup was *"an internal affair"* and that the Greek Government was not involved! He described Makarios' allegations as pure fabrications and Makarios's government as an **oppressive regime** which tortured its opponents.


## THE FIRST TURKISH INVASION
## 20 JULY 1974

When news of the military coup in Cyprus reached **Bulent Ecevit**, the Turkish Prime Minister, he immediately ordered the Turkish forces to be placed on a state of alert. It was a well known fact that the Turkish Government could not tolerate Makarios for his past obstinacy to reach an agreement with Denktash. Now that Sampson had assumed power Turkey wanted to get rid of him because Sampson was well known for his active involvement against Turkish Cypriots especially in the Omorphita riots in December 1963. They considered the Sampson take over of the government as a serious threat to the security of the Turkish Cypriot community.

Two days after the military coup, Ecevit went to London in order to have consultations with the British Prime Minister, as Britain was one of the co-guarantors of the Independence of Cyprus. He arrived on the evening of 17 July for talks with **Harold Wilson**. At the talks, Ecevit had suggested that Britain and Turkey should take joint action in order to restore the status quo. On Wilson's refusal, Ecevit proposed to land forces in Cyprus, through the British bases, and that Britain, as a co-guarantor, had also a duty to intervene.

The British Government refused both proposals and thus failed to abide by its 1960 Treaty obligations in order to help restore the previous status quo. This decision of the British Government, left Turkey to take military action on her own, leading to the well known tragic consequences.

The U.S. State Department had sent Under Secretary **Joseph Sisco** to London in order to talk to Ecevit and try to avert a war between Greece and Turkey. Sisco met Ecevit at the Turkish Embassy in London on 18 July. He was told by Ecevit that Turkey would take military action to remove the Sampson regime, to restore a balance of power and to protect the Turkish community in Cyprus.

Ecevit's visit to London aimed to carry out a possible joint British - Turkish Intervention. The government of Harold Wilson not only refused to take part in order to restore the status quo as it existed before the 15th July 1974, but also did nothing to prevent Ecevit from taking unilateral military action against Cyprus.

On 19 July, while Makarios was taking part in the Security Council debate on Cyprus, Ecevit had telephoned from London to the Commander-in-Chief of the Turkish Army in Adana, giving his authorisation for the invasion of Cyprus. The Turkish Task Force sailed from Mersin at 5.30 p.m. on the 19th July while the debate at the United Nations was still going on.

At about 4.30 to 5.00 a.m. on the 20th July 1974 the Turkish invasion had begun. The Turkish military command had given the name of **Attila** as the code-name of their military operation. Attila was King of the Huns (c. 406 - 453) and his name had become a byword for brutality and savagery. Turkish planes dropped leaflets on Cyprus promising peace and friendship!

The Turkish forces landed near Kyrenia and killed civilians, raped women and looted. Turkish planes dropped napalm bombs on hospitals, homes and hotels and burnt forests . Turkish paratroopers were dropped in the area between the villages of Geunyeli and Mia Milia. By the 23rd July the Turkish army had occupied 3% of the Island's territory and drove 5,000 people out of their homes. Although the United Nations had called for a cease-fire, the Turkish army carried on regardless, capturing and emptying more villages of their inhabitants.

*Turkish Prime Minister Bulent Ecevit gave the order for the invasion which he called "Peace Operation!"*

*The occupied town of Kyrenia*

# UNITED NATIONS RESOLUTION 353

As stated earlier, the UN were still deliberating about Cyprus, when news of the Turkish invasion had reached the Secretary-General. There were already two draft resolutions and after the new developments which followed the military coup, that is the Turkish invasion, the following Resolution (No. 353) was passed on 20th July 1974:

### *Resolution 353   (20th July 1974)*

*1. Calls upon all States to respect the sovereignty, independence and territorial integrity of Cyprus;*

*2. Calls upon all parties to the present fighting as a first step to cease all firing and requests all States to exercise the utmost restraint and to refrain from any action which might further aggravate the situation;*

*3. Demands an immediate end to **foreign military intervention** in the Republic of Cyprus that is in contravention of operative paragraph 1;*

*4. Requests the withdrawal without delay from the Republic of Cyprus of foreign military personnel present otherwise than under the authority of International Agreements including those whose withdrawal was requested by the President of the Republic of Cyprus, Archbishop Makarios, in his letter of 2 July 1974;*

*5. Calls upon Greece, Turkey and the United Kingdom to enter into negotiations without delay for the restoration of peace in the area and constitutional government in Cyprus and to keep the Secretary-General informed.*

What one immediately notices in this Resolution and in all subsequent Resolutions is that **Turkey is not mentioned by name as the country responsible for the invasion and occupation of an independent sovereign republic and Member state of the United Nations!** The Resolution refers to **foreign military intervention.**

## SAMPSON STEPS DOWN AND CLERIDES ASSUMES THE PRESIDENCY

When Sampson was appointed as 'President' by the military Junta, Clerides was contacted by the American Ambassador Roger Davies, who told him that Sampson should step down because he had information that Turkey would invade. Clerides passed this information to Demis Demetriou, Sampson's Foreign Minister but they were assured by the Greek Junta that there was no such evidence. The 'evidence' however, did turn up on 20 July, when Turkey landed its troops on the northern coast.

Three days later, on 23 July 1974 Nikos Sampson stepped down and Glafcos Clerides, as President of the House of Representatives assumed the Presidency of the Republic according to Article 36 of the 1960 Cyprus Constitution. Clerides confessed that he was in a dilemma whether to ask Makarios to return at once to Cyprus, in which case he feared that he himself would be overthrown, and on the other hand, he suspected that if he had continued as Acting President, he feared that he would be accused by the Makarios supporters as working closely with the coup leaders. (*G. Clerides: My Deposition. Vol. 4. p. 26).*

Clerides further states that he was pressurised by the Greek military to be sworn in as the new President by the defrocked Bishop Yennadios. The Constitution provides that the President gives the affirmation before the House of Representatives and not to a priest.

## THE RESTORATION OF DEMOCRACY IN GREECE

Turkey's invasion of Cyprus had meant the end of the seven year dictatorship in Greece. The Junta had collapsed. The Junta's military adventure in Cyprus supported by the EOKA B terrorist organisation had led to Turkey's invasion and to Cyprus' crucifixion. *"Cyprus had become the place of the Golgothas - of crucifixion, which eventually led to the resurrection of Democracy in Greece!"*

For the Junta's President General Ghizikis, there was no

other alternative. When news reached him that Turkey had invaded Cyprus, the Junta suffered a political paralysis. He decided to invite the politicians to an urgent meeting to discuss the situation. It was agreed to ask Karamanlis to return immediately from Paris in order to form a National Government.

Karamanlis returned on 24th July 1974 to a hero's welcome and was seen as the restorer of Democracy. He formed a National Government with himself as Prime Minister and appointed George Mavros as Foreign Minister and his old friend Evangelos Averof as Minister of Defence.

Freedom of speech was restored in Greece and the ban on all the political parties was lifted. Left-wing newspapers were published again and a little later the

Communist Party of Greece, which was banned by the Metaxas dictatorship of 1936 was legalised. Karamanlis formed the *New Democracy Party* and Andreas Papandreou, who had also returned from exile, formed the *PASOK Party (Pan-Hellenic Socialist Movement).*

**Constantinos Karamanlis assumes power in Greece**

General elections were announced for the 17th November 1974, exactly a year after the Polytechnic uprising. As was to be expected, Karamanlis' *New Democracy Party* won 220 out of the 300 seats in Parliament. On 8 December 1974 a plebiscite was held to decide the future of the monarchy. An overwhelming majority (69.18%) voted against the return of the monarchy and Greece was declared a Republic.

# THE TWO CONFERENCES IN GENEVA

### *The first Geneva Conference 25 - 30 July 1974*

The new Foreign Minister George Mavros went immediately to Geneva to attend a Conference of the three guarantor powers. The first Geneva Conference was held between 25 - 30 July and was attended by the three Foreign Ministers James Callaghan, George Mavros and Turan Gunes.

The Conference was held in order to respond to the UN Resolution 353 which called upon all states to respect the independence, sovereignty and territorial integrity of Cyprus, to end foreign military intervention and to withdraw all foreign troops from the Republic of Cyprus. The UN Resolution also called upon Greece, Turkey and the United Kingdom to enter into negotiations without delay for the restoration of peace in the area and constitutional government in Cyprus.

The three Ministers agreed broadly on three things:

*1. To determine a security zone, the evacuation of Turkish enclaves occupied by Greek or Greek Cypriot forces and exchange of military personnel and civilians detained as a result of the hostilities.*

*2. Negotiations to be carried out urgently as provided by Resolution 353 of the Security Council in order to restore peace in the area and the re-establishment of constitutional government in Cyprus.*

*3. The talks to commence on 8th August 1974 at Geneva and the Representatives of the Greek Cypriots and Turkish Cypriots to be invited to participate in the talks with the three Foreign Ministers.*

Although a cease-fire had been agreed between Greece and Turkey on 22nd July (through Joseph Sisco's mediation), the Turkish army had extended its bridgehead from Kyrenia to the Turkish quarter of Nicosia.

In Cyprus, Acting President Clerides was facing a desperate situation: there was still great danger for a civil war to erupt among the pro-Makarios and the anti-Makarios factions. Worst still was the fact that both James Callaghan (the British Foreign Secretary) and Dr Henry Kissinger, the US Secretary of State, would not give Cyprus their support.

Clerides argued that he had received a message from Makarios (via the Foreign Ministry) asking him to have an urgent meeting with Denktash and to make the following offer:

*1. Request the return of the Turkish Vice-President, the Ministers and Members of the House of Representatives, Civil Servants and Police to their posts.*

*2. To offer complete implementation of the Zurich and London Agreements, including those provisions of the Constitution which were termed as unworkable.*

*3. To propose that should either side still consider that certain amendments were needed for better workability of the Constitution, to refer them to a joint committee for examination.*

Makarios had made a dramatic full U -turn. It was Makarios who had proposed and insisted on revising the Constitution and when the Turkish side accepted most of his 13 points he was still adamant and would not make any concessions. Back in 1972, Clerides as the chief negotiator had pleaded with him to give his consent since the Turkish side had agreed on most of his proposals. Makarios had then stubbornly refused and now he was "begging" Denktash to return to the so-called "unworkable" Constitution of 1960!

Clerides, accompanied by the UN Representative and the Commander of the UN Peace-keeping Force, visited Denktash and conveyed to him Makarios' offer. Denktash agreed to discuss the offer with the Ankara Government. Some four or five days later the UN Representative conveyed to Clerides Denktash's and Ankara's reply:

*"The Greek Cypriots refused to implement those agreements for ten years, alleging that they were unworkable and wanted them abolished or drastically changed. Turkey alleged that because of Greek Cypriot attacks on the Turkish community it had been proved that the agreements did not offer adequate protection to the Turkish Cypriots."*

Makarios' delaying tactics during the inter-communal talks

and his refusal to agree for a settlement in 1972, had led to the tragic consequences that we now know. The Turkish side with its army already in Cyprus, was now responding from a position of strength and was preparing to play the same prolonged "cat and mouse" game while the ordinary people continued to suffer the consequences of the invasion!

Clerides was in such a desperate position that between the first and the second Geneva Conference he approached **Sergei Astavin**, the Soviet Ambassador in Nicosia and told him that he was prepared to offer the Soviet Union a base in Cyprus if the Soviet Union was prepared to send some troops to Cyprus as a form of deterrent to Turkey not to attempt to break out of the bridgehead. The reply from the Kremlin was that the Soviet Union would be willing to intervene if the intervention was made jointly with the USA!

Meanwhile, the atrocities of the invading Turkish army continued unabated. Innocent people were killed and women were raped by the invading Turkish soldiers. The Greek Cypriots took reprisals against the equally innocent Turkish people in various parts of the island. The madness of war and ethnic fanaticism and hatred prevailed in the minds of all those who had harboured for many years the ideas of *Enosis* and *Partition*.

# The Second Geneva Conference 8-13 August 1974

As the Nicosia airport was closed, Acting President Clerides flew from the British Base at Akrotiri first to Athens and then to Geneva in order to take part in the Conference. He was accompanied by Tassos Papadopoulos who was a former Minister in the Makarios Government, Michael Triantafyllides, who was President of the Supreme Court and by Polys Polyviou, who was a Lecturer at Oxford University.

During his stop-over in Athens, Clerides met with Prime Minister Karamanlis and the Defence Minister Evangelos Averof. Clerides asked Karamanlis if the Greek Government could help Cyprus militarily if the Geneva Conference ended in failure. The answer was that no Greek reinforcements could be sent either by sea or air because Cyprus was too far away from the nearest Greek air base.

**James Callaghan** chaired the Conference. The Turkish Foreign Minister Turan Gunes insisted that the 1960 constitution was defunct and the new constitution should be based on geographical separation. Clerides argued that Cyprus had a valid constitution and that the duty and purpose of the Conference was to ensure that the two communities return to constitutional order. He added that the Greek Cypriot side was prepared to return to the 1960 Constitution and would welcome the return of the Vice-President and the Turkish Cypriot Ministers and Turkish members of the House and the public servants to their posts.

Denktash then responded rejecting Clerides' offer. He stated among other things the following:

*"For eleven years the Greeks have tried, and did all they could, to destroy the 1960 Constitution. Having harassed the Turks and destroyed hundreds of Turkish villages and rendered thousands of Turks refugees, having tried under the guise of self-determination, to destroy the independence of Cyprus and unite the island with Greece, having brought, with the above objective, 20,000 Greek troops into Cyprus, having established underground organisations with the purpose of destroying the Cyprus Republic...... having done all the above, all that the Greek side could think was to return to the 1960 Constitution."*

Denktash exaggerated with his figures: there were certainly some Turkish villages destroyed but not hundreds. There were certainly about 10,000 Greek troops stationed illegally in Cyprus but not 20,000.

The Greek Foreign Minister George Mavros commented as follows:

*"We cannot accept that the Turkish fait accompli should be the basis on which the problems of the Cyprus Constitution are to be solved; we cannot accept that the occupation of one part of the territory of a sovereign state should be included among the criteria that should influence the solution of the constitutional problem."*

# THE ROLE OF HENRY KISSINGER

At the time of the military coup and the Turkish invasion of Cyprus, **Dr Henry Kissinger**, the American Secretary of State, was also Chairman of the National Security Council. The time of the tragic events coincided with the **Watergate Affair** which led to the resignation of Richard Nixon as President. American Foreign policy was determined by Kissinger who disliked Makarios and did not want to see him return to the Island.

In Geneva, various draft proposals were made by each side. James Callaghan, according to Polyvios Polyviou, who attended the Conference as an adviser to Clerides, kept reminding the Greek Cypriots that Britain was no longer a super-power and could only take decisive action as part of a UN initiative or in support of the Americans.

*British Foreign Secretary James Callaghan (left) and US Secretary of State Henry Kissinger (right).*

Although Callaghan was critical of the Turkish Foreign Minister Gunes for constantly contacting Prime Minister

Ecevit for every move they were making, he himself was in constant touch with Dr Henry Kissinger.

Kissinger told him that the United States would not exert any pressure on Turkey and that he had suggested that an area between 20 - 30% of the territory of Cyprus should come under Turkish Cypriot control. Both Mavros and Clerides spoke to Kissinger on the telephone, who advised them that if they compromised on this territorial arrangement, the US would use its influence to prevent any further movement of the Turkish forces in Cyprus. For Kissinger, Turkey's military action against Cyprus was not interpreted as *" invasion and occupation"* but as an attempt to force the Greek Cypriots to *"compromise on some territorial arrangement!"*

Brendan O'Malley and Ian Craig in their work *The Cyprus Conspiracy - America, Espionage and the Turkish Invasion,* argue contrary to Kissinger's argument that he could do nothing to stop the military coup against Makarios and the Turkish invasion. The authors point out that Kissinger's inaction was no failure of American foreign policy but the realization of a longstanding plan. The authors reveal the explosive strategic reasons why the island was divided, saving its top-secret defence and spying facilities from communist take-over or British defence spending cuts. They argue that Cyprus had become invaluable to Washington, monitoring both Central Asia for Soviet nuclear missile technology and the Middle East for potential military threats. James Callaghan was to confess in an interview with the *Times Higher Education Supplement* in 1999, i.e. 25 years after the invasion, that the US "allowed the invasion" in order to keep spying facilities. He also revealed that:

*" A British task force was sent to Cyprus shortly after the coup in the hope of joint military action with US troops to prevent a Turkish invasion. We nearly went to war with Turkey. But the Americans stopped us."*

During a high level meeting held between the Governments of Greece and Cyprus in order to pursue a common political policy (held in Athens on 30th November and 1st December 1974, Makarios had stated that Kissinger told him that he himself *"was in favour of the establishment of a number of Turkish cantons in the island but was not certain whether the Turkish Government would accept a cantonal solution"*. Clerides also mentioned that he received a telegram from Kissinger stating that *"the Turks wanted a geographical division of a large canton and possibly two or three smaller ones"*.
(C. Karamanlis: Archives, Vol. 8 p. 240).

**Turkey drove these people out of their homes and forced them to sleep in tents or under the trees.**

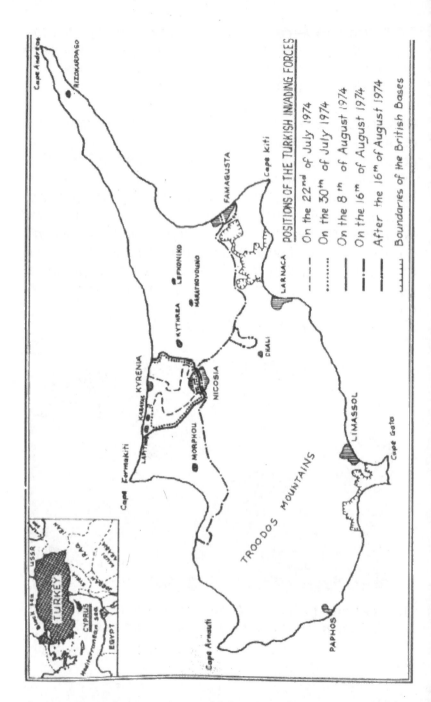

POSITIONS OF THE TURKISH INVADING FORCES

----- On the 22nd of July 1974

......... On the 30th of July 1974

——— On the 8th of August 1974

—·—·— On the 16th of August 1974

—··—··— After the 16th of August 1974

········· Boundaries of the British Bases

Cape Andreas

RIZOKARPASO

FAMAGUSTA

Cape Kiti

LARNACA

LEFKONIKO

MARATHOVOUNO

KYTHREA

DHALI

KARAVAS

KYRENIA

NICOSIA

LAPITHOS

MORPHOU

LIMASSOL

Cape Gata

Cape Kormakiti

TROODOS MOUNTAINS

Cape Arnauti

PAPHOS

BLACK SEA

USSR

TURKEY

CYPRUS

EGYPT

Mediterranean Sea

IRAN

IRAQ

SYRIA

# TURKISH PROPOSAL - DIVISION OF CYPRUS IN CANTONS

Gunes and Denktash, encouraged by the views of Kissinger, were adamant and insisted on the geographical separation of the two communities. On the 12 August Gunes proposed that 34% of the area of Cyprus should be under Turkish Cypriot administration. The Gunes proposal suggested the following:

*1. The Republic of Cyprus is a bi-communal and independent State.*

*2. The Republic will be constituted by one Turkish-Cypriot autonomous zone comprising six districts and by one Greek Cypriot autonomous zone comprising two districts:*

*(a) The Greek Cypriot zone to comprise the Main Greek Cypriot district and (b) the Greek villages in the District of Karpasia.*

*The Turkish Cypriot Main District to cover the area:*

*1. From Panagra, Myrtou. Asomatos, Skylloura, Yerolakkos, (Turkish part of Nicosia), Angastina, Yenagra, Maratha, Styllos, Turkish part of Famagusta and the north-east including Komi Kebir.*

*2. The Lefka region.*
*3. The Polis region*
*4. The Paphos region*
*5. The Larnaca region*
*6. The Turkish villages in the Karpasia region.*

The Turkish proposal had reverted to the old claim for grouping the Turkish villages for administrative purposes something which was rejected by Makarios previously.

On 13 August Clerides had submitted the Greek Cypriot proposal where he stressed the following:

*1. The constitutional order of Cyprus shall retain its bi-communal character.*

*2. Through an appropriate revision to ensure an enhanced feeling of security for both communities.*

*3. Institutional arrangements regarding an agreed allocation of powers and functions.*

*4. Central Government to continue to be based on the Presidential regime.*

*5. Villages and municipalities to be grouped together for administrative purposes.*

*6. Legislative authority over the communal administration to be exercised by the Greek and Turkish members of the House of Representatives.*

The situation was so grave that Clerides, fearing the worst prior to the meeting scheduled for the evening of 13 August, contacted the Soviet observer at the Conference and asked him if the Soviet Government would be willing to help. The last minute "flirt" with the Soviet Union did not work. The Soviet observer repeated what the Soviet Ambassador told Clerides previously, namely that: **"The USSR will only act jointly with the USA."**

On the evening of 13th August Clerides asked the Conference for 48 hours to consider Gunes proposals. He said that he wanted to send a member of his delegation to London to confer with Makarios, whereas he and Mavros were to fly to Athens to confer with Karamanlis. Callaghan, Mavros and Clerides were prepared to return to the negotiating table but Gunes and Denktash were not. The conference broke up at about 3.00 a.m. on the 14th August and at 4.30 a.m. the Turkish military operations and bombing of towns had resumed. The second invasion had commenced.

## THE SECOND PHASE OF THE TURKISH INVASION - 14 AUGUST 1974

On leaving the Geneva Conference, Clerides stopped in Athens on his way back to Cyprus. He asked Karamanlis to send reinforcements to help the defence of Cyprus. Karamanlis had spoken with the Chiefs of the Armed Forces who said that they could not respond, not because they did not want to, but because it was militarily impossible due to the distance.·

Turkish planes bombed lines of communication, military targets as well as towns and villages. The Turkish forces advanced in two directions: they moved East, towards the fertile plain of Mesaoria, Famagusta and the Karpass Peninsula which they occupied and also to the West towards Morphou and Pyrgos. The Turkish army occupied 37% of the territory of Cyprus, which was also the most productive.

About 200,000 people fled to the southern parts in order to

escape, carrying with them only a few personal belongings. Tens of thousands of people found themselves spending many days and nights under the trees and tents, with no sanitation whatsoever and had to rely on the charity of their fellow compatriots for some food and clothing. This was a tragic exodus of biblical proportions. About ***200,000 people expelled from their homes lived in tents***

***one third*** of the population became refugees in their own country.

About 3,000 people were killed, there were numerous rapes and looting of shops and properties was widespread. Many hundreds of people were taken to Turkey as war prisoners and even to this day, (2002) no one knows about the fate of over 1,000 missing persons.

Archaeological sites and treasures were looted. Many antiquities such as statuettes, pottery, copper bronze and gold objects going back 8000 years were looted and sold in foreign markets. Priceless icons and mosaics in Greek churches were stolen and sold or destroyed. Yet the Turkish Prime Minister Bulent Ecevit had the audacity to announce to the world that *"Turkey was not bringing war but Peace to Cyprus! "*

The plundering of Cyprus which Ecevit described as "bringing Peace" reminds one of the words of the Roman Historian Tacitus who once wrote: *"They make a desert and they call it peace."*

*Greek Cypriots taken hostages by the Turkish army*

*The town of Famagusta which fell to the Turks on 14 August 1974 and now a ghost town*

## ETHNIC CLEANSING: TOWNS AND VILLAGES UNDER TURKISH OCCUPATION

In order to implement the "geographical division" of the Island, the Turkish army embarked on an Ethnic Cleansing strategy. ***There was never an area of the Island which was inhabited by one community alone***. There have always been Greek and Turkish villages or mixed villages but ***they were all dispersed in various parts of the Island***. The Turkish Government's plan was to implement the so-called "Attila Line", which cut Cyprus horizontally stretching from Famagusta in the East to Pyrgos in the West. In order to create such "a Turkish area" 160,000 Greek Cypriots and 40,000 Turkish Cypriots were forced to evacuate their 202 towns and villages.

The list below shows all the names of the 202 towns and villages which are under Turkish occupation.

## *Famagusta District*

1. Famagusta
2. Agia Triada
3. Agios Andronikos
4. Agios Georgios
5. Agios Efstathios
6. Agios Elias
7. Agios Theodoros
8. Agios Iakovos
9. Agios Nikolaos
10. Agios Sergios
11. Agios Symeon
12. Agios Hariton
13. Angastina
14. Akanthou
15. Aloa
16. Ardhana
17. Arnadhi
18. Artemis
19. Ashia
20. Avgolidha
21. Afania
22. Acheritou
23. Akhna
24. Vathylakas
25. Vasili
26. Vatyli
27. Vitsadha
28. Vokolidha
29. Gaidouras
30. Galatia
31. Galinoporni
32. Gastria
33. Yenakra
34. Yerani
35. Yialousa
36. Goufes
37. Gypsou
38. Davlos
39. Enkomi
40. Eptakomi
41. Kalopsidha
42. Koilanemos
43. Kontea
44. Kornokipos
45. Korovia
46. Kouklia
47. Knodhara
48. Kridhia
49. Koma tou Yialou
50. Komi Kebir
51. Lapathos
52. Livadhia
53. Leonarisso
54. Lefkoniko
55. Limnia
56. Lythrankomi
57. Lysi
58. Makrasyka

59. Mandres
60. Maratha
61. Marathovounos
62. Melanarka
63. Melounda
64. Milia
65. Monarka
66. Mousoulita
67. Boghazi
68. Neta
69. Ovgoros
70. Ornithi
71. Patriki
72. Peristerona
73. Pighi
74. Pervolia Trikomou
75. Platani
76. Platinissos
77. Prastio
78. Pyrga
79. Rizokarpaso
80. Santalaris
81. Sinta
82. Spathariko
83. Strongylos
84. Stylloi
85. Syngrasi
86. Tavrou
87. Tziaos
88. Trikomo
89. Trypimeni
90. Flamoudhi
91. Psyllatos

## *Nicosia District*

92. Agia Marina
93. Agios Vasilios
94. Agios Georgios
95. Angolemi
96. Ayia
97. Ammadhies
98. Ambelikou
99. Arghaki
100. Avlona
101. Galini
102. Yerolakkos
103. Dhio Potamoi
104. Elia
105. Epicho
106. Exo Metochi
107. Kazivera
108. Kalo Horio
109. Kalyvakia
110. Kanli
111. Kapouti
112. Karavostasi
112. Katokopia
113. Kato Zodhia
114. Gueneli
115. Kokkina
116. Kourou Monasteri
117. Kythrea
118. Kyra
119. Lefka
120. Limnitis
121. Louroudjina
122. Loutros

123. Mandres
124. Massari
125. Mia Milia
126. Bey Kiogiou
127. Mora
128. Morphou
129. Neo Chorio
130. Niketas
131. Xeros
132. Xerovounos
133. Orta Kiogiou
134. Palekythro
135. Pano Zodhia
136. Pentayia
137. Peristerona
138. Petra
139. Petra tou Digeni
140. Potamos tou Kambou
141. Prastio
142. Pyroi
143. Skylloura
144. Syrianohori
145. Trachoni
146. Trachonas
147. Tymbou
148. Filia
149. Chrysidha
150. Chrysiliou

## Kyrenia District

151. Kyrenia
152. Agia Irene
153. Agios Amvrosios

154. Agios Georgios
155. Agios Epiktetos
156. Agios Ermolaos
157. Aghirta
158. Agridhaki
159. Asomatos
160. Vavylas
161. Vasilia
162. Vouno
163. Dhiorios
164. Elia
165. Thermia
166. Kazafani
167. Kalogrea
168. Kambyli
169. Karavas
170. Karakoumi
171. Karmi
172. Karpasia
173. Kato Dhikomo
174. Kiomortsiou
175. Klepini
176. Kormakitis
177. Kontemenos
178. Koutsoventis
179. Krini
180. Lapethos
181. Larnakas Lapethou
182. Livera
183. Bellapais
184. Motidhes
185. Myrtou
186. Orga
187. Paleosofos

188. Pangra
189. Pano Dhikomo
190. Pyleri
191. Sychari
192. Sysklepos
193. Templos
194. Trapeza
195. Trimithi
196. Fterycha

### Larnaka District

199. Arsos
200. Melousia
201. Pergamos
202. Tremetousia

The Turkish invasion had terrible repercussions. As indicated above the human losses and the uprooting of 200,000 people from their homes was a severe blow to everyone. The United Nations passed resolutions in July and in August calling for the withdrawal of foreign troops and for the return of the refugees to their homes but Turkey did not abide by them.

The new Democratic Government in Greece watched the events helplessly. Greece was a guarantor of the Independence of Cyprus but could do very little to help because the Junta had just fallen and the country was politically, economically and militarily still in chaos. Everything seemed to have been in disarray. The British Government also a guarantor of the Independence chose to remain neutral and not to intervene.

Britain alone could have prevented this terrible tragedy because of its two military bases on the Island. The Cypriots felt very bitter about the whole affair and the total apathy of Britain in refusing to fulfill their treaty obligations towards Cyprus. Worst still, the British government agreed to convey a few thousand Turks from the south to the north thus encouraging ethnic cleansing and the permanent partition of the Island.

*Relatives of missing persons*

## A FEDERAL SOLUTION IS AGREED IN ATHENS 30.11 - 01.12.1974

On 30 November and 1 December 1974, talks were held at the Athens Foreign Ministry. Representing the Greek Cypriot side were Makarios, Clerides, Foreign Minister John Christophides, Spyros Kyprianou, Tassos Papadopoulos, Christodoulos Veniamin and Ambassador Nikos Kranidiotis. Representing the Greek Government were Prime Minister Karamanlis, Foreign Minister D. Bitsios, Defence Minister Evangelos Averoff, Deputy Foreign Minister Varvitsiotis and Ambassador Dountas.

Karamanlis chaired the meeting and described the chaotic state which existed in both Cyprus and Greece after the collapse of the Junta. He also stated that when he assumed power on 23rd July, he wanted to send military re-enforcements to Cyprus but the army chiefs were against the idea because of the long distance that separates the two countries. He also suggested to lead personally an armada but again his proposals was not considered feasible.

Clerides then described the chaotic state which existed in Cyprus stating that although the Turks occupied about 40% of the territory, they were also in charge of 75% of the productive area. He also described that there were still many EOKA B supporters carrying guns and the Greek Cypriots were divided. The meeting also discussed the plight of the refugees. Clerides argued that the Turks wanted a solution based on the geographical division of Cyprus. He said that Denktash had told him that if the Greek Cypriots accepted that the Turkish Cypriots could control 25% of the territory then "*we can talk business*"

What Makarios had constantly refused for many years previously, he now realised and was prepared to accept after the Turkish invasion and the tragic consequences that Federation was the only way forward. He argued at this meeting that there were three issues at stake:

1. *Functional Federation* which the Turkish Cypriots had previously accepted but he himself had rejected.

2. *Cantonal Federation* which would mean that the Turkish Cypriots administer some cantons in different areas. The advantage of this solution is that the central government

has more powers.

*3. Bi-zonal Federation.* If the Turks insisted on this type of solution the vast majority of the Greek refugees are not likely to return and live under Turkish administration.

Makarios proposed a *"Multi-regional Federation"* because he argued that this type of solution would avert the danger of a possible Partition of the island. Fearing the future dangers of a possible partition he rejected the Bizonal solution using the argument that it would be best not to sign anything rather than surrender 28% of the territory voluntarily.

The two delegations had also agreed that the maximum size of the territory to be offered should not exceed 25%. At that meeting it was agreed that negotiations should be resumed as soon as possible between Clerides and Denktash. Clerides who had negotiated for many years with Denktash and was often at a point of reaching an agreement (in 1972) when Makarios let him down because he had changed his mind, was not in the mood to continue as negotiator unless Makarios agreed to give him *"Signed Written Terms of Reference on what has been agreed"* at this meeting with the Greek Government. Makarios refused at first and Clerides offered to resign in which case Karamanlis intervened and Makarios was persuaded to accede to Clerides' request.

At the conclusion of the meeting, the Greek Foreign Ministry prepared the text of a Draft whereby the negotiator was instructed to negotiate for the following:

*1. A multi regional federation on a bicommunal basis and*

*with a federal government with substantial powers.*

*2. The extent of the Turkish areas to correspond, as far as possible, to the population ratio, but in no case the total of such areas to exceed 25% of the total area of the island.*

*3. Efforts should be made that Turkish areas should be created, as far as possible, in places where Turkish villages are concentrated.*

*4. The return of all displaced Greek Cypriots.*

*5. Securing the right of ownership and freedom of movement of all the people in the island.*

*6. For those who will not be able to return to their homes, negotiations should take place regarding their rights of ownership.*

*7. Negotiations shall begin from the subject of the powers of the federal government.*

## MAKARIOS RETURNS TO CYPRUS

On 7 December 1974 Makarios returned to Cyprus to a second hero's welcome. The first was in 1959 after his exile by the British. He assumed the Presidency of Cyprus once again when Clerides stepped down. Clerides resumed his post as Leader of the House of Representatives and as negotiator of the Greek Cypriots.

On the same day Makarios addressed the thousands of people outside the Archbishopric who had gathered from all parts of the island to welcome him. He said among other things the following:

*"I thank and pray to God whose providence has saved me from the death planned through the coup and given me the happiness of being once more in my ancestral land and among the people whose love made me their leader.*

*I am profoundly moved because after almost a five-month absence and many tribulations I see Cyprus again and I am, at this moment, among so many thousands of Greek Cypriots who have flooded this place in order to welcome me and express their feelings of love for me. You suppressed today your grief at the major national calamity brought about by the coup, you have, each one of you, bandaged your scars and wounds and come to welcome me, declaring at the same time your confidence in the future of our cruelly-tried country.*

*Many and conflicting are the feelings overwhelming me at this moment. I am glad to be back in Cyprus. But I also grieve that Cyprus is no longer a beautiful and prospering island, as it was until the criminal coup of July 15. It has been reduced to ruins. I grieve that many are absent from today's gathering. They are absent because they have fallen in defending the independence and territorial integrity of our island or have been killed in cold blood by the Turkish invaders.*

*Thousands are absent because thousands are the dead, the missing and those held as hostages. I pay tribute to the sacred memory of our dead and lay on their graves flowers and myrtle, symbols of our love and mourning. I express my profound sympathy to the families of the dead, the missing and the hostages. I also express deep sympathy to the thousands of refugees, to all those who have been forced to leave their homes and properties and become refugees in their own country, refugees living in appalling conditions.*

**Makarios addresses the Greek Cypriots on his return to Cyprus on 7 December 1974**

*The fall of the junta has also facilitated my return to Cyprus. My return means the restoration of constitutional order overthrown by the junta and exploited by Turkey. Turkey put forward internationally the argument that by its military intervention in Cyprus it aimed, as one of the guarantor powers, at restoring constitutional order. From the constitutional point of view, Turkish arguments have now proved to be groundless and unjustified, even though they were mere pretexts right from the outset. For, the occupation by Turkey of a large part of Cyprus territory, the uprooting of thousands of Greeks, and the long chain of other events have nothing to do with the restoration of constitutional order. The Turks evidently aimed at creating faits accomplis through use of force. And we are already confronted with a situation of faits accomplis. We Greek Cypriots, however, are on no account prepared to recognise and accept faits accomplis brought by military operations. We want talks with the Turkish Cypriots for the bridging of our differences, for the finding of a solution to the Cyprus problem. I only say that we shall not accept any solution involving transfer of populations and amounting to partition of Cyprus......*

*I shall not refer to the causes of the conflict, for I do not wish to reopen old wounds which I want to see healed. And for this reason, it is not my intention to persecute my enemies and opponents...... I forgive them all for their sins and grant them amnesty.... In the face of the calamity of Cyprus, there is no room for passions and division....."*

Both Makarios and the House of Representatives expressed their thanks to Glafkos Clerides for his work as Acting President during Makarios's absence. Ezekias Papaioannou, Dr Vasos Lyssarides and Dr Takis Evdokas, leaders of *AKEL, EDEK* and *DEK* respectively, had advised Makarios to form a Government of National Unity and to appoint Ministers from all the political parties based on their parliamentary strength. Tassos Papadopoulos of the *Unfied Party* and Poskotis of the *Progressive Party* had opposed this idea. AKEL even agreed not to propose any members from the AKEL leadeship but persons of left-wing views and gave as an example the name of Costas Partassides, the former Mayor of Limassol.

Makarios was still adamant in his views. He did not want political parties to nominate their representatives in the Cabinet because they would be answerable to their parties and not to himself. Furthermore he used two excuses in order not to form a Government of National Unity:

(a) He held the view that Western powers like the USA who could help in finding a solution, would not approve of a National Unity Government which included Communist members! Makarios the non-aligned leader for so many years all of a sudden remembered the importance of the USA!

(b) He used the excuse that since the *Unified Party* and the *Progressive Party* were against such an idea, there was no full consensus or unanimity of views!

When Karamanlis took over the Government in Greece after the collapse of the Junta he agreed to form a Government of National Unity. Makarios refused to follow his example. In the end he agreed to form a **National Council** which would be an *Advisory Body* and consist of the leaders of all the Political Parties. The first meeting of the National Council was held on 21st January 1975 and it was agreed that it would have jurisdiction on all the aspects of the Cyprus problem both on matters of substance and tactics.

*Hundreds of Greek-Cypriot war prisoners taken to Turkey as hostages. Many of them are still missing.*

## INTER-COMMUNAL TALKS RESUMED
## 19th DECEMBER 1974

On 19 December 1974 Makarios gave Clerides the *"Signed Written Terms of Reference"* to resume negotiations (based on what was agreed in Athens on 30th November and 1st December). The intercommunal talks between Clerides and Denktash resumed on the afternoon of the same day (19th December).

The talks were held at Denktash's office in the presence of UN Special Representative Mr Weckmann-Munoz. During these meetings which continued until 10 February 1975 a number of Humanitarian issues were also raised such as the issue of missing persons and living conditions of the enclaved people in the North.

During their first meeting (19. 12. 1974) Denktash wanted to ascertain for himself that Clerides had the proper power and authority to act on the Greek Cypriots behalf and to sign for anything should they come to an agreement. He asked Clerides for clarifications on a number of points:

(a) He expressed his doubts about the sincerity of intentions of Makarios towards the Turkish community. He said that he was not convinced that the Archbishop is genuinely interested in finding a solution of the Cyprus problem on a partnership basis because he wanted Cyprus to remain a Hellenic island and considered the Turks as a minority.

(b) He wanted to know whether Clerides considered himself as the representative of the Archbishop or of the Greek Cypriot community.

(c ) He wanted to know whether Clerides had any power to sign on anything that was mutually agreed.

*(G. Clerides: My Deposition, Vol. 4. pp. 147 - 150)*

On 11 February 1975 Clerides issued a paper describing the **Principles Proposed on the Constitutional Aspect of the Cyprus Problem**. The Greek paper briefly suggested the following:

*(a) Cyprus should be an independent sovereign republic.*

*(b) The constitution shall be that of a bicommunal multiregional federal state.*

*(c) The areas to be under the Turkish Cypriot administration*

*shall correspond approximately to the present ratio of the Greek and Turkish population of the island.*

*(d) The Central Government of the Federal State shall have substantial powers.*

Some of the main points of the Turkish paper were the following:

*(a) Cyprus should be an indpendent and secular state.*

*(b) The Constitution shall be for a Bicommunal and biregional Federal State.*

*(c ) Federal laws cannot discriminate against the members of the Turkish and Greek Federated States and shall be so made as not to make it possible for one national community to overpower the other in economic and political fields.*

## "TURKISH FEDERATED STATE"

On 13 February 1975 Denktash declared the occupied parts in the North as the **Turkish Federated State of Cyprus**. The Turkish Cypriot administration elected Denktash as "President". The United Nations Security Council met on 20th February 1975 and discussed this latest development. Glafcos Clerides, President of the House of Representatives and Greek Cypriot negotiator called on the Council to take urgent and firm measures in order to prevent the destruction of the independence of Cyprus. In his statement he also disclosed the proposals he had handed to the Turkish Cypriot side.

On 12 March 1975 the Security Council unanimously adopted a Resolution which expressed:

"*Regrets at the unilateral decision of 13 February 1975 declaring that a part of the Republic of Cyprus would become 'a federated Turkish state'.*

The Resolution called for an urgent endorsement of General Assembly **Resolution 3212** endorsed by Security Council **Resolution 365 (1974**).

## THE 1975 VIENNA TALKS

Following the above UN Resolution, the UN Secretary-General Dr Kurt Waldheim arranged for new Cyprus inter-communal talks to be held in Vienna. The first round of talks was held on 28 April, the second round on 5 - 9 June and the third on 24 - 27 July 1975. It was during the third round of talks in Vienna that it was agreed that some 9,000 Turkish Cypriots should be moved to the North and that the 10,000 Greek Cypriots who were already living in the North should be allowed to stay.

A fourth round of talks was arranged to be held at the UN headquarters in New York on 8 - 10 September. It was previously agreed in Vienna that the two sides should present their set of proposals for a settlement. Clerides gave the proposals of the Greek Cypriots but the Turkish side failed to come up with any proposals stating that it was impossible to do so because of the Turkish senate elections in October. Makarios and Clerides wanted the Secretary-General to apportion blame on the Turkish side for failing to keep their promises but he would not agree to

338

that. Denktash on the other hand threatened that if the Greek Cypriot side refused to agree to a date for a fifth round of talks it would mean the end of talks, he would take further action and would make the separation complete and final.

Makarios and Clerides decided that the inter-communal talks should not be resumed unless the Turkish side agreed to submit in advance of the talks written proposals on the territorial issue. This proposal was turned down by the Turks and the talks were not resumed.

## MAKARIOS MEETS KISSINGER AND GROMYKO IN NEW YORK

In September 1975 Makarios visited New York. He met and had talks with USSR Foreign Minister Andrei Gromyko and Dr Henry Kissinger. He thanked Kissinger for his reference on Cyprus during his address to the UN General Assembly. Dr Henry Kissinger supported the following principles:

*(a) A settlement must preserve the independence, soverignty and territorial integrity of Cyprus.*

*(b) It must ensure that both the Greek-Cypriot and the Turkish-Cypriot communities can live in freedom and have a large voice in their own affairs.*

*(c ) The present dividing lines cannot be permanent. There must be agreed terriorial arrangements which reflect the economic requirements of the Greek Cypriot community and take account of its self-respect.*

*(d) There must be provision for the withdrawal of foreign military forces other than those present under the authority of international agreements.*

*(e) There must be security for all Cypriots; the needs and wishes of the refugees who have been the principal victims and whose tragic plight touches us all must be dealt with speedily and with compassion.*

In the meantime, during the early part of 1975, several thousands of Turks from mainland Turkey were brought to Cyprus and re-housed in the homes of Greek Cypriots. This was the first attempt to change the island's demographic character.

On 20 November 1975 the UN General Assembly after debating the Cyprus problem passed by 117 votes in favour to 1 vote against (Turkey) and 9 abstentions adopted **Resolution 3395**. The Resolution re-affirmed the content of the previous resolutions, demanded the withdrawal without further delay of all foreign armed forces and foreign military presence and personnel from the Republic of Cyprus, and the cessation of all foreign interference in its affairs. It also called **"for the safe return of all refugees to their homes and to settle all other aspects of the refugee problem".**

# THE NATO MEETING IN BRUSSELS, THE RESIGNATION OF CLERIDES

On 12 December 1975 during a meeting of NATO Foreign Ministers, Bitsios and Caglayangil, the Foreign Ministers of Greece and Turkey met privately and agreed to re-activate the inter-communal talks. It was also agreed that the Greek Cypriots should be the first to put proposals on the territorial aspect. This was confirmed by Makarios during the National Council meeting on 28th January 1976.

Prior to the commencement of the fifth round of inter-communal talks, which were scheduled to be held in Vienna on 17 February 1976, Denktash raised two issues:

(a) The status of the negotiator. He wanted to know whether Clerides represented the Greek Cypriot community or whether he represented the Government and the National Council.

(b) He was prepared to go to Vienna without advisers and that he would not participate if Clerides attended the talks with advisers.

The issues for discussion were: (a) the territorial aspect, (b) the question of federation and (c ) the powers of the Central Government. The two sides agreed to meet again in April and to come up with concrete proposals regarding the territorial and other issues.

Although it was previously agreed that the Greek Cypriot side would submit proposals on the terriorial aspect first, Clerides did submit the proposals first, a few days prior to the talks, but he committed the "*cardinal sin.*" He submitted the proposals to Denktash but kept it secret from Makarios. As we shall see below, Clerides was to pay heavily for this "secrecy" because he was accused of "political treachery", that he was negotiating behind the back of the Government etc. A little later the Cyprus Government itself published the very same proposals which Clerides handed to Denktash. On the territorial issue the proposal was that *"the total area which will be under Turkish Cypriot administration should extend to 20% of the territory of the Republic"*.

The Turkish side leaked the news that Clerides had "secretly" handed the proposals to them to a British journalist. Clerides was criticised for making a secret agreement and resigned as chief negotiator and also from his position as President of the House of Representatives. He was replaced by **Tassos Papadopoulos**. After the resignation of Clerides, Denktash decided to downgrade the status of the talks and appointed **Umit Suleiman** as the Turkish Cypriot negotiator.

Clerides admitted that he had taken a calculated risk but what he could not understand was why, because Makarios and the National Council had already agreed at the National Council meeting on 28th January 1976 that they should be the first to submit proposals. What he also considered strange was the fact that both Makarios and the National Council authorised his successor, Tassos Papadopoulos to give proposals first on a map. (*G. Clerides: My Deposition, Vol 4. p. 407 - 8*).

The criticism waged against Clerides was so great that his political opponents in Government tried to politically "ostracise" him. Makarios offered him the post of Permanent Representative of Cyprus at the U.N. but he turned it down.

# THE 1976 ELECTIONS IN CYPRUS AND THE USA

On 20 June 1976 "Presidential elections" were held in the occupied areas. Rauf Denktash received 41,059 votes and his opponent Ahmet Berberoglou polled 11,869. In the Parliamentary elections, Denktash's National Unity Party won 30 out of the 40 seats in the Legislative Assembly.

Parliamentary elections were also held in the free areas of the Republic on 5 September 1976. Clerides had formed the *Democratic Rally Party* and contested the September 1976 elections. The coalition of the other parties (AKEL, Democratic Party and EDEK) blocked Clerides and his Party from winning any seats even though the Democratic Rally polled 24.1% of the vote. Such was the animosity of Makarios and the other parties towards Clerides that they amended the electoral system to that of the first-past-the-post so that Clerides' party would not manage to win a single seat.

Of the 35 seats in Parliament (allocated for the Greek Cypriots, the other 15 seats were allocated for the Turkish Cypriots but they had never attended since 1964), 21 went to Spyros Kyprianou's *Democratic Party*, 9 went to Papaioannou's *AKEL Communist Party*, 4 went to Vassos Lyssarides' *EDEK Socialist Party* and the other seat went to Tassos Papadopoulos who stood as an independent candidate.

In the November 1976 US Presidential elections the victory of Democrat leader Jimmy Carter had raised the hopes of the Greek Cypriots for a solution to the Cyprus problem. Prior to his election he had made promises that he will try to help resolve the problem. When news of his victory was announced, the joy and the expectations of the Greek Cypriots was such that church bells rang all over the island.

*The three evicted monks at St Barnabas Monastery*

Meanwhile Denktash and the Turkish army of occupation continued with their ethnic cleansing. They wanted to remove from the occupied parts in the north every historical trace of the Greek Cypriots. On 20 December 1976 the Denktash administration evicted three old Monks from the Monastery of St Barnabas, near Famagusta.

The monks, the 82 year old Abbot Stephanos, his 77 year old brother Barnabas and 82 year old Nektarios, who had lived in the monastery for the past 60 years were evicted. The historic monastery was built in 477 AD at the spot where St Barnabas was buried. St Barnabas and St Paul preached the new Christian faith in Cyprus in 45 AD. The monastery was destroyed by the Saracens in 649 and the present one was built in 1756.

# THE MAKARIOS - DENKTASH 1977 SUMMIT

At the beginning of Januray 1977 Denktash wrote to Makarios asking to meet him to discuss the Cyprus problem. The meeting was held on 27th January. Makarios said that he was willing to examine any form of federal solution, multiregional or bizonal. On the territorial issue Makarios proposed 20% (based on the population ratio) but Denktash proposed 32.8% (based on ownership of land). They also discussed the following issues:

(a) Freedom of Movement.
(b) Right to property.
(c) Right of settlement.
(d) Right of refugees to return to their homes.
(e) Right to work.
(f) Right to reside.

On 12 February 1977 Makarios and Denktash met in the presence of U.N General Secretary Dr Kurt Waldheim. The 1977 High Level Agreement set the "guidelines" for the negotiations, stating that the aim:

*The establishment of an independent, non-aligned and bi-communal federal republic, with the powers and functions of the central federal government being such as to safeguard the unity of the country having regard to its bicommunal character.*

These summit agreements were perhaps Makarios's final and biggest blunder. *The issue at stake was the invasion and occupation by Turkey of 37% of the territory of Cyprus.* This was the real issue which was taken to the United Nations. By agreeing to discuss the nature of the constitution *prior to the departure of the Turkish occupying forces in Cyprus, Makarios had committed a fatal mistake*.

The United Nations adopted these "high level agreements" and the issue at stake was no longer the invasion and occupation of Cyprus by Turkey but the format of a final agreement to be reached between Makarios and Denktash!

Meanwhile, in Cyprus there was great pressure on the Government to bring to justice all those involved in the military coup. Many people complained about Makarios' amnesty to those EOKA B' criminals, who by their action, helped to bring the Turkish invaders.

Nikos Sampson rejected Makarios' offer of amnesty and refused to "repent" for his involvement in the military coup in 1974. Sampson's refusal led to his prosecution and sentence to 20 years imprisonment in 1977. He was the only Cypriot to be prosecuted and jailed in connection with the 1974 coup. Two years later (in 1979) he was granted a parole for medical reasons. He lived in France for the next 11 years returning to Cyprus in 1990 to serve the remainder of his sentence and was released in 1993. He died in May 2001 at the age of 66.

**Makarios, Dr Waldheim and Denktash**

# THE DEATH OF MAKARIOS
## 3rd AUGUST 1977

Makarios died on the 3rd August 1977. His funeral was attended by thousands of people and by foreign dignitaries. He was buried near Kykko Monastery on the Troodos mountains where he was once a monk. His grave has become a place of pilgrimage for many Greek Cypriots. His death certainly marked the end of an era.

Makarios began his political career soon after the Greek Civil War, that is, at a time when most of the Greek governments were subservient to British and American interests. He was often advised and warned of the obstacles to achieve *Enosis.* Yet he stubbornly insisted, together with Grivas, ignoring the existence of the 18% Turkish community on the island. Both leaders (Makarios and Grivas) not only ignored the Turkish community but also called for the abstention of the left-wing Greek Cypriots who traditionally constituted about 33% of the population.

Makarios began his political career by being a very stubborn leader for insisting on *Enosis* at a time when even the Greek Governments were advising him against the idea. He compromised on Independence when he realised that there was no other alternative. He tried to amend the Constitution without consulting the Turkish Vice-President and the three guarantors. He simply presented them with his 13 proposals. Even when Clerides managed to get Rauf Denktash to agree on most of the 13 proposals, Makarios changed his mind and wanted to abolish the post of Vice-President!

347

*The grave of Makarios near Kykko Monastery. The inscription reads: "Thousands of Makarios will continue your struggle."*

He ended his political career by making unbelievable compromises. Had he agreed in 1972 with the Turkish Cypriots on the issue of local government, the course of Cypriot history would have been very different. Both Makarios and Grivas were hostages to their oaths and their nationalism. The Cypriot people have been paying for their leaders' mistakes as well as for the barbarous and illegal Turkish invasion and occupation.

# THE KYPRIANOU ADMINISTRATION
# 1977- 1988

Makarios was succeeded by **Spyros Kyprianou** as President and by the Bishop of Paphos **Chrysostomos** as Archbishop. Kyprianou was at the time, the President of the House of Representatives and according to the Constitution in the absence or death of the President of the Republic, the President of the House of Representatives assumes office until elections are held.

The new President, Spyros Kyprianou, was born in Limassol in 1932. He studied law in England and from 1952 to 1956 he acted as Makarios' Secretary in London. In 1960 he was appointed Foreign Minister and was a close colleague of the Archbishop. On his inaugural speech, Kyprianou had promised to pursue the policies of the late President both at home and abroad. In 1978 he was elected President (unopposed) for a period of five years.

Two years after the Makarios - Denktash High Level Agreements to establish a Bi-communal Federal Republic, President Kyprianou met with Mr Rauf Denktash in May 1979, again under the auspices of the U.N. Secretary-General. The 1979 High Level Agreements went further by including:

*"Respect for human rights and fundamental freedoms of all citizens, the demilitarization of the Island, adequate guarantees for the independence, sovereignty and territorial integrity of the Republic, and priority for reaching agreement on the resettlement of Greek Cypriot refugees in Famagusta."*

In Britain there was a change of Government in 1979 and the Conservative Party led by Margaret Thatcher came to power. In Greece the PASOK Socialist Party of Andreas Papandreou came to power in 1981.

*Kyprianou, Waldheim and Denktash in 1979*

President Kyprianou and Foreign Minister Nikos Rolandis arranged many visits in Europe, the USA and other parts of the world in order to promote a just solution to the Cyprus problem. Kyprianou met President Regan, Prime Minister Thatcher, newly elected socialist leader Andreas Papandreou and many others.

In the 1981 General elections in Cyprus, the system of proportional representation was adopted and the results for the 35 seats were as follows:

AKEL (Communist Party) :  12
Democratic Rally (Conservative) : 12
Democratic Party : 8
EDEK (Socialist Party) : 3

In the occupied areas the strength of the UBP (National Unity Party) was reduced, although it had a majority in the Assembly.

In February 1983 Presidential elections were held.  Spyros Kyprianou was re-elected with AKEL's support. The results were as follows:

| | | | |
|---|---|---|---|
| Spyros Kyprianou | 173, 791 | or | 56.45% |
| Glafcos Clerides | 104, 294 | or | 33.93% |
| Vassos Lyssarides | 29,307 | or | 9.53% |

In the occupied areas,  Dr Fazil Kutchuk who was elected unopposed  as Vice-President of the Republic since 3rd December 1959, had stepped down on 18 February 1983. In fact after the inter-communal troubles of December 1963, he had left the Government with the three Turkish Ministers and the  15 Turkish Cypriot MPs. Dr. Kutchuk was born in Nicosia in 1906 and died in London (at the Westminster Hospital) on 15 January 1984  aged 78.

*The author with President Kyprianou in London*

In 1980 Michael Foot was elected Leader of the Labour Party. The large Cypriot community in Britain as well as most Cypriots in Cyprus had placed their hopes on an election victory for Michael Foot in the 1983 General Election since Margaret Thatcher had not applied Britain's Treaty obligations towards Cyprus nor did she exercise any pressure on Turkey to abide by the UN Resolutions. Michael Foot had promised at a Greek Institute function in North London that if he was elected Prime Minister then he would restore Justice to Cyprus. To the great disappointment of all Cypriots, Michael Foot lost the election.

*The author with Michael Foot (then Leader of the Labour Party), Lord Brockway and Lord Caradon at the Greek Institute function in North London 1983*

## DENKTASH DECLARES UDI
### *"Turkish Republic of Northern Cyprus"*

On 15 November 1983 Rauf Denktash declared the occupied parts of Northern Cyprus as the **Turkish Republic of Northern Cyprus.** In his address to the Turkish Assembly in Nicosia, Denktash stated:

*"We hereby declare before the World and before History the establishment of the Turkish Republic of Northern Cyprus as an Independent State.*

*On this historic day, we extend once again our hand in peace and friendship to the Greek Cypriot people.*
*The two Peoples of the island are destined to co-exist, side by side.*

*We can, and must, find peaceful, just and durable solutions to all our differences, through negotiations on the basis of equality.*

*The proclamation of the new State will not hinder, but facilitate the establishment of a genuine federation.*

*The new Republic will not unite with any other State.*

*The new State will continue to adhere to the Treaties of Establishment, Guarantee and Alliance."*

Denktash was asking the international community to accept and recognise the Turkish army's invasion and occupation of the northern parts of the Republic in 1974 which resulted in the forceful removal of 200,000 Cypriots from their homes in order to create his "new state."

Denktash's action was denounced by the United Nations. The Security Council rejected the Declaration and called upon all member states not to recognise it and to respect the sovereignty of the Republic of Cyprus (Resolution 541). The European Parliament in its Resolution of 17 November 1983 condemned the action taken by the Turkish Cypriot sector to declare an independent Turkish Cypriot State in Cyprus and called on all parties concerned to support the initiative of the UN Secretary-General. Turkey was the only country that recognised Denktash's pseudo-state.

In May 1984 the U. N. Security Council Resolution 550 called for the handing over by the Turks of the city of Varosha (Famagusta) to U.N. administration and the return of its original inhabitants to their homes. Intercommunal "Proximity Talks" resumed in September 1984 and a high level meeting took place between the UN Secretary

General, President Kyprianou and Denktash in New York in January 1985 which ended in failure.

In the fifth Parliamentary elections in the free parts of the Republic held on 8 December 1985 the Parliamentary seats were increased from 50 to 80, i.e. 56 seats for the Greek-Cypriots and 24 seats for Turkish-Cypriots. The latter, however, had not taken part since the inter-communal troubles of December 1963 and elected their own Legislative Assembly which at first consisted of 40 members and later increased to 50 members. The results were as follows:

| | |
|---|---|
| Democratic Rally | 19 seats |
| Democratic Party | 16 seats |
| AKEL (Communist) | 15 seats |
| EDEK (Socialist) | 6 seats |

In the Turkish occupied areas in the 1985 elections, in an attempt to eliminate smaller political parties, only parties breaching the 8% barrier were awarded seats.

After the disagreements between AKEL and President Kyprianou, the AKEL leadership decided to support in the February 1988 Presidential elections an Independent candidate *George Vassiliou*.

Vassiliou was a successful businessman but was not very well known for his political views. In an effort to stop Kyprianou to be re-elected and to prevent Clerides from being elected the left-wing AKEL together with the Socialist Party EDEK supported the candidacy of George Vassiliou.

The results of the February 1988 Presidential elections

(second round after Kyprianou was eliminated in the first round), were as follows:

George Vassiliou        167,834   or  51.63%
Glafcos Clerides        157,228   or 48.37%

# THE VASSILIOU ADMINISTRATION
# 1988 - 1993

The new President **George Vassiliou** was born in Famagusta in May 1931 and studied at the Universities of Geneva, Vienna and Budapest where he obtained a doctorate in Economics. He later specialised in marketing and market research in the U.K. In 1962 he established the Middle East Market Research Bureau which is the largest organisation of its kind in the Mediterranean and the Middle East.

Although Vassiliou was elected with AKEL and EDEK's support his Cabinet was not made of AKEL and EDEK leading members. Vassiliou kept George Iacovou who served as Foreign Minister in the Kyprianou government.

In April 1988 **Ezekias Papaioannou** who had been one of the longest serving Communist leaders, died at the age of 80. In the leadership contest that followed a young person was chosen: **Demetris Christofias**. It was later stated that Christofias was the "*personal choice*" of the late Papaioannou, because he had argued that Christofias was young, educated and active.

*Demetris Christofias, leader of AKEL since 1988 and President of House of Representatives 2001*

Christofias was born in Kato Dhikomo, Kyrenia, on 29 August 1946 and studied History in Moscow where he obtained his doctorate. He was General Secretary of EDON - the Youth section of AKEL (1977-87) and member of the Central Committee of AKEL (1982). He was also elected MP for the Kyrenia district and in 2001 he was elected President of the House of Representatives.

The "old" colleagues of Papaioannou (Andreas Fantis, Pavlos Dinglis, Andreas Ziartides and some others) immediately split ranks with AKEL. They left the party and formed the ADISOK. Ziartides also relinquished his position as Secretary General of the left wing Trade Union PEO (Pancyprian Labour Federation) and was replaced by Avraam Antoniou.

The new President made a number of visits to some European capitals as well as to the USA in order to re-activate the efforts to solve the Cyprus problem.

At the invitation of the UN Secretary-General President Vassiliou and Turkish Cypriot Leader Denktash commenced talks in Geneva on 15 September 1988. In July 1989 following the presentation of proposals by both sides and further intensive negotiations, the Secretary-General submitted a "Set of Ideas" but Denktash and the Turkish Governmentr demanded the withdrawal of these proposals.

In March 1990 a High-level meeting in New York failed because Denktash raised new pre-conditions for a separate right to "self-determination" and the introduction of the term *"peoples"* instead of *"communities"*. The Security Council with its Resolution 649 rejected these demands.

In the occupied areas Rauf Denktash was elected as "President" in 1990.

The May 1991 Parliamentary elections in the free areas of the Republic were as follows:

| | | |
|---|---|---|
| Democratic Rally - Liberals | 35.8% | 20 seats |
| AKEL - Left New Forces | 30.6% | 18 seats |
| Democratic Party | 19.5 % | 11 seats |

| EDEK Socialist Party | 10.9% | 7 seats |
| ADISOK - New Left | 2. 4% | - |

In August 1991 US President George Bush announced that Greece and Turkey agreed to attend a meeting on Cyprus in September. In October 1991 the Secretary-General rejected Mr Denktash's new demands for the recognition of separate sovereignty of the Turkish Cypriot Community, including the right to secession.

In April 1992 the report of the European Commission on Human Rights condemned Turkey for massive Human Rights violations in Cyprus.

In 1992 the former Egyptian Foreign Minister **Boutros Boutros-Ghali** was appointed Secretary - General of the UN. Proximity talks between Vassiliou and Denktash were held in June and July 1992 and in August the Secretary-General's Report to the Security Council included an Annex entitled **"Set of Ideas and Map on territorial adjustments"**. The Security Council adopted unanimously Resolution 774.

# THE GHALI "SET OF IDEAS" AUG. 1992

The **"Set of Ideas on an overall framework agreement on Cyprus"** consisted of nine sections:

*1. Overall Objectives 2. Guiding Principles 3. Constitutional aspects of the Federation, 4. Security and Guarantee, 5. Territorial Adjustments, 6. Displaced Persons, 7. Economic Development and Safeguards, 8. Transitional Arrangements, 9. Notification to the United Nations.*

In the Section *Guiding Principles,* the Set of Ideas recommended among other things the following:

*The Federal Republic will be one territory composed of two politically equal federated states with one sovereignty;*

*The Republic will be secular and have its own flag.*

*Each federated state will be administered by one community and will decide on its own governmental arrangement. The federal Government cannot encroach upon the powers and functions of the two federated states.*

*Security, law and order and the administration of justice in its territory will be the responsibility of each federated state.*

In the Territorial Adjustments a map of Cyprus was provided which recommended the return to the Greeks, the towns of Varosha (Famagusta) in the east and Morphou in the west together with some villages near these two towns. The Turkish occupied area of 37% would be reduced to about 28%. Boutros-Ghali stated that there were about 160,000 displaced Greek Cypriots and about 45,000 Turkish Cypriots. Compensation would be offered to those displaced persons who did not wish to return at the 1974 value of their property plus inflation.

The *Ghali Set of Ideas* were discussed by both sides but in the end both sides were not willing to compromise on a solution based on the Ghali ideas.

In the occupied areas Denktash had a major falling out with his "Prime Minister" Dervis Eroglu. Eroglu had accused Denktash as "too flexible on the issue of a political

*President George Vassiliou and Mr Rauf Denktash*

settlement". As a result 10 pro-Denktash MPs left Eroglu's *National Unity Party* and formed the new *Democratic Party* under the leadership of Hakki Atun and Serdar Denktash.

On 20 January 1993 the European Parliament adopted a resolution supporting the U.N. initiative on Cyprus.

In the February 1993 Presidential elections, Vassiliou was once again supported by AKEL and hoped to win a second term of office. After the first round, when Spyros Kyprianou, leader of the Democratic Party and Vassos Lyssarides leader of Socialist EDEK were eliminated, a number of their supporters opted to support the candidacy of Glafcos Clerides.

# THE CLERIDES ADMINISTRATION
## 1993 - 2003

*Glafcos Clerides* had won the February 1993 election by just over 2,000 votes. Some bitter words were exchanged between some of the supporters of AKEL and Socialist EDEK, the first accusing the latter for giving their votes to a Conservative politician.

The results were as follows:

| | | |
|---|---|---|
| Glafcos Clerides | 178,945 | or 50.31% |
| George Vassiliou | 176,769 | or 49.69% |

The new President *Glafcos Clerides* was born in April 1919. As we have already seen, he played a major part along with Makarios in shaping the island's history since 1955. He was President of the House of Representatives for many yearsas and also Acting President after the from 23 July until 7 December 1974 when Makarios was absent from Cyprus due to the Military coup. When he assumed the Presidency he relinquished the leadership of the Democratic Rally Party because he stated that he wanted to be seen as the President of all Cypriots and not of a section of Cypriots. The leadership of the Democratic Rally was assumed by Yiannakis Matsis.

In May 1993 a new round of talks began in New York and in October the Commonwealth Heads of Government Meeting took place in Cyprus.

In December 1993 a snap election in the occupied areas resulted in a dead heat between Eroglu's National Unity Party with 17 seats and the Democratic Party with 15 seats. This deadlock was later broken when the Democratic Party formed a coalition with Ozker Ozgur's CTP with 13 seats.

On 13 July 1994 the existence of a confidential UN Report exposing the policy of ethnic cleansing enforced by Turkey against the enclaved Greek Cypriots in occupied Cyprus was given great publicity. Five days later, on 18 July Denktash threatened to integrate the occupied areas with Turkey.

On 28 August 1994 the Turkish Assembly in the occupied areas announced that *it has abandoned federation as a solution.*

In 1995 the USA backed Cyprus' application to join the European Union and President Clinton appointed Richard Beattie as his Special Envoy on Cyprus.

In April 1995 "Presidential" elections were held in the occupied areas and Denktash's chief opponent was his former ally Dervis Eroglu. Denktash managed to win the election due the support he received from CLP and RTP members. Ozker Ozgur the CTP leader was "Deputy Prime Minister" in the Coalition Government but when he realised that Denktash was not genuinely concerned for a political settlement and continued obstructionism he resigned and was replaced by Mehmet Ail Talat.

*Turkish Cypriot leader Rauf  Denktash (born 1924)*

On 13 August 1995 the illegal regime in the occupied areas introduced 'legislation' for the distribution of "title deeds" for the transfer of property belonging to Greek Cypriot refugees to Turkish Cypriots and  Turkish settlers.

In January 1996 PASOK MPs elected **Costas Simitis** as the new Prime Minister shortly after the death of Andreas Papandreou. A week after his election as PM, Simitis faced a serious  crisis in the Aegean when Turkey made territorial claims on the Greek island of Imia.

In May 1996 **Sir David Hannay** was appointed by the John Major Government as the UK Special Representative on Cyprus. He had many talks with both leaders but failed to break the existing deadlock.

In the May 1996 Parliamentary elections the results were as follows:

| | | |
|---|---|---|
| AKEL - Left New Forces | 33.00% | 19 seats |
| Democratic Rally - Liberals | 34.47% | 20 seats |
| Democratic Party | 16.43% | 10 seats |
| EDEK - Socialist | 8.13% | 5 seats |
| Free Democrats | 3.69% | 2 seats |
| New Horizons | 1.71% | |
| ADISOK - New Left | 1.44% | |
| Ecologists | 1.00% | |

In June 1996 President Clerides met with President Bill Clinton and British P.M. John Major who both expressed support for a peaceful settlement through the UN Resolutions.

On 2 August 1996, the *European Motorcyclists Federation* and the *Cyprus Motorcycle Association* organised a ten day ride from Europe to commence from the former divided city of Berlin and to end in occupied Kyrenia in Cyprus. Some 120 motorcyclists took part. The ride and demonstration in Cyprus planned for 11 August aimed at freedom of movement and an immediate end to the division of Cyprus.

After driving across Europe, the final phase of the motorcyclists rally in Cyprus was cancelled at the Government's advice, on the basis of information that the Turkish occupation forces were intent on violence to prevent the demonstrators entering the occupied area.

On 11 August and despite the Cyprus Government warning demonstrations took place along the cease-fire line outside Dherynia (near Famagusta). Turkish forces and Members of the Grey Wolves Turkish nationalists organisations brutally killed Tassos Isaac and wounded 41 others.

On 14 August 1996 following the funeral of Tassos Isaac who was beaten to death on 11 August, a small group of Greek Cypriots who attempted to pay tribute to the dead man near the place where he was killed were fired at by Turkish troops. A young man Solomos Solomou who tried to climb the flag pole in order to bring down the occupiers' flag was shot and killed.

*Tassos Isaac murdered near Dherynia, August 1996*

The United Nations and the European Parliament condemned these brutal killings. The resolution adopted by the European Parliament on 19 September 1996:

*"Condemned the murders of the two young Greek Cypriots by the Turkish army of occupation and members of the unlawful Denktash regime.*
*Expressed its deep concern at the indiscriminate use of violence by the Turkish occupying forces during a peaceful*

*demonstration for the reunification of the island.*

*Called on Turkey to take all necessary measures to identify, arrest and bring to justice all those implicated in the murders*

**Solomos Solomou shot by Turks as he tried to
remove the Turkish flag, near Dherynia, August 1996**

Although the Resolution was a positive one it was perhaps "naive" of the European Parliament to expect Turkey to comply with it. How could such a Government respond positively since that very Government was responsible for invading and occupying 37% of the territory of Cyprus and driving mercilessly 200,000 Cypriots out of their homes? How could a Government which had inflicted so much pain and sorrow to so many people, for so many years, to feel remorse, all of a sudden, for the additional death of two more innocent people?

As it was to be expected, the Turkish army of occupation not only ignored the appeals from the United Nations and the European Parliament,  but on 13 October 1996 committed a further atrocity.  Petros Kakoullis, a refugee from Lefkoniko,  was shot dead by Turkish soldiers while collecting snails in the buffer zone.

In 1996 the Cyprus Government negotiated the purchase from Russia of S-300 surface-to-air missiles. The Ankara Government  threatened with reprisals if this agreement was not cancelled.

In January 1997 Clerides visited Athens to discuss with Simitis the latest developments of the Cyprus problem and also the Turkish threats on the proposed purchase of Russian S-300 missiles.

In 1997 Kofi Annan became the new Secretary-General of the U.N. and in April he appointed Diego Cortovez of Ecuador as his Special Advisor.

The USA Government appointed on 4 June 1997 **Richard Holbrooke** as the Presidential Representative on Cyprus. He had several meetings with both leaders but did not succeed to break the existing  deadlock.

Direct  talks between Clerides and Denktash were held on 9 - 13 July 1997 first at Troutbeck, a resort near New York and then on 11-15 August at Glion-sur-Montreux, in Switzerland.

Presidential elections were held on 15 February  1998 and the left wing party  AKEL  backed the candidacy of  **George Iacovou**, the former Foreign Minister. The results were as follows:

| Glafcos Clerides | 206,879 | or 50.82% |
| George Iacovou | 200,222 | or 49.18% |

Soon after his election for a second term as President, Clerides appointed former President George Vassiliou as Cyprus chief negotiator for the island's accession to the European Union and also made proposals for the participation of the Turkish Cypriots in the accession negotiations.

On 29 June 1998 the UN Security Council passed a Resolution (1179) re-affirming the Council's position that a Cyprus settlement must be based on a *"State of Cyprus with a single sovereignty and international personality and a single citizenship".*

On 31 August, Rauf Denktash, the Turkish Cypriot leader proposed the establishment of "a Cyprus Confederation".

After talks with the Greek Government, President Clerides announced on 29 December 1998 his decision not to proceed with the purchase of the Russian S300 surface-to- air- missiles. The decision was greeted with relief from many quarters.

On 29 June 1999 the UN Security Council passed Resolution 1250 which called for UN sponsored negotiations to be urgently arranged.

Following the terrible earthquake which struck north-western Turkey on 17 August 1999, the Cyprus Government approved the sending of aid to Turkey worth

$100,000.

On 19 and 20 November 1999 President Bill Clinton accompanied by Secretary of State Madeleine Albright visited Athens. In his speech Clinton stressed the importance of Greece and Turkey improving their relations and that Turkey will be accepted in the European Union when she resolved her differences with Greece. He also referred to the Turkish occupation of the northern parts of Cyprus and said that *"The present status quo in Cyprus is unacceptable."*

New UN-sponsored "Proximity Talks" were held with the aim of opening the way for the permanent settlement of the Cyprus problem. There were five such meetings held in New York and Geneva between 3 December 1999 and October 2000 but they all ended in deadlock.

*Denktash and Clerides with the Secretary-General Kofi Annan, New York , 1999*

Kofi Annan, the UN Secretary-General appointed **Alvaro de Soto** as his Special Adviser on Cyprus. Alvaro de Soto made his first visit to Cyprus on 29 February 2000 and he also visited the occupied areas, including the Monastery of Apostolos Andreas.

On 10 May 2001 the European Court of Human Rights in a 126 page judgement, found Turkey guilty of gross human rights violations in the occupied areas of Cyprus.

In the May 2001 General elections, the results were as follows:

| | | |
|---|---|---|
| AKEL - Left New Forces | 34.71% | 20 seats |
| Democratic Rally | 34.00% | 19 seats |
| Democratic Party | 14.84% | 9 seats |
| KISOS - EDEK - (Social Dem.) | 6.51% | 4 seats |
| United Democrats | 2.59% | 1 seat |
| New Horizons | 3.00% | 1 seat |
| ADIK | 2.16% | 1 seat |
| Ecologists | 1.98% | 1 seat |

For the first time in the history of Cyprus, a left wing leader, the leader of AKEL **Demetris Christofias**, had been elected President of the House of Representatives in June 2001.

On 26 September 2001 the UN Security Council issued a statement blaming the Turkish Cypriot side for rejecting Kofi Annan's invitation to new talks on the Cyprus problem.

In November 2001 Prime Minister Ecevit announced that "Turkey decides about the future of Cyprus and not Denktash."

Finally, at the request of Denktash, a meeting was held in Nicosia between the two Cypriot leaders on 4 December

2001. The UN Special envoy Alvaro de Soto also attended this meeting. At the end of the meeting de Soto read the following statement:

*"At the meeting held today, 4 December 2001, between H.E. Mr Glafcos Clerides, the Greek Cypriot leader, and H.E. Mr Rauf Denktash, the Turkish Cypriot leader, at the residence of the UN Chief of Mission and in the presence of Mr Alvaro de Soto, the Special Adviser to the Secretary-General on Cyprus, the two leaders agreed to the following:*

*That the Secretary-General, in the exercise of his mission of good offices, would invite the two leaders to direct talks; That these talks will be held in Cyprus starting in mid-January 2002 on UN premises; That there will be no pre-conditions; That all issues will be on the table; That they will continue to negotiate in good faith until a comprehensive settlement is achieved; That "nothing will be agreed until everything is agreed".*

On 5 December 2001, Clerides was the guest of Denktash, in the Turkish part of Nicosia. Clerides had also invited Denktash to his residence on 29 December 2001. It was agreed that formal talks will commence on 16 January 2002.

The Clerides-Denktash meetings have been greeted by both the Athens and Ankara Governments as positive steps in the right direction. Alvaro de Soto stated soon afterwards, that he was hopeful that a solution to the long standing Cyprus problem could be achieved in six months. Denktash speaking to the Anatolia news agency said that "Cyprus was a difficult issue and the two sides were poles apart. He expressed the hope that a solution will be found in 2002.

# CYPRUS AND THE EUROPEAN UNION

In July 1990 Cyprus applied formally for EEC Membership and the application was referred to the Commission. On 30 June 1993, the European Commission recognised the European identity and character of Cyprus. The Commission also confirmed that Cyprus satisfies the criteria for membership and is suitable to become a member of the Communities.

Discussions between the Cyprus government and the Commission began in November 1993 and were completed in February 1995.

In June 1994, during the Greek Presidency of the European Union Summit, held in Corfu, it was decided that the next phase of enlargement would include Cyprus and Malta.

On 15 July 1997, the Commission issued **Agenda 2000**, a document that looks into the possible effects of enlargement on the EU. The Commission reaffirmed its 1993 Opinion on Cyprus and noted *"Cyprus' advanced level of development and economic dynamism"*. It also added that *"if progress towards a settlement is not made before the negotiations are due to begin, they should be opened with the government of the Republic of Cyprus, as the only authority recognised by international law."*

On 12 March 1998, President Clerides invited the Turkish Cypriot community to nominate representatives to be included as full members of the Cypriot team negotiating

Cyprus' accession to the EU. The invitation was communicated by the British Presidency to the Turkish Cypriot leadership, who rejected it for not providing for separate negotiations with the illegal regime in the occupied area.

The European Commission issued *"Reports on Cyprus Progress towards Accession"* in 1998, 19989 and 2000 and confirmed that Cyprus was a functioning market economy which continued to grow strongly and was operating at full employment.

By July 2001, 23 out of the 29 chapters screened have been provisionally closed and the remaining six are expected to be closed within the first six months of 2002. Cyprus has complied with all its commitments and the harmonisation process will be completed by the target date 1 January 2003, so that Cyprus can accede to the EU by that date.

On 26 October 2001 European Commission President Romano Prodi said in Nicosia that Cyprus is well advanced in its preparation for European Union membership and will be among the first new member group.

# POLITICAL PARTIES

## 1. GREEK CYPRIOT POLITICAL PARTIES

The **AKEL** *(Anorthotiko Komma Ergazomenou Laou)* the Communist Party which is the oldest party (the original Communist Party of Cyprus K.K.K. was founded in 1926 and AKEL its successor, was founded in 1941. The current General Secretary of AKEL is Andros Kyprianou.

The **DESY** *(Demokratikos Synagermos)* Democratic Rally, is the Conservative Party and was founded by Glafcos Clerides in 1976. When Clerides assumed the Presidency of the Republic, the Party was led by Yiannakis Matsis. The current leader is Averof Neophytou.

The **DEKO** *(Demokratiko Komma)* Democratic Party, a party of the Centre, was founded in May 1976 by former President of the Republic Spyros Kyprianou. The current leader is Nikos Papadopoulos.

The **EDEK-KISOS** *(Kinima Social-Demokraton)* Movement of Social Democrats, is the successor of the **EDEK - KISOS** Party which was founded in 1969 and was led by Dr Vassos Lyssarides. In 2000 the EDEK was renamed Social Democratic Movement. The current leader is Marinos Sizopoulos.

**EUROPEAN PARTY** – The current leader is Demetris Sillouris.

**THE GREEN PARTY** – The current leader is George Perdikis.

## 2. TURKISH CYPRIOT POLITICAL PARTIES

Although the electorate in the occupied areas is approximately 120,000 there are currently nine political parties. From 1974 when Turkey invaded Cyprus until the late 1980s there has been very little opposition. The current political parties are the following:

1.    *Republican Turkish Party (CTP)* Current leader Ozkan Yorgancioglu.

2.    *National Unity Party (UBP)* Current leader Huseyin Ozgurgun.

3.    *Democratic Party (DP)* Current leader Serdar Denktsash.

4.    *Communal Democracy Party (TDP)* Current leader Mustafa Akkinci.

*The two political dinosaurs who dominated Cypriot politics for more than 40 years, Clerides (right) and Denktash (left) in Nicosia 4 December 2001*

# INTERNATIONAL SUPPORT FOR THE RE-UNIFICATION OF CYPRUS

When Turkey invaded Cyprus in July and August 1974 the international community expressed its solidarity with Cyprus. Governments from all over the world have condemned Turkey's invasion and occupation of part of the Republic of Cyprus, a member state of the United Nations.

In Britain, the USA, Australia, the former Soviet Union, the Non-aligned countries, many Parliamentarians have strongly criticised Turkey's violation of the Independence and sovereignty of Cyprus. The Cypriot communities all over the world have campaigned with the full support of many British MPs (from all parties) and Members of the House of Lords, US Senators and Congressmen, Members of the European Parliament, for the removal of the Turkish troops from Cyprus and for the return of all refugees to their homes.

In Britain, Lord Fenner Brockway a long-time friend of Cyprus, a Labour MP in the early 1930s until 1964 when he was elevated to the House of Lords, actively campaigned in the 1950s along with 80 other British MPs, who belonged to the *Movement for Colonial Freedom*, for Cyprus' right to Self-determination. Lord Brockway was interviewed by this author on 13 February 1975.

Lord Caradon (formerly Sir Hugh Foot was the last British Governor of Cyprus 1957-1960 and later British Ambassador at the United Nations) and subsequently Chairman of the *Friends of Cyprus* Committee also actively campaigned for Cyprus' re-unification. Lord Caradon was interviewed by this author on 26 July 1976. This author also had talks on Cyprus with many British MPs. Brockway, Caradon, Bethel, Barbara Castle, Lena Jegger and others spoke out in support of Cyprus both in the House of Lords and elsewhere criticising the failure of the British Government to meet its Treaty obligations towards Cyprus. Senators and Congressmen in the USA were critical of the US administration for not stopping Turkey, a NATO member, to invade Cyprus. Many Australian, Canadian and European Parliamentarians spoke in their national parliaments in support of Cyprus. The interviews with Brockway and Caradon were published in the *Greek Review,* (Spring 1975 and Summer 1976).

Turkey's invasion of Cyprus was condemned by the international community. The numerous Resolutions adopted by the United Nations speak for themselves. They called for the removal of all foreign troops and the return of all the refugees back to their homes.They also condemned the creation of the "pseudo state" in the occupied areas of the north.

Turkey has repeatedly ignored both UN and European Union Resolutions. The only super-power, the USA does not exercise any pressure because Turkey is treated as an important member of the NATO Alliance and until recently (1991) was considered as an important bastion against the former Soviet Union. For the USA, the American air bases in Turkey served a useful purpose against Iraq and most recently against Afghanistan. More important still is the production of oil in that region. It seems that the economic and strategic interests of both the USA and Britain are more important than the violation of the Human rights of some 200,000 Cypriots. With the collapse of the Soviet Union the hegemony and monopoly of international power now rests swith the USA and the European Union and it is with the latter that the Cypriots now rest their hopes and aspirations for the re-unification of their country when they become full members in 2004.

*The author with Lord Brockway 13.2.75 at the House of Lords*

*The author with Lord Caradon  26.7.76 at the House of  Lords*

# THE 1998 PRESIDENTIAL ELECTIONS

On the 8th February 1998 Presidential elections were held and there were seven candidates and in the first round the candidates obtained the following votes:

*Glafcos Clerides* candidate of the right wing Democratic Rally 40.06%.

*George Iacovou* the candidate supported by the left wing AKEL and the Democratic Party 40.61%.

*Vassos Lyssarides,* candidate of the socialist EDEK 10.59%.

*Alexis Galanos* independent candidate but supported by some Democratic Party members 4.04%

*George Vasiliou* of the United Democrats (and former president) 3.00%

*Nikos Koutsou* (New Horizons Party) 0.91%

*Nikos Rolandis* (Liberal Party) 0.78%

In the second round of the elections which was held on the 15th of February 1998, there were two candidates and they obtained the following votes:

*Glafcos Clerides* 206,879 or 50.8% of the vote and

*George Iacovou* 200,222 or 49.2% of the vote.

Clerides wanted to form a Government of National Unity but AKEL turned down his proposal. Clerides went ahead and offered two cabinet posts to the EDEK Party, two cabinet posts to the Democratic Party and one Cabinet post to the Liberal Party. Spyros Kyprianou continued to be President of the House of Representatives and the new Government spokesman was Christos Stylianides.

Clerides kept Yiannakis Kasoulides as Foreign Minister and he also appointed ex-president George Vasiliou in charge of the Cyprus-EU negotiations.

## GREEK PRESIDENT AND TURKISH P.M. VISIT CYPRUS

On 25th June 1998 the President of Greece Kostis Stefanopoulos visited Cyprus. This was the first official visit by a Greek president since the establishment of the Cyprus

Republic in 1960. He was accompanied by Foreign Minister Theodoros Pangalos and other officials and they were given a warm welcome by the Greek Cypriots.

A month later, on 20th July 1998 the Turkish P.M. Mesut Yilmaz visited the occupied parts of Northern Cyprus in order to celebrate the 24th anniversary of the Turkish invasion of the island. He was also accorded a warm welcome by the Turkish Cypriots.

## THE S-300 MISSILES

On 29th December 1998 Clerides who had ordered the S-300 missiles from the Soviet Union supposedly to protect Cyprus from any further Turkish aggression, after much pressure from the USA and NATO had decided to back down.

Originally, the missiles were to be stationed at the military air base called "Andreas Papandreou" in Paphos. Clerides eventually agreed with the Greek Government and the S-300 missiles were stationed on the island of Crete.

## BILL CLINTON VISITS GREECE

In June 1997 the American Secretary of State Madeleine Albright had met in Washington with Cyprus Foreign Minister Yiannakis Kasoulides and told him that the American Government is greatly concerned and wants to see a settlement of the Cyprus problem. As a result of this interest the Clinton administration had appointed Ambassador Richard Holbrooke as the special envoy of President Clinton on Cyprus.

President Bill Clinton was in Istanbul in November 1999 where he attended the Conference about European Security. He was accompanied by his Secretary of State Madeleine Albright as well as by his wife Hilary and daughter Chelsea. During his visit there he met with the Ecumenical Patriarch Vartholomeos.

He then visited Athens from 19-20 November and was given a very warm welcome. During a reception in his honour he spoke of the links of Greece and the USA and described himself as a philhellene and also described the existing state of affairs in Cyprus as unacceptable.

## New Cyprus talks in New York and Geneva

On 2nd November 1999, Kofi Annan, the Secretary-General of the UNO announced that he had appointed the Peruvian Alvaro de Soto as his new Special Envoy for Cyprus.

Kofi Annan had invited Clerides and Denktash to New York for separate talks on 3rd December 1999. Four items were discussed: 1. The issue of government. 2. The issue of security. 3. The issue of property and 4. The issue of territorial adjustment.

The second round of talks was held in Geneva from the 31st January to 8th February 2000. The two leaders had diametrically opposite views and as there was no agreement a third round of talks was arranged in Geneva from the 5th July to 4th August 2000. Clerides was in favour of a federation but Denktash insisted for a Confederation.

A fourth round of talks followed in September 2000 in New York and a fifth round in Geneva from 1-10th November 2000. Although a sixth round of talks was arranged for January 2001 Denktash refused to attend.

## Parliamentary Elections May 2001

On 27th May 2001 the Parliamentary elections were held and the results were the following:

| | | |
|---|---|---|
| AKEL (Communist) | 34.7% and | 20 seats |
| Democratic Rally | 34.0% and | 19 seats |
| Democratic Party | 14.8% and | 9 seats |
| EDEK (Socialist) | 6.5% and | 4 seats |
| New Horizons | 3.0% and | 1 seat |
| United Democrats | 2.6% and | 1 seat |
| ADIK | 2.2% and | 1 seat |
| Green Party | 2.0% and | 1 seat |

## Death of Ploutis Servas

In February 2001 the veteran Communist leader and intellectual Ploutis Servas died. Servas was born in Limassol in 1907 and in the 1930s studied Political Science in Moscow. He was Secretary of the Cyprus Communist Party and also Mayor of Limassol.

In 1941 he organised a conference of left wing Cypriots and founded the new party called AKEL which succeeded the Cypriot Communist Party. Servas was the first General Secretary of AKEL and remained in that position until 1947. In that year he was replaced by Fifis Ioannou and from 1949 AKEL was led by Ezekias Papaioannou who remained leader until his death in 1988.

Servas was a prolific writer. He wrote numerous books such as "The Prague Spring", "Cyprus Tragedy", "Old and New China", "Responsibilities of the Cyprus Problem" and many more. He died in 2001 but because he did not want to have a church service and wanted to be cremated his body was brought to London and was cremated at the New Southgate Crematorium in February 2001.

## Municipal Elections 2001

The Municipal Elections which were held on 16 December 2001 had the following results and Mayors:
Nicosia - Michael Zambelas. Limassol - Demetris Kontides.
Larnaca - Andreas Moyseos. Paphos - Feidias Sarikas.

Famagusta - Kikis Kazamias. Agia Napa - Barbara Pericleous. Paralimni - Nikos Vlittis.

In these Municipal elections AKEL won 10 municipalities, the Democratic Party won 6, the Democratic Rally won 5, EDEK won 5 and Independents won 7.

## Demetris Christofias – New leader of AKEL

When Ezekias Papaioannou the General Secretary of AKEL died in 1988 there were two candidates competing for this post: One was Demetris Christofias, an active leader in the Youth Section of AKEL called EDON (who was later said to be the favourite candidate of Papaioannou) and the other candidate was Pavlos Dhinglis.

Demetris Christofias won in the election that followed and some of the old members in the AKEL Central Committee such as Andreas Fantis, Andreas Ziartides, Pavlos Dinglis and some others left AKEL and formed a new party which they called ADISOK – Renewed Democratic Socialist Movement.

## New Talks at Nicosia airport

On 16 January 2002 the Cyprus talks among President Clerides and Denktash were resumed at the dis-used Nicosia airport and the talks were chaired by the UN Special Envoy Alvaro de Soto. The talks were intensified and were held three times a week.

On 14 May 2002 the General Secretary of the UNO Kofi Annan visited Cyprus and had extensive meetings with the two leaders and tried to persuade them to find a compromise solution. In the efforts of Kofi Annan to help the two leaders to reach a compromise settlement the British Lord David Hanney and the American diplomat Thomas Weston were recruited to exert their influence on the two leaders in June 2002.

## Death of Spyros Kyprianou 2002

Spyros Kyprianou, the former President died on 12 March 2002. He was also the founder of the Democratic Party and when President Makarios died he became his successor.

He had studied Law in London and was a close ally of Makarios and was for a number of years Foreign Minister. In 1979 he had signed an Agreement with Turkish Cypriot leader Raouf Denktash confirming what was agreed in the 1977 summit between Makarios and Denktash. The two leaders had agreed to form a Bi-communal Federation in Cyprus.

## The Kofi Annan Plan 2002

Kofi Annan was determined to help find a solution to the Cyprus Probem. With his associates he prepared a Plan for s settlement which became known as the "Kofi Annan Plan". The main provisions of the Plan were the following:

1. Cyprus should consist of two states – the Greek Cypriot and the Turkish Cypriot.

2. The Parliament should consist of the Upper House –which should consist of 48 Members (24 from each state) and the House of Representatives would consist a proportional number of Members according to the size of each community.

3. In the territorial issue the Greek Cypriots would control 71.5 % and the Turkish Cypriots 28.5%.

4. Cyprus would be demilitarised but Greece and Turkey as guarantors will each have 9,999 troops on the Island.

5. The Presidency would rotate every 10 months.

The Plan was revised five times and each time was made worse for the Greek Cypriots. The fifth and final version of the Plan was made on April 1st 2004, and had some recommendations which were not so favourable to the Greek Cypriots. The government of Clerides accepted the Plan and so did the majority of Turkish Cypriots but the other Greek Cypriot parties expressed their strong opposition.

# THE TASSOS PAPADOPOULOS ADMINISTRATION 2003 - 2008
## The Presidential Elections of February 2003

In the Presidential elections of 16 February 2003 there were ten

*Tassos Papadopoulos –*
*President 2003 – 2008*

candidates. Four of them were leaders of parties such as Glafcos Clerides, Tassos Papadopoulos, Alekos Markides and Nikos Koutsou. The other six candidates stood as independent. In this election AKEL and EDEK supported the candidacy of Papadopoulos.

The results were as follows: Tassos Papadopoulos 213.353 votes or 51.51%, Glafcos Clerides 160,724 or 38,89%, Alekos Markides 27,404 or 6.62% and Nikos Koutsou 8,771 or 2.12%. This result meant that Papadopoulos was elected from the first round because he managed to get over 50% of the votes.

Papadopoulos was born in Nicosia in 1934 and studied Law in London. He took an active part in the EOKA struggle of 1955-59 and was a close supporter of Makarios. He succeeded Spyros Kyprianou as leader of the Democratic Party in 2000.

## Opening of the dividing "borders"

In April 2003 the Turkish Cypriot leader Raouf Denktash decided to open the "borders" which divided the Island since 1974. The two "border" openings were at Ledra Street in Nicosia and in Pergamos near Pyla. A third opening was made a few days later at Strovilia.

*Queues of people waiting to cross the Border line to visit their villages and homes.*

The decision to open the dividing lines had such an emotional and dramatic impact which reminded everyone the collapse of the Berlin Wall. By the end of May 2003, about 400,000 Greek Cypriots and Turkish Cypriots had crossed the dividing lines because they wanted to see their homes and villages after 29 years.

What was disappointing however was the fact that those who wished to cross the line to visit their homes and villages had to show either their passports or their Identity Cards. What was even worse and upsetting was the fact that they had to knock on the doors of their own houses in order for some person to open to them. Some of the Turkish settlers who lived in the refugees' homes even refused to open the doors.

The new President was very much against the Kofi Annan Plan. He opposed many of its recommendations. The 5th Revised Plan stated that in the territorial adjustments it stipulated that only 18% Greek Cypriots could live in the Turkish Cypriot state. They could not buy properties – not even their own properties. The flag of Cyprus would be abolished and in its place there would be a new flag with horizontal stripes of blue, white, yellow and red colours.

On the 7th April 2004 Papadopoulos made a moving speech on Cyprus television where he called upon all Greek Cypriots to say NO to the referendum on the 24th April 2004.

The referendum was held among the two communities on the 24th April 2004 and the results were as follows:

The Greek Cypriots said NO to the Plan by 75.83% and 24.17% said Yes.

The Turkish Cypriots said YES to the Plan by 64.91% and 35.09% said No.

The Kofi Annan Plan was rejected because it was not accepted by both communities.

## Cyprus joins the European Union

On the 1st May 2004 President Papadopoulos was in Dublin to attend the official ceremony for Cyprus accession to the European Union. In Cyprus in all the government buildings was now flying the Cyprus flag together with the EU flag.

A month later, on the 13 June the first Euro elections were held in Cyprus for the six seats in the Euro-Parliament. The six seats went to 2 Democratic Rally, 2 to AKEL 1 to DEKO and 1 to Yiannakis Matsis.

## Turkish Cypriot Elections in 2005

*Mehmet Ali Talat*

"Presidential" elections were held in the occupied areas on 17 April 2005. The leader of the Republican Party of Mehmet Ali Talat obtained 55,943 votes or 55.6%. Dervis Eroglu of the Party of National Unity obtained 22,869 votes or 22.73%. Mustafa Arapagioglu of the Democratic Party obtained 13,302 votes or 13.22%.

Mehmet Ali Talat was elected "President" of the occupied parts of Northern Cyprus and a week later succeeded Raouf Denktash as the leader of the Turkish Cypriot Community.

Talat was born in Kyrenia in July 1952 and studied Mechanical Engineering at Ankara Polytechnic.

## Parliamentary Elections

On 21st May 2006 there were  Parliamentary elections in the Republic of Cyprus. The results were as follows:

AKEL  obtained  31.16%  and 18 seats
DESY  obtained  30.33%  and 18 seats
DEKO  obtained  17.91%  and 11 seats
EDEK  obtained  8.91%  and 5 seats
EUROKO  5.73%  and 3 seats
Green Party  1.95%  and 1 seat

## The Agreement of 8th July 2006

In March 2006 President Papadopoulos met with Secretary General Kofi Annan in Paris and agreed with him to resume the inter-communal talks with Mehmet Ali Talat the new Turkish Cypriot leader.  The two leaders met on the 8th July 2006 and both accepted that the current status-quo was unacceptable. They agreed on the following five points:

1. Commitment to reunite Cyprus on the basis of a bi-zonal, bi-communal federation with political equality based on the UN Security Council Resolutions.
2. Recognition of the fact that the status-quo is not acceptable.
3. Commitment of a commonly accepted solution without any further delays.
4. Immediate start of inter-communal talks on matters of substance.
5. Commitment of creating the appropriate climate so that this new procedure will have a positive result.

## New Archbishop of Cyprus

After the death of Archbishop Chrysostomos I, there were four candidates competing for the vacant position. These were: The Bishop of Paphos also called Chrysostomos, the Bishop of Limassol Athanasios, the Bishop of Kition (Larnaca) also called Chrysostomos and the Bishop of Kykko Nikeforos.

The Bishop of Paphos Chrysostomos was elected Archbishop on 5th November 2006 as Archbishop Chysostomos II.

## New UN Secretary-General

*Ban Ki Moon*

In January 2007 Ban Ki Moon took over from Kofi Annan as the new Secretary General of the United Nations. The new Secretary General was born in South Korea in 1944 and previously was Foreign Minister of South Korea.

In a speech he made in Brussels on 23rd January 2007 he promised to urge the two community leaders in Cyprus to implement their agreement of 8th July 2006.

## Cyprus introduces the Euro - AKEL withdraws support from Papadopoulos

The European Union accepted the application of Cyprus to introduce the Euro as its main currency and as from 1st January 2008 Cyprus replaced the Cyprus pound and adopted the Euro.

On 8th July 2007 AKEL withdrew its support to the Papadopoulos government using various accusations that Papadopoulos was supposedly not being "co-operative" and "stubborn". As a result of this, the four Ministers who came from AKEL had resigned from the Government.

390

# THE CHRISTOFIAS ADMINISTRATION 2008 - 2013
## The Presidential Elections of 2008

There were three main candidates in the 17th February 2008 elections. Ioannis Kasoulides – representing the Conservative DESY party who obtained 33.51% of the votes.

Demetris Christofias representing AKEL and obtained 33.29% of the vote.

*Demetris Christofias with Mehmet Ali Talat*

Tassos Papadopoulos leader of the Democratic Party obtained 31.79% of the vote.

In the second round Kasoulides competed against Christofias and the results were:

Demetris Christofias obtained 53.36% of the votes and Ioannis Kasoulides 46.64%.

Christofias was the first Communist leader ever to be elected as President of Cyprus. As soon as he came to power he had arranged to have meetings with Mehmet Ali Talat. When they met in Nicosia on 21st March 2008 they agreed to set up technical committees and had their first meeting on 3rd September 2008 in the presence of Alexander Downer the UN Secretary-General Special Representative in Cyprus.

Christofias Cabinet included the following:

Markos Kyprianou - Foreign Affairs
Harilaos Stavrakis - Finance

Neoklis Silikiotis - Interior
Costas Papacostas - Defence

On 15 December 2008 Tassos Papadopoulos died suffering from lung cancer at the age of 74.

On 20th December 2008 Christofias had announced that he was stepping down from the AKEL leadership and on the 21st January 2009 there were elections to replace him.

*Andros Kyprianou – New leader of AKEL*

There were only two candidates: Andros Kyprianou and Nikos Katsourides. Of the 105 votes of the Central Committee Andros Kyprianou obtained 57 votes and Nikos Katsourides 48 votes.

### Elections in Greece – October 2009

In the General elections held in Greece on 4th October 2009 the PASOK party of George Papandreou had won. PASOK had won 160 seats out of the 300 seats of the Greek Parliament. Papandreou visited Cyprus and agreed to work together with Christofias in order to find a peaceful settlement of the Cyprus problem.

On the 7th January 2010 the Turkish Cypriot leader Talat had given Christofias a list of five proposals which had the full

392

backing of the Ankara Government. These were the following:

1. The Greek Cypriot President should be for three years and the Turkish Cypriot for two years.
2. The Council of Ministers should consist of 12 Members seven of them will be Greek and five will be Turkish.
3. In the Legislative power there should be equal representation in the Upper House.
4. In Administrative matters the proportion of representation will be 4:3
5. In international relations the two states will be free to sign their own agreements.

These proposals were rejected by the Greek Cypriot side.

Intensive talks continued during January and March 2010 and three parties the Democratic Party, the Socialist EDEK and the Green Party were insisting that Christofias should withdraw his offer concerning the stay of 50,000 mainland Turks and also his offer of alternating the Presidency.

## Turkish Cypriot Elections April 2010

In the "Presidential" elections held in the occupied parts on 18th April 2010 Mehmet Ali Talat lost to Dervis Eroglou. Eroglou obtained 50.38% and Talat 42.85% and so Eroglou became the new leader.

*Turkish Cypriot leader Dervis Eroglu*

Dervis Eroglu was born in Famagusta in 1938 and studied medicine in Istanbul. He was the leader of the National Unity Party and was appointed "Prime Minister" four times in the occupied Northern Cyprus. He was "President" for five years 2010-2015 and had several meetings with President Christofias in order to solve the Cyprus problem.

## The Cyprus Economy 2012-2013

The economy of Cyprus was getting from bad to worse. The Laiki Bank (Cyprus Popular Bank) in September 2012 had 16% of the share of the market in loans and 14.5% share of deposits. The Bank made a series of large loans, many to Greek companies prior to and during their financial crisis.

What followed has been described as "billions handed out in bad loans created a financial time-bomb". After the bank collapsed, it was rescued by the Cypriot government, which took 84% ownership on 30 June 2012 and as of March 2013 it was dismantled as part of the **2012-2013 Cypriot financial crisis.**

On 25 March 2013, a €10 billion international bailout by the Eurogroup, European Commission (EC), European Central Bank (ECB) and International Monetary Fund (IMF) was announced, in return for Cyprus agreeing to close the country's second-largest bank, the Cyprus Popular Bank, imposing a one-time bank deposit levy on all uninsured deposits there, and possibly around 48% of uninsured deposits in the Bank of Cyprus (the island's largest commercial bank), many held by wealthy citizens of other countries (many of them from Russia) who were using Cyprus as a tax haven. No insured deposit of €100,000 or less would be affected.

Thousands of people who had invested over 100,000 euros in the Laiki Bank or the Bank of Cyprus, lost millions of pounds as they were only allowed to keep 100,000 Euros. Those who were aware of the financial situation managed to get their money out of Cyprus in time, especially to Switzerland.

Some Cypriots blamed the Christofias administration and others blamed the previous right wing governments. Financial corruption existed for many years in all political parties and governments. Back in 2007 the former Central Bank Governor Christodoulos Christodoulou was implicated in the payment of 1m euros and his omission to declare it to the taxman landed him a five-month prison term.

Recently the Focus Maritime Corporation which belonged to Greek ship owner Michalis Zolotas had revealed that they donated 850,000 Euros to AKEL and 650,000 to Desy. AKEL flatly denied the allegation and DESY said that they only acknowledged receipt of 50,000 euros from a group of ship owners.

## Historic Meeting between Papandreou and Erdogan

*George Papandreou and Tayyip Erdogan*

In May 2010 the Turkish Prime Minister Tayyip Erdogan with ten of his Ministers made an official visit to Athens and discussed various bilateral matters with Greek Prime Minister George Papandreou.

During this meeting Papandreou suggested that both countries' should reduce their Defence spending by 25%. Erdogan was accompanied by ten of his Ministers who also signed agreements with their Greek counterparts.

Both the meetings of Papandreou and Erdogan in Athens as well as the meetings of Christofias with Eroglu in Cyprus indicated that some progress was being made in the Greek - Turkish relations and high hopes were raised for a lasting settlement in Cyprus.

## The Explosion at Evangelos Florakis Naval base

On 11th July 2011, 98 containers of explosives that had been stored for 2 ½ years in the sun in the Evangelos Florakis Naval base near Zygi - Mari, self-detonated and killed 13 people and injured 62. Among the dead was Andreas Ioannides Commander of the Navy.

As a result of the incident Costas Papacostas the Cypriot Defence Minister and the Commander-in-Chief of the National Guard both resigned. Angry demonstrations outside the Presidential Palace and in other parts of Cyprus were held calling for the resignation and trial of President Christofias because they considered him responsible for what had happened.

## Elections in Greece

In January 2015 elections were held in Greece. The two main partties competing for power were the conservative New Democracy led by Antonis Samaras and the left wing party called SYRIZA led Alexis Tsipras.

Alexis Tsipras won 149 seats out the 300 seats in the Greek Parliament and formed an alliance with the Party of Independent Greeks led by Panos Kamenos.

Tsipras was born in July 1974 and studied Civil Engineeding at the Athens Technical University. He was active in the Communist Youth Movement and soon rose to prominence and stood as a candidate for the Mayor of Athens and won 10% of the vote.

The time he was elected Prime Minister coincided with the financial problems of Greece and he made numeroys visits to Brussels and other European capitals and met German Chancellor Angel Merkel, French President Francois Hollande and many other European leaders. He also attended the Davos Economic Forum. He visited Cyprus and had talks with President Anastasiades and other Cypriot political leaders offering Greece's full support for a fair and just solution to the Cyprus problem.

Tsipras was re-elected in September 2015 and won 145 seats. Once again he had a coalition government with the Independent Greeks.

*Nikos Anastasiades and Alexis Tsipras in Davos, Switzerland, 2016.*

Turkey has agreed to stem the flow of migrants to Europe in return for cash, visas and renewed talks on joining the EU in a deal which the Turkish prime minister called a "new beginning" for the uneasy neighbours.

Leaders of the 28 European Union states met Turkish premier Ahmet Davutoglu in Brussels on 6th March 2016 to give their collective political blessing to an agreement hammered out by diplomats over the past few weeks.

Donald Tusk the European Council President stated at a News Conference that "We agreed that (Turkey's) accession process needs to be re-energised," with Turkish Prime Minister Ahmet Davutoglu and European Commission President Jean-Claude

Juncker following a summit with the EU's 28 heads of state and government.

*President Anastasiads with Turkish PM Ahmet Davutoglu and European Council Leader Donald Tusk.*

Cyprus hopes for a solution have been re-ignited because currently Turkey is refusing to abide by some EU rules and Cyprus has the right of veto in case Turkey continues to occupy parts of its territory.

# GREEK CYPRIOT POLITICAL LEADERS

## Democratic Rally - Δημοκρατικός Συναγερμός

Averof Neophytou was born in Argaka in the district of Paphos in July 1961. He studied Economics and Accounting at the New York Institute of Technology. He was the Mayor of Polis Chrysochous from 1991-96 and Minister of Communications and Works in the government of Glafkos Clerides from 1999 to 2003.

He was also Deputy President of the Democratic Rally until the election of Nikos Anastasiades to the Presidency. He has been President of the Democratic Rally since 2013.

*Averof Neophytou - Leader of Democratic Rally*

The Democratic Rally (Desy) a Conservative party together with AKEL a Communist party are the two largest political parties in Cyprus.

## Democratic Party selects Nicholas Papadopoulos as leader

In 2013 the Democratic Party selected Nicholas Papadopoulos (son of former President Tassos Papadopoulos) as its new leader. The previous leader was Marios Garoyian. Nicholas Papadopoulos was born in 1973 and studied Law at the University College London. He was elected a Member of Parliament in 2006. The Democratic

*Nicholas Papadopoulos*

Party was founded by Spyros Kyprianou in the 1970's and in recent years it has become the third largest party.

## The Alliance of Citizens - Yiorgos Lillikas

Yiorgos Lillikas was born in 1960 in Panayia village in Paphos (the same village as Makarios was born). He studied Political Science in Lyon in France and he was later elected as an MP collaborating with AKEL. When Tassos Papadopoulos won the election in 2003 he was appointed Minister of Commerce and Industry and Tourism and in 2006 was appointed Foreign Minister. When AKEL decided to break their support to Papadoulos, Lillikas and the other three Ministers connected with AKEL resigned. Later Lillikas found a new movement which he called "Symmahia Politon" which translates as the "Alliance of Citizens".

*Yiorgos Lillikas*

## The European Party

Demetris Syllouris was born in Potamia, Nicosia in 1953. He studied Civil Engineering at the North East London Polytechnic. He was a Member of Parliament for DESY (Democratic Rally) 1991-2001 and Parliamentary spokesman for DESY from 2001-2004. He became the leader of the European Party a right wing party in 2005. In the European Parliament Elections of 2014 Evroko formed an alliance with the Democratic Rally.

*Dimitris Syllouris*
*leader of EVROKO*
*(European Party)*

# THE ANASTASIADES ADMINISTRATION 2013 –2018

*Nikos Anastasiades*
*the new President*

Nikos Anastasiades was born in Pera Pedi village in 1946. He studied Law at the University of Athens and did postgraduate studies in shipping law at the University College London. He was leader of the Democratic Rally from 1997- 2013.

**Presidential elections** were held in Cyprus on 17 February 2013. A runoff was held on 24 February 2013. Nicos Anastasiades of the Conservative Democratic Rally (DESY) won the election.

The other candidates were Stavros Malas of the Progressive Party of Working People (AKEL); Praxoula Antoniadou of the United Democrats and Giorgos Lillikas of Movement for Social Democracy (EDEK).

Nikos Anastasiades of DESY obtained 236,965 votes or 57.48 and Stavros Malas of AKEL obtained 175,267 votes or 42.52%.

The Cabinet of Anastasiades consisted of 13  people seven from the Democratic Rally (DESY) and six people from other parties.  Yiannakis  Kasoulides  remained  Foreign Minister, Socrates Hasikos became Minister of Interior, Harris Georgiades as Minister of Finance and Costas Kadis as Minister of Education.

Anastasiades supported the Annan Plan in the referendum. The start of peace negotiations between Nicos Anastasiades and his

Turkish Cypriot counterpart began in October of 2013, attracting the interest of international media and world leaders including Barack Obama. In February 2015 President Nicos Anastasiades. agreed to make Cypriot ports available to Russian military ships and planes.

On 18th September 2015 Anastasiades met British P.M. David Cameron and discussed the Special European Council on the migration crisis, the Cyprus settlement talks and the UK's EU renegotiation agenda.

**Turkish Cypriot Elections 2015**

Mustafa Akinci was elected as "President" of the occupied parts of Northern Cyprus in April 2015. He was born in Limassol in 1947 and studied architecture at the Middle East Technical University.

He was the first elected Mayor of the Nicosia Turkish Municipality and served for 14 years - from 1976 to 1990. During his 14 years of Mayorship, he collaborated with the then Nicosia Greek Cypriot Mayor Lellos Demetriades on the implementation of the Nicosia Sewerage Project and the Nicosia Master Plan.

In 2003 Akinci and Demetriades were awarded the prestigious 'Europa Nostra Medal of Honour' in recognition of their consistent and successful efforts for Nicosia and its citizens during particularly difficult times, and for the preservation of the historical and architectural environment of the Walled City.

Akinci also played a vital role in the establishment of the Union of Turkish Cypriot Municipalities, of which he then became the first president. In 2003, Akinci established the Peace and Democracy Movement. The main aims of the party were the promotion of reunification of Cyprus based on the proposed Annan Plan and the consequent EU accession of a reunified Cyprus. As of 2015, Akinci continued to view European integration very favourably.

# TURKISH CYPRIOT POLITICAL LEADERS

*Mustafa Akinci - new Turkish
Cypriot leader 2015 -2020*

Mustafa Akinci was born in Limassol in 1947 and studied Archi-tecture at the Middle East Technical University. He became the first elected Mayor of the Turkish part Nicosia and he worked closely with the Greek Mayor of Nicosia Lellos Demetriades.

In 2003, Akinci esta-blished the Peace and Democracy Move-ment. The main aims of the party were the promotion of reuni-fication of Cyprus based on the proposed Annan Plan and the consequent EU accession of a reunified Cyprus. In 2015, Akıncı was elected "President" with 60.5% of the vote. He succeeded Dervis Eroglu. Akinci is considered a progressive and moderate politician.

*Ozkan Yorgancioglu leader of the CTP Party*

Ozkan Yorgancioglu was born in Lempa in Paphos in 1954 and studied at the University of Istanbul. He is the leader of the Turkish Republican Party and since the 2nd September 2013 is the "Prime Minister" in the occupied parts of Northern Cyprus.

*Huseyin  Ozgurgun leader of  UBP*

Huseyin Ozgurgun was born in Nicosia in 1965 and is the current leader of UBP  the National Unity Party. He studied in Ankara. He was previously the "Foreign Minister" in the occupied parts of Northern Cyprus. He succeeded Irsen Kucuk who was a nephew of Dr Fazil Kucuk who was the first Vice-President of the Republic of Cyprus.

*Serdar Denktash leader of the Democratic Party*

Serdar Denktash is the only surviving son of Rouf Denktash the former Turkish Cypriot leader. He was born in Nicosia in 1959 and studied at the London College of Printing and then he studied Economics at the University College Cardiff but he never completed his studies. He was elected an MP in the Turkish Cypriot "Parliament" and also served as "Minister" of Tourism.

# EPILOGUE

In July 2016, 42 years have been completed since the Greek military coup and the Turkish invasion. About 200,000 people were driven away from their homes and settled in various parts of the Island.

In 2004 Cyprus had joined the European Union in the hope that Europe will help to restore the re-unification of Cyprus but this has not happened. Numerous resolutions were passed by the United Nations calling upon Turkey to withdraw its troops from Cyprus but again the resolutions fell on deaf ears.

Hundreds of meetings had taken place between the Greek Cypriot and the Turkish Cypriot leaders but all of them had ended in total disagreement. The Kofi Annan Plan was rejected by the Greek Cypriots because it would not have allowed many Greek Cypriots to return to their homes but it was accepted by the Turkish Cypriots.

Sadly, whatever agreement is reached, it would not fulfil the aspirations and wishes of all Cypriots because Cyprus will not be the same island that it was in July 1974. The proposal to divide Cyprus into two zones (one Greek and one Turkish) and calling it A Bi-zonal Bi-Communal Federation is another disguised form term for "Partition". Tragically, many thousands of Greek and Turkish refugees will not be able to return to their villages. The tragedy is that whole communities have been destroyed because its members have been scattered in various parts of the island.

In 2016 those who were born in 1974 will be 42 years old and know very little about their parents' villages and perhaps not all of them would wish to go back to those villages especially if they already have their own families in other parts of the island. It seems that this was a deliberate policy and strategy by the Turkish Government to "bite time" because time would work in their favour.

As already outlined in this work, there were many, too many

tragic mistakes, made by both sides. The leadership of both sides were "hostage" to their nationalism and saw themselves first and foremost as "Greeks" and "Turks" and not as "Cypriots".

In recent years the Greek and Turkish Governments have tried to improve their relations but the unsolved problem of Cyprus still remains the major stumbling block. The Cyprus Government had hoped by joining the European Union they would be able to force Turkey to abide by the EU rules and regulations and to withdraw from Cyprus. They believe that if Turkey wants to be a member of the EU then they could not justify a Member-state invading and occupying part of another member-state.

The election of the moderate politician Mustafa Akinci as leader of his Community, had raised hopes among Greek and Turkish Cypriots because he was in favour of re-unification.

Both Anastasiades and Akinci expressed high hopes that the year 2016 will be the year of a final and peaceful settlement. This however remains to be seen.

*Nikos Anastasiades the UN Special Envoy Espen Barth Eide and Mustafa Akinci.*

# BIBLIOGRAPHY

Adams, T.W. *AKEL: The Communist Party of Cyprus* (Hoover Institution Press, USA, 1971)

AKEL, *Chronicle of Contemporary Cypriot Tragedy,* (in Greek) Nicosia 1975

Alastos, D. *Cyprus in History* (Zeno, London, 1976)

Alastos, D. *Cyprus Guerrilla: Grivas, Makarios and the British* (Heinemann, London 1960)

Asmussen J: *Cyprus at War - Diplomacy and Conflict during the 1974 crisis,* London, 2008

Attalides, M. *Nationalism and International Politics* (Q Press, Edinburgh, 1979)

Averof-Tositsa, E. *A History of Missed Opportunities: Cyprus 1950 - 1963* (2 volumes, Athens 1981 - in Greek)

Birand, M.A. *Pazaremata* (Bargaining) (Floras, Athens, 1985).

Bitisios, D.S. *Beyond the Froniters 1974 - 1977* (Athens 1982, in Greek)

Bitisios, D.S. *Sto Orio ton Kairon,* Nea Synora-Livanis, Athens 1997

Christodoulou, M. *Poreia mias Epochis* (Floras, Athens, 1987)

Chrysostomides, K. *Sto telos tis archis.* Kastaniotis, Athens 1997

Cobham, CD. *Excerpta Cypria* (C.U.P. 1908, rep. 1969)

Clerides G.: *Documents of an era* 1993-2003 (in Greek), Nicosia 2007

Clerides, G. *Cyprus - My Deposition,* 4 vols. Nicosia 1992

Coufoudakis, V. (Ed) *Essays on the Cyprus Conflict,* Pella, New York, 1976

Craig, I & O'Malley B. The Cyprus Conspiracy, London 1999

Crawshaw, N. *The Cyprus Revolt,* Allen & Unwin, 1978

Denktash Rauf. *The Cyprus Triangle,* Allen & Unwin 1982

Drousiotis, M. EOKA - *The Dark Side,* Athens 1998

Drousiotis, M. *Apo to Ethniko Metopo stin EOKA B,* Nicosia 1994

Foley, C. *Island in Revolt,* Longmans, London 1962

Foley, C. *Legacy of Strife,* Penguin Books 1964

Foot, H. *A Start in Freedom* Hodder & Soughton, 1964

408

Grekos, Costas. *History of Cyprus,* Nicosia, 1982

Grivas, G. *Reminiscences of EOKA's Struggle (1955-59),* Athens 1961 (in Greek)

Hadjidemetriou, K. *Istoria tis Kyprou,* Nicosia, 1979

Hannay, D.: *Cyprus - The Search for a Solution,* Tauris, London 2005

Hitchens, C. *Hostage to History,* Verso, 1997

Holland, R. *Britain and the Revolt in Cyprus,* Oxford 1998

Hunt, D.: *Memoirs - Military and Diplomatic,* Trigraph London 2006

Hunt, D.(Ed). *Footprints in Cyprus,* London 1982

Ignatiou, M. *The Rome Seminar,* Athens 1989

Ioannides, CP. *Realpolitik in the Eastern Mediterranean,* Pella, New York, 2001

Kakaounakis, N. *2650 Days of Conspiracy* 2 vols. Athens 1976

Karageorghis, V. *Cyprus - From the Stone Age to the Romans,* Thames & Hudson, 1982

Karamanlis C. *Archives - Documents,* Athens

Katsis, A. *From EOKA to Independence* (Greek), Limassol, 1981

Katsis, A. *From Independence to the Turkish invasion,* (Greek) Nicosia, 1977

Katsourides, Y.: *The History of the Communist Party in Cyprus,* London 2014

Kizilyurek N. *Oliki Kypros,* Nicosia, 1990

Kranidiotis, N. *Kypros: Dyskola Hronia 1950-60,* Athens 1981

Kyprianos (Archimandrite): *Chronological History of Cyprus,* Nicosia 1933

Kyrris, CP. *History of Cyprus,* Nicosia 1985

Leonidou, L. George Grivas Dighenis: A Biography (2 vols, Nicosia, 1995-97)

Luke, H. *Cyprus under the Turks 1571-1878* (Humphrey Milford, London 1921)

Luke, H. Cyprus: *A Portrait and an Appreciation* (G. Harrap, London 1965)

Maier, F.G. *Cyprus from the earliest times to the present day* (Elek, London 1968)

Mallinson W: *Cyprus - A Modern History,* Tauris, London 2009
Mallinson W: *Cyprus - Diplomatic History and Clash of Theory in International Relations,* Tauris, London 2010
Mayes, S. *Cyprus and Makarios* (London 1960)
Mayes, S. *Makarios-A Biography,* Macmillan Press, 1981
Mirbagheri, F. *Cyprus and International Peacemaking,* London 1998
Orr, C.W. J. *Cyprus under British Rule,* London 1972

Panteli, S. *A New History of Cyprus,* London 1984
Panteli, S. *The Making of Modern Cyprus,* London, 1990
Papadopoulos, L.G. *To Kypriako Zitima - Keimena,* University Studio Press, Salonica, 1999
Papageorgiou, S. *Apo tin Zyriche ston Attila* (3 vols) Athens
Papageorgiou, S. *Makarios* Athens 1976
Papageorgiou, S. *Archives of the EOKA Struggle,* Nicosia 1984
Papandreou, A. *Democracy at Gunpoint,* Penguin, 1970
Polyviou, P. *Cyprus, Conflict and Negotiation,* London 1980
Press and Information Office: *Resolutions adopted by the United Nations on the Cyprus Problem 1964 - 1999,* Nicosia, 1999

Serafim-Loizou, E. *O Apeleftherotikos Agonas tis Kyprou 1955-1959,* Nicosia, 1982
Servas, P. *Efthynes,* 5 volumes, Athens 1985 - 95
Servas, P. *Koine Patrida,* Nicosia, 1997
Spanos Ch. J. *EOKA - Etsi polemoun oi Ellines* (2 vols), Nicosia 1996
Spyridakis, C. *A Brief History of Cyprus,* Nicosia, 1964
Stephens, R. *Cyprus: a Place of Arms,* London 1966

Vanezis, P. *Makarios: Faith and Power,* London 1971
Vanezis, P. *Makarios:Pragmatism & Idealism,* Lon. 1974
Vanezis, P. *Makarios: Life and Leadership,* London 1979
Venizelos K. & M. Ignatiou: *The secret files of Kissinger (in Greek),* Athens 2002
Vlachos, A. *Dheka Chronia Kypriakou,* Estia, Athens, 1980

Woodhouse, C.M. *Something Ventured,* London 1982

Xydis, Linardatos, Hadjargyris: *O Makarios kai oi Symmachoi tou,* Athens

# INDEX